The Sacred Effusion

THE SACRED EFFUSION

Reflections on Ziyārat ʿĀshūrā of
Sayyid al-Shuhadā al-Ḥusayn b. ʿAlī عليه السلام

Volume 1

Written by Shaykh Muhammad M Khalfan

Foreword by Dr. Hasnain Walji
Introduction by Shaykh Abbas M H Ismail

British Library Cataloguing in Publication Data
A catalogue record for this book is available from the British Library

ISBN 978-1-898449-73-7

Published by:
The World Federation of Khoja Shia Ithna-Asheri Muslim Communities
Registered Charity in the UK No. 282303
The World Federation is an NGO in Special Consultative Status with the Economic and Social Council (ECOSOC) of the United Nations

Islamic Centre, Wood Lane, Stanmore, Middlesex, United Kingdom, HA7 4LQ
www.world-federation.org

Cover Design & Layout by the Islamic Publishing House (www.iph.ca)

Printed in Canada
By Friesens Corporation – www.friesens.com

Table of Contents

TRANSLITERATION TABLE

The method of transliteration of Islāmic terminology from the Arabic language has been carried out according to the standard transliteration table mentioned below.

ء	ʾ	ض	ḍ
ا	a	ط	ṭ
ب	b	ظ	ẓ
ت	t	ع	ʿ
ث	th	غ	gh
ج	j	ف	f
ح	ḥ	ق	q
خ	kh	ك	k
د	d	ل	l
ذ	dh	م	m
ر	r	ن	n
ز	z	و	w
س	s	ي	y
ش	sh	ه	h
ص	ṣ		

Long Vowels		Short Vowels	
ا	ā	ـَـ	a
و	ū	ـُـ	u
ي	ī	ـِـ	i

سبحانه وتعالى - Free from imperfections and Exalted is He

صلى الله عليه وآله - Prayers be upon him and his family

عليه السلام - Peace be upon him

عليها السلام - Peace be upon her

HUMBLE PRESENTATION

This nondescript humbly presents this work to Majmaʿ al-Nurayn (Confluence of the Lights of Nubuwwa and Wilāya), Ḥaḍrat Fāṭima al-Zahrā عليها السلام

Muhammad M. Khalfan
Rajab al-Asamm 1430 AH [lunar]
Holy Proximity of Ḥaḍrat Maʿṣūma عليها السلام
Qum al-Muqaddasa
Islamic Republic of Iran

Foreword

By Dr. Hasnain Walji

بسم الله الرحمن الرحيم

In the Name of Allāh, the
Most Gracious, the Most Merciful

Ziyārat al-ʿĀshūrā: A potent antidote to reawaken our hearts.

This is an age where the very purpose of our existence has been obscured by the glut of materialism. We seem to be engulfed in a quagmire that deflects our energy away from his divinely intended purpose. Our true fulfillment can only come through inner light, when the heart is awakened to seek it's divinely intended purpose.

This seminal work on Ziyārat ʿĀshūrā, aptly named *The Sacred Effusion*, by Shaykh Muhammad Khalfan, is a beacon for the seeker to seek the Sacred and the Divine. With his characteristic insight, the venerable Shaykh guides us to understand how Ziyārat ʿĀshūrā can be a potent antidote to reawaken our hearts to the real purpose of our existence and not remain a mere habitual or ritual recitation.

As one reads the words so passionately penned by the author, one cannot help but visualize and ponder upon the origin of the very word *Ziyārat*, which originates from the word *zawr,* which means to deflect or turn away. The context becomes all the more evident when we read that the Arabic word *zūr* refers to a lie - because it deflects from the path of truth. This sets the scene for the reader to contextualize the very essence of the spiritual and moral aspects of the Ziyārat - that when visiting the shrines of the Maʿṣūmīn, or reciting the Ziyārat we momentarily 'turn away' from our worldly existence and gravitate towards an inner state of seeking none other than Allāh. The essence of the Ziyārat, as elucidated by the author is that the *zair* who recites the *Ziyārat* must imbibe the spirit and attain the cognizance of the sublimity of Ziyārat ʿĀshūrā to enable him to align himself with the spirit of the visited one.

The author eloquently elucidates that the crux of the Ziyārat ʿĀshūrā are the concepts of al-Tawallī and al-Tabarrī. He writes:

> Besides its ample merits, it is a program of revolution for the sleeping masses. The crux of the Ziyārat is al-tabarrīʾ and al-tawallī, which can correctly be translated as 'fleeing from imperfection' and 'seeking perfection', or in beautiful words of every Muslim: Lā ilāhaillallāh - Besides Allāh - the Only Beloved, there is no other ilāh (beloved). The name Allāh exemplifies all the perfect attributes of the Divine Essence, which the human being has been molded to appreciate and naturally seek. The Holy Qurʾān says: '...the innate nature of Allāh, upon which the human beings were molded.' (30:30). Therefore the Ziyārat in reality is a call to the unsullied innate disposition (fiṭra) of the human being.

The oft-repeated salutation of *Assālamu 'Alayka Yā Abā 'Abdillāh,* assumes an everlasting impression upon our minds when we read how we must manifest our intentions to unite with his lofty ideals, and in cursing his opponents how we must demonstrate our revulsion at the worldly desires of his enemies. If we truly make that salutation with that understanding, it helps us align ourselves with the spirit of Imām al-Ḥusayn عليه السلام and we have fulfilled and are true to the words we recite in the *Ziyārat:*

> So I ask Allāh, who ennobled me by knowing you and knowing your friends, and enabled me to seek remoteness from your enemies, to place me in your company in this world and the Hereafter.

This allows us to seek nearness to Allāh through the Ziyārat rather than to be only motivated to gain personal benefits. Unquestionably, many traditions of the A'imma عليهم السلام promise us that by the recitation of Ziyārat ʿĀshūrā our needs would be fulfilled. For example Imām Jaʿfar as-Ṣādiq عليه السلام guided Safwān thus:

> When you are confronted with some adversity, then seek redress of your grievances from Imām al-Ḥusayn عليه السلام with this Ziyārat and Allāh never reneges on His word.

However, the real question that we are encouraged to ponder upon is *"What is our real need that we should ask for?"* It helps us create an awareness of our own selves so that we can assess the true value of our neediness. Cited is an inspiring example of asking for one's real need is of Shaykh ʿAbd al-Karim Ḥairī, the founder of the Ḥawza of Qum. It is said that during the Ziyārat at the Ḥaram of Imām al-Ḥusayn عليه السلام he was seen weeping and telling the Imām عليه السلام: *"O dear master, I have become a mujtahid but I want to become a human being."*

Thus the *Ziyārat*, must go beyond the seeking of mundane material benefits and rise to the lofty sublimities of cognition and self awareness to awaken us from the sluggishness caused by the excesses of hubbe-duniya. To do so is to realize the ultimate purpose of Ziyārat. After all who can be a better symbol than Imām al-Ḥusayn عليه السلام whose supreme sacrifice on the day of ʿĀshūrā, symbolized the highest manifestation of Tawheed - that Besides *Allāh- the Only Beloved, there is no other ilāh (beloved).*

Hasnain Walji
Plano Texas, March 2009

Preface

By Shaykh Muhammad M Khalfan

All praises belong exclusively to Allāh, and may His peace and benedictions be on Muḥammad, the most perfect epitome of Divine Attributes and his infallible progeny, the Ahl al-Bayt, who are rightfully known as the ships of salvation, whosoever boards their ship, earns eternal felicity, and whosoever lags behind and is indifferent drowns and attains eternal damnation.

Al-Qandūzī, the Hanafite narrator of traditions, in his radiant collection *Yanābī' al-Mawadda* (lit. Fountains of Constant Love) narrates a tradition from Abū Dharr al-Ghiffārī who narrates from the Holy Prophet ﷺ:

إِنَّ مَثَلَ أَهْلِ بَيْتِي فِيكُمْ مَثَلُ سَفِينَةِ نُوحٍ، مَنْ رَكِبَهَا نَجَا وَمَنْ تَخَلَّفَ عَنْهَا هَلَكَ

> The similitude of my progeny among you is that of the ship of Noah ؑ; whosoever boards it is saved, and whosoever lags behind would perish[1]

The ship of al-Ḥusayn ؑ, however, according to another tradition is more rapid: Once a companion of Imām al-Ṣādiq ؑ asked him about the prophetic tradition "Surely al-Ḥusayn is the lamp of guidance and the ship of salvation" saying: "Aren't you [the Ahl al-Bayt ؑ] ships of salvation [too]?" The Imām ؑ replied:

---

1 Al-Qandūzī, *Yanābī' al-Mawadda*, v.2, p.90

كُلُّنَا سُفُنُ النَّجَاةِ إِلاَّ أَنَّ سَفِينَةَ الْحُسَيْنِ أَوْسَعُ وَأَسْرَعُ

> All of us are ships of salvation, save that the ship of al-Ḥusayn عليه السلام is **more spacious and faster.**[2]

This tradition is also endorsed by great mystic scholars who can appreciate the sublime secrets of religion. The late mystic-scholar Āyatullāh Mīrzā Tabrizī in his monumental prayer manual *al-Murāqabāt* says:

> It should be known that the door of al-Ḥusayn عليه السلام is the door of comprehensive mercy, rapid response and approval. And he [the Imām] would say during his life time: 'The similitude of doing good is rain water which covers both the virtuous as well as the sinful.'[3]

Sayyid Ḥaddād al-Mūsawī a great Shīʿite saint and a contemporary of ʿAllāmah al-Ṭabāṭabāʾī, is reported to have quoted their mentor in practical gnosis, Āyatullāh Qāḍī al-Ṭabāṭabāʾī as having said:

> My teacher, Marḥūm Qāḍī (may his spirit be sanctified) said to me that it is impossible for a human being to attain the station of *tawḥīd* [proximity to God] without the path of Sayyid al-Shuhadāʾ.[4]

And ʿAllāma al-Ṭabāṭabāʾī is reported to have said:

> That Ḥaḍrat [i.e. Imām al-Ḥusayn عليه السلام] has great

---

2 Sayyid ʿĀdil al-ʿAlawī, *Risālāt Islāmiyya*, v.6 p. 183

3 Āyatullāh al-Tabrīzī, *al-Murāqibāt*, p.286

4 Sayyid ʿAlī al-Mūsawī al-Ḥaddād, *ʿĀrifun fī al-Riḥāb al-Qudsiyya*, p.47

> attention towards the wayfarers of the path of God in removing the veil and impediments of the 'path of God'.[5]

One of the excellent ways of establishing contact with Imām al-Ḥusayn عليه السلام is through offering salutations to his exalted personality (*Ziyārat*). This can be achieved either in front of his radiant tomb in Karbalā, or in the environs of one's house observing some specific etiquettes.

The secret however is that the *zā'ir*, one who performs the *Ziyārat*, must yearn to the attain the apex of the meaning of what he recites and unite with the spirit of the *mazūr* (the visited one). The grand Āyatullāh Jawādī Āmulī in his masterpiece '*Adabe Fināye Muqarrabān*' says:

> *Ziyārat* is the mystical presence of the fervent lover (*'āshiq*) in the dwelling of the Beloved; it is the visitor's passionate encounter of the abode of the visited one; it is the lover's expression of intense love and consideration for the beloved; it is when the enamored one sincerely gives his heart in the alley of the possessor of the heart...[6]

The present commentary tries to examine and reflect on one of the well-known *ziyārāt* that many of the Muslims recite with great zeal and devotion. Most of the Shī'a Muslims express their veneration and sorrow when they recite this sublime *Ziyārat* on the day of 'Āshurā'. However, the Infallible Imāms of the Ahl al-Bayt عليهم السلام have taught us to recite it very often. Besides its ample merits, it is a program of revolution for the sleeping masses. The crux of the *Ziyārat* is *al-tabarrī'* and *al-tawallī*, which can correctly be translated as 'fleeing from imperfection' and 'seeking perfection', or in the beautiful words of every Muslim *Lā ilāha illa Allāh* -Besides Allāh- the Only Beloved, there

---

5 Hādī Hāshimiyān, *Daryāye 'Irfān*, p.97

6 Āyatullāh Jawādī Āmulī, *Adab-e-Fināye Muqarribān*, v.1, p. 17

is no other *ilāh* (beloved). The Name Allāh exemplifies all the perfect attributes of the Divine Essence, which the human being has been molded to appreciate and naturally seek. The Holy Qur'ān says:'*...the innate nature of Allāh, upon which the human beings were molded...*'(30:30). Therefore the *Ziyārat* in reality is a call to the unsullied innate disposition (*fiṭra*) of the human being.

In expressing veneration and seeking the higher levels of peace for Imām al-Ḥusayn ﵇ we are trying to unite with his ideas, thoughts and towering volition, and in cursing his opponents, who overtly declared themselves to be Muslims and believers, but were extensions of the hypocrites, we are trying to flee from all their ideas, thoughts and actions. Hence this recital trains the reciter to overhaul himself and unite with the spirit of the sacred Imām ﵇. In fact, as we shall come to observe in this *Ziyārat* later, one of the beautiful supplications taught to us when expressing our greetings to the Imām is to seek spiritual harmony with the Imām ﵇ in both this world as well as the Hereafter. We say later in this *Ziyārat*

فَأَسْأَلُ اللهَ الَّذِي أَكْرَمَنِي بِمَعْرِفَتِكُمْ وَمَعْرِفَةِ أَوْلِيَائِكُمْ وَرَزَقَنِي الْبَرَاءَةَ مِنْ أَعْدَائِكُمْ أَنْ يَجْعَلَنِي مَعَكُمْ فِي الدُّنْيَا وَالآخِرَةِ

So I ask Allāh, who ennobled me by knowing you and knowing your friends, and enabled me to seek remoteness from your enemies, to place me in your company in this world and the Hereafter.

Understanding the aforementioned obliges every high-spirited seeker of truth to aim for the achievement of the crux of the *Ziyārat* rather than be selfishly motivated to gain personal benefits. The rewards of the *Ziyārat* which are both sacred and sublime should not be the only factor to lead us to recite it. It is the natural love for the Imām ﵇ who exemplifies the Divine Attributes in himself that should transport us to recite this humble presentation. In fact some traditions, as we shall soon consider, clearly state that whosoever visits Imām al-Ḥusayn ؑ in Karbālā is as if he has visited Allāh at His Throne.[7]

Another very important point to bear in mind is that because the reciter of this *Ziyārat* has been guaranteed by the Imāms ؑ that his needs would be fulfilled, he must be very careful in distinguishing 'that which is really a need' from 'that which is not really a need'. The great saint Āyatullāh Ḥaddād al-Mūsawī, a contemporary of ʿAllāma al-Ṭabāṭabā'ī, would see people clinging onto the radiant enclosure where Imām al-Ḥusayn ؑ is buried, and instead of seeking their real needs, asking for those things that would increase the burden that they had already accumulated. He is reported to have said:

> إنَّ أكْثَرَ النَّاسِ حِيْنَمَا يَذْهَبُوْنَ إلى زِيَارَةِ العَتَبَاتِ المُقَدَّسَةِ يَقِفُوْنَ مَاسِكِي الضَّرِيْحِ فَيَتَوَسَّلُوْنَ بِالإمَامِ ؑ لِحَوَائِجِهِمْ المَادِّيَّةِ فَيَحْمِلُوْنَ ثِقْلاً عَلى ثِقْلِهِمْ وَلَمْ يَسْئَلُوا الإمَامَ ؑ بِأنْ يَأْخُذَ مِنْهُمْ ثِقْلَهُمْ وَهُوَ التَّعَلُّقُ بِالدُّنْيَا، بَلْ يَسْئَلُوْنَهُ بِأنْ يُعْطِيَهُمْ بَيْتاً أوْ وَلَداً أوْ زَوْجاً أوْ سَيَّارَةً، وَمَا سَمِعْنَا عَنْ أحَدٍ دَخَلَ بِخِدْمَتِهِ وَقَالَ لَهُ خُذْ مِنِّي كَذَا وَكَذَا

> When most of the people visit the holy shrines, they stand holding fast onto the enclosures of the graves and ask the Imām ؑ to mediate on their behalf, so that their material needs are fulfilled. Consequently, they add a burden over their burden. They do not ask the Imām ؑ to remove their burden which is 'attachment to the world'; rather they ask for a

7 Ibn Qūlawayh, *Kāmil al-Ziyārāt*, p. 147

> house, an off spring, a wife or a car; and never have we heard from anyone who entered in his service, and asked him: 'Relieve me from such and such a thing.'[8]

In one of his lessons on practical ethics (*akhlāq*), Āyatullāh Mujtahidī (may Allāh elevate his status) narrates the following incident:

> حاج شیخ عبدالکریم حائری (ره) را در حرم امام عليه‌السلام دیدند که گریه می‌کند و به امام می‌گوید: **آقا جان من مجتهد شده‌ام، ولی می‌خواهم آدم بشوم.**
>
> Ḥāj Shaykh 'Abd al-Karīm Ḥā'irī [the founder of the Islamic Seminary of Qum] was seen in the ḥaram of Imām al-Ḥusayn عليه‌السلام weeping and telling the Imām عليه‌السلام: O dear master, I have become a juristconsult *(mujtahid)*, but I want to become a [perfect] human being.[9]

Some traditions clearly teach us about the ultimate purpose of *Ziyārat*. Observe the following:

1. Ṣafwān bin Mihrān is reported to have said:

> عَنْ اَبِيْ عَبْدِ اللّٰه عليه‌السلام قَالَ: مَنْ زَارَ قَبْرَ الْحُسَيْنِ عليه‌السلام وَهُوَ يُرِيْدُ اللّٰهَ عَزَّ وَجَلَّ شَيَّعَهُ جَبْرَئِيْلُ وَمِيْكَائِيْلُ وَاِسْرَافِيْلُ حَتَّى يَرِدَ إِلى مَنْزِله.
>
> Imām al-Ṣādiq عليه‌السلام said: 'Whosoever visits the grave of al-Ḥusayn عليه‌السلام while ***he seeks Allāh***, the Invincible

8 Sayyid Alī al-Mūsawī al-Ḥaddād, *'Ārifun fī al-Riḥāb al-Qudsiyyah*, p. 146

9 See the following website:
http://www.tebyan.net/Religion_Thoughts/TheLearned/Contemporary/2008/1/29/59850.html

and Exalted, Jibrā'īl, Mīkā'īl, and Iṣrāfīl accompany him until he returns back to his house."[10]

2. Mu'ammar is reported to have said: I heard Zayd bin 'Alī عليه السلام saying:

مَنْ زَارَ قَبْرَ الْحُسَيْنِ بْنِ عَلِيٍّ عليه السلام لاَ يُرِيْدُ بِهِ إلاَّ اللهَ تَعَالى غَفَرَ لَهُ جَمِيعُ ذُنُوْبِهِ وَلَوْ كَانَتْ مِثْلُ زَبَدِ الْبَحْرِ، فَاسْتَكْثِرُوْا مِنْ زِيَارَتِهِ يَغْفِرُ اللهُ لَكُمْ ذُنُوْبَكُمْ.

Whosoever visits the grave of al-Ḥusayn bin 'Alī عليه السلام while he ***does not seek thereby save Allāh,*** *Allāh* would forgive all his sins even if they be like the foam of the ocean; therefore, visit him often, and Allāh would forgive your sins.[11]

Seeking 'Allāh' as mentioned in the abovementioned narrations refers to yearning for Allāh's proximity, which in reality is perfecting oneself to attain the attributes of Almighty Allāh. If this is the purpose behind *Ziyārat*, the visitor would naturally struggle for a complete unity with religion and divine values.

Before we begin the commentary of this radiant *Ziyārat*, which is also reckoned to be among the sacred traditions[12] *(aḥādīth qudsiyya)*, and understand both its particular as well as its universal import, it is imperative to generally know the significance of *Ziyārat*, and its exalted purpose.

Meaning of Ziyārat

The word *'Ziyārat'* is derived from the word "*zawr*" which means to

10 Ibn Qūlawayh, *Kāmil al-Ziyārāt*, p. 274

11 *Ibid.*

12 Ibid., p.333

deflect or draw away from something. A lie is called *zūr* because it deflects from the path of truth. The *zā'ir* is known to be so, because he deflects from other than "the one he intends to visit". That is why some lexicographers translate "*Ziyārat*" to mean intention *(qaṣd)*, for the one who deflects from other than a certain entity intends the entity. Al-Fayūmī, a well-known lexicographer in his authoritative lexicon *al-Miṣbāḥ al-Munīr* says:

و(الزِّيَارَةُ) فِي الْعُرْفِ قَصْدُ الْمَزُورِ اِكْرَامًا لَهُ
وَاسْتِئْنَاسًا بِهِ

> The conventional meaning of *al-Ziyārat* is to intend the one to be visited, for his veneration and intimacy.[13]

And it is said that the reason why *Ziyārat* is referred to as visiting the saintly human beings, is because it is to deflect from the material routine and draw away from the corporeal world and incline towards the world of spirit, while one is present in the corporeal environment and maintains one's bodily form.[14]

Sometimes *Ziyārat* is translated as *'ittiḥād al-zā'ir bi-al mazūr'* (the unity of the visitor with the visited one). In simpler words: 'to color oneself with the attributes of the visited one'. This definition does not contradict the former definitions, for 'seeking and uniting with the attributes of the *mazūr* (visited one)' is nothing but 'deflecting and drawing away from attributes contrary to the *mazūr*'. In a subtler expression, we can say '*Ziyārat* is to flee from imperfection while struggling for perfection'.[15]

Allusions of this reality can also be gotten from the Qur'ānic verse:

---

13 Aḥmad al-Fayūmī, *al-Miṣbāḥ al-Munīr*, p. 136

14 Āyatullah Jawādī Amulī, *Adabe Fināye Muqarribān*, v.1, p. 23

15 It is important to note that fleeing from imperfection is the same as fleeing towards perfection.

'*And flee towards Allāh*' (51:50). Imām al-Ṣādiq عليه السلام is reported[16] to have commented on this verse saying "*ay ḥujjū*" (It means 'perform *ḥajj*'). And the literal meaning of *ḥajj* is *qaṣd* (intention). In a conversation he had with his son Zayd bin 'Alī, Imām Zayn al-'Ābidīn عليه السلام says:

> وَمَعْنَى قَوْلِهِ عَزَّ وَجَلَّ: ﴿فَفِرُّوا إِلَى اللَّهِ﴾ يَعْنِي حُجُّوا إِلى بَيْتِ اللَّهِ، يَا بُنَيَّ إِنَّ الْكَعْبَةَ بَيْتُ اللَّهِ فَمَنْ حَجَّ بَيْتَ اللَّهِ فَقَدْ قَصَدَ إِلى اللَّهِ...
>
> And the meaning of Allāh's speech "*And flee to Allāh...*" is *Ḥujjū ilā baytillāh* (Intend the house of Allāh); O my dear young son, surely the Ka'ba is the house of Allāh; therefore, whosoever intends the house of Allāh, has surely intended Allāh...[17]

Therefore *ḥajj*, as it is correctly conveyed, is not only '*ḥajju bayt Allāh al-Ḥarām*' (intending the sacred House of Allāh), but *ḥajj Allāh* (intending Allāh) as the verse explicitly conveys: *fa firrū ila Allāh* (so escape towards Allāh). And escaping towards Allāh is seeking His noble attributes and fleeing from the contrary. And *ḥajj* if perfomed with its proper etiquettes, as the experts of the kernel of Islamic law mention, enables one to attain such noble attributes.

Some narrations explicitly say that doing *Ziyārat* of the Holy Prophet صلى الله عليه وآله وسلم and the infallible Imāms عليهم السلام is like doing the *Ziyārat* of Allāh. Consider the following traditions:

> عَنْ زَيْدِ الشَّحَّامُ قَالَ: قُلْتُ لأَبِي عَبْدِ اللَّهِ عليه السلام: مَا لِمَنْ زَارَ رَسُولَ اللَّهِ صلى الله عليه وآله وسلم؟ قَالَ: كَمَنْ زَارَ اللَّهَ

16 'Allāma al-Ṭabrasī, *Tafsīr Majma' al-Bayān*, v.9, p. 268

17 'Allāma al-Majlisī, *Biḥār al-Anwār*, v.3, p. 321

عَزَّ وَجَلَّ فَوْقَ عَرْشِهِ . . .

Zayd al-Shaḥḥām is reported to have said: I asked Abū ʻAbdilāh (al-Ṣādiq ﵇): What is the reward for one who visits the Messenger of Allāh? The Imām ﵇ said: ʻIt is like one who has visited Allāh at His throne (*ʻarsh*).ʼ[18]

عَنْ زَيْدٍ الشَّحَّامِ، عَنْ اَبِيْ عَبْدِ اللهِ ﵇ قَالَ: مَنْ زَارَ قَبْرَ الْحُسَيْنِ بْنِ عَلِيٍّ ﵇ عَارِفًا بِحَقِّهِ كَانَ كَمَنْ زَارَ اللهَ فِيْ عَرْشِهِ . . .

Zayd al-Shaḥḥām is reported to have said: Abū ʻAbdillāh (al-Ṣādiq ﵇) said: Whosoever visits the grave of al-Ḥusayn ﵇ with the knowledge of his status is like one who visits Allāh at His Throne.[19]

عَنْ جَابِرٍ اَلْجُعْفِيِّ، قَالَ: دَخَلْتُ عَلَى جَعْفَرِ بْنِ مُحَمَّدٍ ﵇ فِيْ يَوْمِ عَاشُوْرَآء، فَقَالَ لِيْ: هَؤُلَاءِ زُوَّارُ اللهِ وَحَقٌّ عَلَى الْمَزُوْرِ اَنْ يُكْرِمَ الزَّائِرَ . . .

Jābir al-Juʻfī is reported to have said: I came to Jaʻfar bin Muḥammad (al-Ṣādiq ﵇) on the day of ʻĀshurāʼ, and he said to me: ʻThese people are the visitors of Allāh (*zuwwār Allāh*), and it is the right of the *mazūr* to honor the *zāʼir*...[20]

The above traditons confer the implication that because the Imāms (عليهم السلام)

18 Shaykh al-Kulaynī, *Al-Kāfī*, v.4, p. 585. It should be noted here that ʻthroneʼ does not refer to the material throne for Almighty Allāh is greater than such limitations.

19 Ibn Qūlwayh, *Kāmil al-Ziyārāt*, p. 324

20 *Ibid.*

are manifestations of Allāh's sublime names,[21] visiting them and seeking their proximity is the same as seeking the proximity of Almighty Allāh. Proximity here, we should understand, does not refer to any kind of physical closeness. Rather, it refers to spiritual proximity. In other words, as the *zā'ir* (one who deflects from other than the attributes of the *mazūr*) draws spiritually closer to the Imām عليه السلام he in reality embellishes himself with the attributes of Almighty Allāh which the Imām عليه السلام exemplifies according to his *limitations*. The Imāms عليهم السلام, however, are sheer manifestations (*maẓāhir*) of Allāh's names and thus no attribute independently belongs to other than Allāh. The Holy Qur'ān says:

﴿اَللّٰهُ لاَ إِلَهَ إِلاَّ هُوَ لَهُ الأَسْمَآءُ الحُسْنَى﴾

> Allāh, other than Him there is no God; and to Him alone belong the Beautiful Names...(20:8)

Notice here that instead of Allāh saying 'The Beautiful Names belong to Allāh' He says 'To Him alone belong the Beautiful Names'. In grammatical terminology, the predicate is brought before the subject. And whenever this happens, it signifies restriction. In other words 'To Him alone [and no one else] belong the Beautiful Names'.

Those who are able to appreciate the secrets of prayer tangibly comprehend this reality in the state of *rukū'* when they vision that no one other than Almighty Allāh has any perfection whatsoever. Imām Khumaynī in his Etiquettes of Prayer says:

اِعْلَمْ اَنَّ عُمْدَةَ اَحْوَالِ الصَّلاَةِ ثَلاَثَةٌ، وَسَائِرُ
الاَعْمَالِ وَالاَفْعَالِ مُقَدِّمَاتُهَا وَمُهَيِّئَاتٌ لَهَا، الاَوَّلُ:
اَلْقِيَامُ. وَالثَّانِيْ: اَلرُّكُوعُ. اَلثَّالِثُ: السُّجُوْدُ. وَاَهْلُ

---

21 A reference to the tradition of Imām al-Ṣādiq عليه السلام: *Naḥnu al-Asmā' al-Ḥusnā* 'We are the Most Beautiful Names of Allāh.'

الْمَعْرِفَةِ يَرَوْنَ هَذِهِ الثَّلاَثَةَ إِشَارَةً إِلى التَّوْحِيْدَاتِ الثَّلاَثَةِ. . .وَفِي الرُّكُوْعِ تَرْكٌ لِرُؤْيَةِ النَّفْسِ عَلى حَسَبِ مَقَامِ الصِّفَاتِ وَالاَسْمَاءِ وَرُؤْيَةِ لِمَقَامِ اَسْمَاءِ الْحَقِّ وَصِفَاتِه

Beware that the main states of prayer are three, and the rest of the acts serve as introductory and preparatory phases: (1) *qiyām*, (2) *rukū'*, and (3) *sujūd*. And the men of gnosis reckon these three acts as the three kinds of unity...and in the state of *rukū'* one cannot behold himself in terms of attributes and names, and beholds God's exclusive station of Names and Attributes. [In other words, he sees that every kind of attribute or name belongs only to God].[22]

Ziyārat of Believers

Islam highly encourages one to visit one's Muslim brother or sister. However, it does not emphasize on any kind of *Ziyārat* whatsoever. It encourages meaningful *Ziyārat* - *Ziyārat* with a purpose and aim. Observe the following traditions:

Imām al-Ṣādiq عليه السلام is reported to have said:

قَالَ تَزَاوَرُوا فَإِنَّ فِي زِيَارَتِكُمْ إِحْيَاءً لِقُلُوبِكُمْ وَذِكْراً لأَحَادِيثِنَا وَأَحَادِيثُنَا تُعَطِّفُ بَعْضَكُمْ عَلَى بَعْضٍ فَإِنْ أَخَذْتُمْ بِهَا رَشَدْتُمْ وَنَجَوْتُمْ وَإِنْ تَرَكْتُمُوهَا ضَلَلْتُمْ وَهَلَكْتُمْ فَخُذُوا بِهَا وَأَنَا

22 Imām Khumaynī, *al-Ādāb al-Ma'nawiyya li al-Ṣalāt*, p. 523

بِنَجَاتِكُمْ زَعِيمٌ

> Visit one another, for verily in your visitation is the revival of your hearts, and a remembrance of our speeches; our speeches make you harbor affection for one another; and if you act according to them, you would be guided and saved, and if you shun them, you would go astray and perish; therefore follow them while I guarantee your salvation.[23]

And Imām al-Bāqir عليه السلام is reported to have said:

تَزَاوَرُوا فِي بُيُوتِكُمْ فَإِنَّ ذَلِكَ حَيَاةٌ لِأَمْرِنَا رَحِمَ اللَّهُ عَبْداً أَحْيَا أَمْرَنَا

> Visit one another in your homes for surely in that is the revival of our affair; may Allāh's Mercy be upon one who revives our affair.[24]

It should be noted that the revival of the affair discussed in the above traditions is nothing but the revival of Islamic values, for the Ahl al-Bayt عليهم السلام are protectors of Islamic values and to remember them and their teachings is to elevate the human spirit in reality. One should not conjecture that there is any personal gain that these infallible leaders of truth derive from such gatherings. Rather it is their followers who benefit.

Another important point to bear in mind is that 'the revival of their affair' cannot be merely achieved by thoughts and words. We must sow the seeds of resolution in our visitations in order to reap the fruits of applying the teachings of the Ahl al-Bayt عليهم السلام.

So far *Ziyārat* has been reduced to visitation in the earthly abode. The

---

23 ʿAllāma al-Majlisī, *Biḥār al-Anwār*, v. 17, p. 258

24 Ibid., v. 17, p. 352

Islamic worldview, however, due its sharp and accurate cognition of reality, as taught by the Holy Qur'ān, the Holy Prophet ﷺ and his infallible successors, does not limit *Ziyārat* to the corporeal world. It rather believes that human beings can communicate with those who have transcended this limited world of matter and can listen to them as well. In our daily prayer, we address the Holy Prophet ﷺ as follows:

أَلسَّلاَمُ عَلَيْكَ أَيُّهَا النَّبِيُّ وَرَحْمَةُ اللّٰهِ وَبَرَكَاتُهُ

> Peace be unto you O Prophet and may Allāh's mercy and blessings be on you.[25]

This statement presumes the presence of the *mukhāṭab* (the addressee). And therefore we believe that the Prophet ﷺ is present and can behold our presence too.

One of the important etiquettes of entering the shrine of the Holy Prophet ﷺ and the infallible Imāms of the Ahl al-Bayt عليهم السلام is to read the well-known *idhn al-dukhūl* (recital of permission to enter). The *zā'ir* (visitor) adopts a very humble attitude, and appreciating the presence of the Holy Prophet ﷺ seeks his permission to enter his sanctuary. In this well-known recital, we say:

. . . وَاَعْلَمُ اَنَّ رَسُولَكَ وَخُلَفَائَكَ عليهم السلام اَحيَاء عندك
يُرزَقُونَ، يَرُونَ مَقَامِي وَيَسْمَعُونَ كَلاَمِي،
وَيَرُدُّونَ سَلاَمِي. . .

> ...and I know that Your Apostle and vicegerents (upon whom be peace) are alive, receiving sustenance in Your proximity, they see where I stand presently, and hear my speech and respond to my

25 Ayatullāh al-Sīstānī, *Minhāj al-Ṣāliḥīn*, v.1, p. 226

salutation...[26]

Unlike those who consider the human being as an entity which perishes after the worldly death, Islām teaches mankind that death is a purgatory and bridge to the realm beyond. In fact, to be more accurate, death is "tearing of some veils" from the higher reality of every thing. Great people like Imām ʿAlī عليه السلام, due to their intense purity, could boldly claim that they can behold the ultimate form of the reality of this world while they still exist in this earthly abode. In one of his famous dictums, Imām ʿAlī عليه السلام is reported to have said:

لَوْ كُشِفَ الغطاء مَا ازْدَدْتُ يقينًا

> If the curtains were unveiled nothing would be added to my conviction.[27]

The tearing of veils, however, should not be considered as being limited to the Prophets عليهم السلام and infallible Imāms عليهم السلام. Those human beings who are entirely submissive to the laws of Almighty Allāh and have purified their hearts can also relatively enjoy such exalted positions. In fact, Almighty Allāh calls the human beings to appreciate the kernel of this world in the following verse:

﴿أَوَلَمْ يَنْظُرُوا فِي مَلَكُوتِ السَّماوات وَالأرْضِ﴾

> And do they not look into the kernel of the heavens and the earth? (7:185)

Hence there is an invitation to tear the veils that we have created for ourselves by sinning. In another interesting dictum of the Holy Prophet صلى الله عليه وآله we are told:

---

26 Shaykh ʿAbbās Qummī, *Mafātīḥ al-Jinān*, new ed., p. 380

27 ʿAllāma al-Majlisī, *Biḥār al-Anwār*, v. 40, p. 153

لَوْلا أنَّ الشَّياطِينَ يَحُومُونَ عَلَى قُلُوبِ بَنِي آدَمَ
لَنَظَرُوا إلَى مَلَكُوتِ السَّماوَاتِ

Was it not for the Satans circling around the hearts of the off-spring of Adam, they surely would have beheld the kernel of the heavens.[28]

Therefore, the more purity we enjoy, the better we can communicate with those exalted spirits who have left this material world, are alive in the real sense of the word, and due to their exalted station of existential mediation (about which we shall soon discuss in detail) can influence the world of contingent existence and even benefit us in different ways. There have been ample narratives indicating how people visited the shrines of the Ahl al-Bayt ﻋﻠﻴﻬﻢ السلام and solved very great problems in their lives.

Our aim of *Ziyārat*, however, must transcend seeking personal benefits. It is therefore important to first decipher the purpose of *Ziyārat*, and the reason why our holy Imāms ﻋﻠﻴﻬﻢ السلام would teach us particular recitals for visiting the tomb of their grandfather Imām al-Ḥusayn عليه السلام. Of course this does not mean that one should not seek personal benefits from the great personalities, but one must at least have realized the ultimate purpose of *Ziyārat*. It is through such realization, dear readers, that rain falls from the hearts and embraces every human being, rather every creature beyond time and place. Such realizations tear the veils of the past and future, and release the human being into the world of perpetual bliss and ecstasy. Soon the reader shall understand the words of this nondescript, for the world of Ahl al-Bayt ﻋﻠﻴﻬﻢ السلام is a world yet unknown. Their followers have no share save appreciating the tip of the iceberg:

Imām ʿAlī عليه السلام is reported to have said to Abū Dharr:

28 ʿAllāma al-Majlisī, *Biḥār al-Anwār*, v. 6, p. 332

اعْلَمْ يَا أَبَا ذَرٍّ أَنَا عَبْدُ اللَّهِ عَزَّ وَجَلَّ وَخَلِيفَتُهُ عَلَى عِبَادِهِ لا تَجْعَلُونَا أَرْبَاباً وَقُولُوا فِي فَضْلِنَا مَا شِئْتُمْ فَإِنَّكُمْ لا تَبْلُغُونَ كُنْهَ مَا فِينَا وَلا نِهَايَتَهُ

Know O Abū Dharr that I am [only] a slave of Allāh and His vicegerent over His servants; do not consider us as lords and you may say whatever you want about our merits, for you cannot appreciate the essence of our perfection, nor its zenith...[29]

And in another tradition he ﷺ is reported to have said:

لا يُقَاسُ بِآلِ مُحَمَّدٍ ﷺ مِنْ هَذِهِ الأُمَّةِ أَحَدٌ

...None from this *umma* can be compared with the progeny of Muḥammad (upon whom be peace)...[30]

The Purpose of Ziyārat

One of the fundamental requisites of understanding the purpose of *Ziyārat* is to have a correct worldview. If we realize the purpose of human creation, and submit our volition to our intellectual decision, our deeds would be directed towards our eternal salvation. The purpose of human creation according to Qur'ān and Sunna is to worship Almighty Allāh:

﴿وَمَا خَلَقْتُ الْجِنَّ وَالإِنْسَ إِلاَّ لِيَعْبُدُونِ﴾

And I have not created the jinn and the men save that they worship me alone. (51:56)

And worship without knowledge carries no meaning. This is because

29 Ibid., v. 62, p. 7

30 *Ibid.*, v. 32, p.11 7

worship is not a mere exercise without any sense of devotion. *'Ibādah* in the literal sense is defined as:

العِبَادَةُ هِيَ نَصبُ الْعَبْدِ نَفْسَهُ فِي مَقَامِ الْمَمْلُوكِيَّة لِرَبِّهِ

> *'Ibāda* is when the servant places himself in the position of being a bondsman of his Lord.[31]

And this cannot transpire without the knowledge of the Creator. It is by appreciating His real ownership[32] of the entire world of creation, His knowledge over all things, His omnipotence and omnipresence that the human being is overtaken and humbles himself down before Allāh. He also realizes that the true Lord and Master is none but his Creator, and thus he places himself in the station of being an obedient slave of Almighty Allāh. Imām al-Ḥusayn عليه السلام, underlining the clear link between knowledge and worship is reported to have said:

إِنَّ اللَّهَ جَلَّ ذِكْرُهُ مَا خَلَقَ الْعِبَادَ إِلاَّ لِيَعْرِفُوهُ فَإِذَا عَرَفُوهُ عَبَدُوهُ فَإِذَا عَبَدُوهُ اسْتَغْنَوْا بِعِبَادَتِهِ عَنْ عِبَادَةِ مَا سِوَاهُ...

> Surely Allāh ﷻ did not Create His servants except for knowing Him, and when they know him, they would worship Him, and when they worship Him, it would suffice them from worshipping other than Him...[34]

---

31 ʿAllāma al-Ṭabāṭabā'ī, *Tafsīr Al-Mīzān*, v.1, p.24

32 Readers must differentiate between real ownership in which the existence and subsistence of an entity is entirely dependent on the owner, and legal ownership in which the existence and subsistence of a property is independent of the owner.

34 ʿAllāma al-Majlisī, *Biḥār al-Anwār*, v.23, p.83

The worship that results from prior knowledge reaps knowledge itself. Knowledge before worship, however, is mostly intellectual (*ʿaqlī*) and conceptual (*taṣawwurī*). It is the result of rationally establishing the existence of God and His attributes as well as the utter poverty and dependence of the entire creation on His infinite existence. Having realized this the impartial servant worships with veneration and awe. If such worship was out of sincerity, then he is availed with a higher form of knowledge, which is beyond the realm of intellect. It is known in the language of traditions as '*yaqīn* (conviction)' and 'the vision of the heart' which is knowledge by presence (*al-ʿilm al-ḥuḍūrī*). Perhaps the following verse of the Qurʾān alludes to the close link between worship and conviction:

﴿وَاعْبُدْ رَبَّكَ حَتَّى يَأْتِيَكَ الْيَقِينُ﴾

> And worship your Lord so that conviction comes to you[35]

In some of the *ziyārāt* taught to us by the infallible Imāms عليهم السلام we are taught to address the Imāms declaring that they had attained the exalted station of *yaqīn* through sincere worship. Consider the following examples:

1. In one of the *ziyārāt* of the Holy Prophet ﷺ we are taught by Imām ʿAlī عليه السلام to address his noble being as follows:

. . . وَأَشْهَدُ أَنَّكَ قَدْ نَصَحْتَ لأُمَّتِكَ، وَجَاهَدْتَ فِي
سَبِيلِ رَبِّكَ، وَعَبَدْتَهُ حَتَّى أَتَاكَ الْيَقِينُ . . .

> ...And I bear witness that you gave counsel to your nation and struggled in the way of your Lord, and worshipped Him until conviction (*al-yaqīn*) came to

35 Holy Qurʾān, 15:99

you...[36]

2. In another *Ziyārat* we address Imām al-Ḥusayn ﷺ as follows:

. . . يَا أَبَا عَبْدِ اللهِ أَشْهَدُ أَنَّكَ قَدْ بَلَّغْتَ عَنِ اللهِ

عَزَّوَجَلَّ مَا أُمِرْتَ بِهِ وَلَمْ تَخْشَ أَحَدًا غَيْرَهُ

وَجَاهَدْتَ فِيْ سَبِيْلِهِ وَعَبَدْتَهُ صَادِقًا حَتَّى أَتَاكَ

الْيَقِيْنُ . . .

...O Abā 'Abdillāh, I bear witness that surely you conveyed what you were ordered by Allāh (the Invincible and Majestic) and other than Him you never feared anyone, and you struggled in His way, and worshipped Him truthfully until conviction (*al-yaqīn*) came to you...[37]

3. In one of the *ziyārāt* of Imām al-Riḍā ﷺ we are taught to address him as follows:

. . . أَشْهَدُ أَنَّكَ قَدْ أَقَمْتَ الصَّلاةَ وَآتَيْتَ الزَّكَاةَ

وَأَمَرْتَ بِالْمَعْرُوْفِ وَنَهَيْتَ عَنِ الْمُنْكَرِ وَعَبَدْتَ

اللهَ مُخْلِصًا حَتَّى أَتَاكَ الْيَقِيْنُ، السَّلامُ عَلَيْكَ يَا أَبَا

الْحَسَنِ . . .

...I bear witness that you kept prayer upright and gave the poor tax and invited to what was good and forbade the evil and worshipped Allāh sincerely until conviction (*al-yaqīn*) came to you; peace be

---

36 al-Ḥimyarī al-Qummī, *Qurb al-Isnād*, p. 382

37 Shaykh al-Kulaynī, *al-Kāfī*, v.4, p. 573

upon you O Abā al-Ḥasan...[38]

There are stages of *yaqīn.* The *yaqīn* spoken about in the above traditions is beyond the comprehension of the likes of me and you. Obviously it is a level of knowledge by presence, but beyond our description.

Having realized the fundamental role of sincere worship, our *ziyārāt,* which also rank among acts of worship, should serve as catalysts to earn the exalted station of appreciating the truth by the vision of the heart. Such a state is only possible for a person who is utterly submissive to Allāh. The *Ziyārat* therefore should teach the *zā'ir* the lesson of utter submisssion to Allāh. In other words, the *Ziyārat* should be a means of uniting the *zā'ir* with Abū ʿAbdillāh (an appellation depicting Imām al-Ḥusayn عليه السلام's utter submission to Allāh). And this can easily be attained after we understand the meaning of the *Ziyārat* and exemplify its teachings in ourselves. If we read the *Ziyārat* for our lower ambitions in life, there would be no difference between us and the laity who have busied themselves with the world of matter. Therefore we should bear an exalted aspiration and aim for a great transformation in order to unite with the spirit of al-Ḥusayn عليه السلام.

Readers do appreciate that the reason why the allies of contemporary formalists hamper us from expressing our sorrow near the graves of the infallible leaders, is because they have realized the revolution it can create in the hearts.

Imām al-Ḥusayn عليه السلام is a symbol of uprising against falsehood even at the cost of the sacrifice of every possession. Our *Ziyārat* which is an endeavor of unity and harmony with his noble spirit, therefore, should be a declaration of readiness rather than a mere transaction or habitual recitation.

---

38 Shaykh al-Ṣadūq, *'Uyūn Akhbār al-Riḍā* عليه السلام, v.1, p. 302

Introduction

By Shaykh Abbas M H Ismail

Ziyārat: External Proof

The Holy Qur'ān is clear in its explication of the reason for which the jinns and humans were created: to worship Allah[1] ﷻ which can only be done with any real quality after we come to know Him.[2] Our fundamental aim is thus inextricably linked to gaining gnosis of Him. This task is by no means a simple one as the Qur'ān clearly states that He is incomparable to any thing we may already know, and therefore unknowable in His entirety.[3]

But far from being an oppressive ruler over His subjects and setting them a task doomed to failure, Allāh ﷻ desires that humans fulfil their potential and attain salvation by achieving closeness to Him. He has therefore, through His undiminishing mercy, granted His servants access to numerous avenues to be able to reach at least some level of gnosis:

﴿يَا أَيُّهَا الَّذِينَ آمَنُوا اتَّقُوا اللَّهَ وَابْتَغُوا إِلَيْهِ الْوَسِيلَةَ
وَجَاهِدُوا فِي سَبِيلِهِ لَعَلَّكُمْ تُفْلِحُونَ﴾

O you who believe! Be mindful (of your duty) to

1 Holy Qur'ān, 51:56
2 Al-Ṣadūq, *'Ilal al-Shara'i*
3 Holy Qur'ān, 42:11

> Allāh and seek means of nearness to Him, and struggle in His way, so that you may be successful.[4]

Of these avenues and means, the most effective is to seek the intercession and guidance of the Fourteen Infallibles and to obey them.[5] The Qur'ān mentions that by obeying the Messenger, one would have thereby followed Allāh ﷻ.[6] The same applies when considering the family of the Prophet, the Ahl al-Bayt ﷺ, whose obedience may also be included in the category of being a valid act of servitude to Allāh ﷻ.[7] By this argument, the seemingly difficult duty upon the shoulders of humans at first consideration, i.e. the worship of Allāh ﷻ through His gnosis, is made somewhat manageable by the adherence of humans to the obedience and love of the Prophet ﷺ and his holy family, the Ahl al-Bayt ﷺ; by loving and obeying the Prophet and his family, humans are fulfilling both a Qur'ānic injunction of seeking a means to the nearness of Allāh ﷻ, as well as correctly identifying this means as being none other than the Fourteen Infallibles.

Ziyārat: An Internal Inclination

Allāh ﷻ has created the human with an innately ordained disposition towards goodness,[8] known as *fiṭrah* in Arabic.[9] This *fiṭrah*, even whilst confined to the realm of the corporeal world, continuously yearns and seeks goodness and is instinctively attracted and naturally inclined to honouring and respecting those instances of goodness it perceives, whether the acts are current and live, or have happened in the past and belong to legends of history, such as members of the Ahl al-Bayt ﷺ.[10]

Therefore, through both external instruction via the Qur'ān and the

---

4 Ibid. 5:35
5 M. Ṭahrīrī, *Simaye Mukhbitin,* Mishkat, Tehran, 2000, pp.13-14
6 Holy Qur'ān, 4:80
7 Ibid. 42:23, 33:33
8 J. Amoli, *Adab e Finaye Muqarraban*, Isra, Qum, 2002, p.55
9 Holy Qur'ān, 30:30
10 J. Amoli, *Adab e Finaye Muqarraban*, Isra, Qum, 2002, p.18

lives of the Infallibles, and through the internal proof, the *fiṭrah,* the connection with the Ahl al-Bayt ﷺ is a fundamental part of human existence and assists to fulfil an inherent metaphysical need within us of seeking closeness to Allah through noble characteristics perceived in extra-ordinary personalities.

Ziyārat and a Link to *Ḥajj*

When describing the Islamic forms of worship two terms are often used: *'Ibādah* and *Dhiyāfah.* The term *'Ibādah* generally relates to the outer, jurisprudential nature of our acts of worship whilst *Dhiyāfah* can often refer to the inner, spiritual dimensions.[11] As an example, our Ramaḍān supplications, (our *'Ibādah)* seek for Allāh ﷻ to grant us the chance to perform the Ḥajj pilgrimage, *"... In this year and every year ..."*[12] The Ḥajj, which is the resulting *Dhiyāfah* at Allāh ﷻ's house in Makkah, actually takes place three months later in the month of Dhu al-Ḥijjah.

A close consideration of this will demonstrate that Allāh ﷻ's initial pleasure was for us to ask of Him in Ramaḍān to grant us Ḥajj. In prescribing to us what our supplications should be in Ramaḍān through set prayers, Allāh ﷻ enables His to become aware of what his Master has to offer. The Wise Lord, in commanding His subjects to ask of Him, is able to show us the magnanimity of His banquet and the lofty aspirations we may have of Him. Thus, every subsequent supplication of the servant will improve as he is now aware of what the Host of hosts can grant to him and these two elements become inseparable – i.e. each instance of seeking is accompanied by a higher level of giving, and thus the circle continues between Master and slave. This may be the true meaning behind this excerpt of Du'ā al Iftitā:

وَ لاَ يزيده كثرة العطاء إلاَّ جوداً وَ كرماً

And His excessive giving does not increase in Him,

11 J. Amoli, *Sahbaye Safa,* Mashar, 2001, p.26
12 A. Qummī, *Mafātīḥ al-Jinān*

> except (from the point of view of) generosity and kindness.[13]

When considering the *Ziyārat* of the Infallibles, a similar conclusion seems to hold true. The Infallibles, through their positions as intermediaries and avenues between Allāh ﷻ and His subjects, are able to encourage the elevation of people's wants and desires beyond mere material wishes. Just as Allāh ﷻ has a banquet He wishes to share, so too the Infallibles; their banquet is to assist humans to reach levels of divine proximity.

The importance and weight of this is adequately portrayed in some of the legal opinions expressed by eminent Muslim jurists of previous generations. Both ʿAllāmah Ḥillī and Sheikh Ṭūsī have been cited as having declared it to be compulsory for Ḥajj pilgrims to perform the *Ziyārat* of the Holy Prophet in Medina, and have even permitted the Islāmic ruler to force people to do so if they do not perform the *Ziyārat* of their own volition.[14] The Holy Prophet has declared:

من أتى مكة حاجاً و لم يزرني إلى المدينة جفاني

> Whoseover comes to Makkah as a Ḥajj pilgrim and does not visit me in Medina has shunned me.[15]

Such is the importance placed upon *Ziyārat* that even after performing the rites of Ḥajj and after seeking proximity to Allāh ﷻ in Makkah, ʿArafah, Muzdalifa and Mina, the pilgrim is still expected to pay respects to the Holy Prophet. This is a view common in both Shīʿa and Sunni sources.[16]

Walāyah* and *Ziyārat

Al-Kulaynī reports in al-Kāfī from Imām al-Bāqir عليه السلام:

13 Ibid.
14 J. Amoli, *Adab e Finaye Muqarraban*, Isra, Qum, 2002, p.32
15 M. Najafi, *Jawahir al-Kalam*, volume 20
16 See A. Amini, *al-Ghadīr,* volume 5

عَنْ أَبِي جَعْفَر قَالَ بُنِيَ الإِسْلامُ عَلَى خَمْسٍ عَلَى الصَّلاةِ وَ الزَّكَاةِ وَ الصَّوْمِ وَ الْحَجِّ وَ الْوَلايَةِ وَ لَمْ يُنَادَ بِشَيْءٍ كَمَا نُودِيَ بِالْوَلايَةِ

Islam has been founded upon five: Prayers, Alms-giving, Fasting, Pilgrimage and Walāyah. And nothing has been emphasised the way emphasis has been placed on Walāyah.[17]

The cited hadith suggests that of all the acts of worship, it is the *Walāyah* of Allāh ﷻ, and the Ahl al-Bayt ﻋﻠﻴﻬﻢ ﺍﻟﺴﻼﻡ, that is the most important. Hence one of the most important etiquettes of the act of *Ziyārat* is to establish a firm connection with the visited one. It is at this juncture that our acts may transform from mere *'Ibādah* to something similar to *Dhiyāfah.*

Whilst recognising the host and his kindness it would be foolish not to be cautious of other false hosts and adversaries of the Infallibles. By distancing ourselves from these people, we engage in *Tabarrī,* a pre-requisite to *Tawallī* – seeking closeness to the Infallibles. *Tabarrī* is a key theme among the reliable *ziyarāt* supplications. Ziyārat al-ʿĀshūrāʾ is emphatic upon this point, and urges the reader to seek distance from not only the direct adversaries of the Infallibles that confronted the Infallibles in their lifetimes, but even all previous usurpers and oppressors, spanning generations, and their supporters and partisans.[18] This demonstrates that for our visitation to truely carry the colour of *Walāyah,* the *Walāyah* we profess must be comprehensive and absolute.

The folly of not adhering to this is eloquently portrayed by the Master of eloquence, Amīr al-Muʾminīn, ʿAlī. Al-Majlisī quotes in Biḥār al-Anwār:

17 M. al-Kulaynī, *al-Kāfī*
18 J. Amoli, *Adab e Finaye Muqarraban*, Isra, Qum, 2002, p.62

> إنّ رجلاً قدم على اميرالمؤمنين عليه السلام فقال: يا اميرالمؤمنين! إنّي أُحبّك و أُحبّ فلاناً – و يسمى بعض أعدائه – فقال عليه السلام: أما الآن فأنت أعور فإما أن تعمى و إما أن تبصر
>
> Indeed a man approached Amīr al-Mu'minin عليه السلام and said: "Verily I have love for you and I also love so and so" – and he named one of his (the Imām's) adversaries – he (Imām) replied: "At this moment you are as though you possess one eye (and your vision is incomplete). So either you should choose blindness or complete vision."[19]

In the Imām's words, such a person is incomplete and must address his course of action lest he were to become completely attached to falsehood, thereby becoming utterly lost.

Sincerity and *Ziyārat*

Islāmic ethical discourse stresses the importance of one's intention and sincerity as a defining factor in the classification of the quality of any action. The purer the intention of the actor in performing the act, the more reward and benefit will be gained from that action. In this regard, people are of different grades and qualities. Whilst the outer action may actually seem identical and uniform, the inner realities and benefits may be tremendously different due to the difference in the purity and sincerity of the intention. It is only in the non-corporeal realm where such realities exist in their truest form. The ḥadith reports that comment upon this reality are manifold. We cite one such report to grant light to our discussion:

---

19 M. al-Majlisī, *Biḥār al-Anwār,* volume 27

عن البزنطي قال: قرأت كتاب أبي الحسن الرضا عليه السلام: أبلغ شيعتي أنّ زيارتي تعدل عندالله عزّ و جلّ ألف حجّة. قال: فقلت لأبي جعفر عليه السلام: ألف حجّة؟ قال عليه السلام: إي والله ألف ألف حجّة لمن زاره عارفاً بحقه

Al-Bazanṭī narrates, "I read in the letter of Abū al-Ḥasan al-Riḍā عليه السلام: Tell my Shīʿas that verily the rewards of my Ziyārat, according to Allāh the Mighty and Glorious, is equal to one thousand Ḥajj pilgrimages. So I said to Abū Jaʿfar (Imām al-Jawād) عليه السلام: A thousand Ḥajj pilgrimages? He (as) said to me: Yes, by Allāh! A thousand thousand (a million) Ḥajj pilgrimages for he who performs his Ziyārat whilst understanding his rights."[20]

An Intellectual Spark

The truly balanced servant must however realise the potential granted him by Allāh ﷻ in being able to utilise all the divine bounties and be wary of satanic traps. It may be all too easy for one to assume that sincerity is sufficient; however, if one is simply unaware of the inner realities of wayfaring and its etiquette, then it is possible the intellect is under-utilised and mere sincerity, whilst praiseworthy, will lead to a lesser outcome. The Qur'ān, when describing the Messenger's mission, speaks of both *Tazkiya* (purification) as well as *Ta'līm* (education).[21] Such accuracy in one's intake of education will result in the realisation that each one of the noble acts, *Ṣalāt, Ṣawm, Zakāt, Ḥajj, Walāyah,* has no outer, worldly existence, but rather these entities exist in their truest and most radiant form in the non-corporeal realm. If each of these were

20 M. Majlisi, *Bihar al-Anwar,* volume 99
21 J. Amoli, *Sahbaye Safa,* Mashar, 2001, p.29

to be understood, considered and treated as living entities (albeit in the non-material realm), capable of speech, form and interaction, one's approach to them would surely be of a particularly focused, respectful and determined nature.[22]

Together with these realities, the true realities of the visited ones, i.e. the Infallibles that are the intermediaries for initial receipt and subsequent channeling of divine grace, can not err nor do they suffer any imperfection; and although they exist in their most majestic form as light-ordained celestial beings in another sphere, they are able to influence matters in the physical world through their specially ordained mastership granted by Allāh ﷻ and dependent upon His permission.

Following these principles, a wayfarer can coach and train himself to be mindful and intensely aware of such truths and when he is able to do so he will witness an active manifestation of the Qur'ānic injunction:

﴿وَلِلَّهِ الْمَشْرِقُ وَالْمَغْرِبُ فَأَيْنَمَا تُوَلُّوا فَثَمَّ وَجْهُ اللَّهِ إِنَّ اللَّهَ وَاسِعٌ عَلِيمٌ﴾

> To Allāh belongs the east and the west, so whithersoever way you turn there will be the face of Allāh...[23]

Such an outlook will be truly appreciative of the divine at all times and places.

There is a possibility for the opposite to also become true. The Qur'ān offers a stark warning:

﴿بَلَى مَنْ كَسَبَ سَيِّئَةً وَأَحَاطَتْ بِهِ خَطِيئَتُهُ فَأُولَـٰئِكَ أَصْحَابُ النَّارِ هُمْ فِيهَا خَالِدُونَ﴾

22 Ibid. p.30
23 Holy Qur'ān, 2:115

Indeed whoever does evil and his sins surround him
on every side, such shall be the inmates of the fire,
and they shall remain therein forever.[24]

Such a person will no longer be able to perceive the divine and the 'face
of Allāh', rather his outlook will be satanic and evil: whithersoever this
person may turn he would perceive the face of Shayṭān; evil would
envelop him and he would descend into a spiral of negativity, blocked
senses, narrow mindedness and a skewed sense of reality. It may be that
he is accepting of all things he perceives as utmost truth, or even worse,
he may deny all true things as utter falsehood.[25]

Thus, the individual wayfarer, in seeking a companion, a means, and an
avenue to the Absolute Truth, must be conscious of the choice of whom
he visits and must approach the visitation with a true gnosis and
recognition of the visited one, as well as a heart of sincerity, and thereby
be completely balanced and guided.

Marḥūm Tustari declares:

وتفاوتت التأثيرات بتفاوت المعرفة بحق الامام
الحسين عليه السلام فقد ورد في الروايات التقييد بكونه
عارفا بحق الامام الحسين صلوات الله تعالى عليه

And the difference in the benefits (of the *Ziyārat*) is
due to the difference in the levels of recognition (in
the people reciting the *Ziyārat*) of the rights of
Imām al-Ḥusayn ؏, as the narration mentions the
condition (for benefiting from the *Ziyārat*) is to be
aware of the rights of Imām al-Ḥusayn, blessings of
Allāh, the High, upon him.[26]

---

24 Ibid. 2:81
25 J. Amoli, *Sahbaye Safa*, Mashar, 2001, p.31
26 J. Tustari, *al-Khasais al-Husayniyyah*, p.164

A Mystical Firebrand

Having now realized the intrinsic beneficial nature and the importance of ziyarah it befits the wayfarer and the slave of the visited one to reflect upon the inner meanings of the act of *Ziyārat.* The etymology of the word stems from زور , originally meaning 'to move away' from a thing. Aḥmad Ibn Fāris comments that the term is used to refer to the act of *Ziyārat* because when a person visits another, he has effectively moved his attention away from everyone and everything else to concentrate upon the visited one. Fayumi adds that Ziyārat involves honouring the visited one and making a bond with them.[27] Āyatullāh Jawādī Amolī suggests that the turning away may also be from the material world of bodies and quiddity towards the celestial realm of souls and spirits.[28]

The *Ziyārat* should therefore transport us into a higher level of consciousness and spiritual being. Freedom from the world of matter is essential if we are to reach the heights of our potential. An interesting narration quoted by Marḥūm Tustari encapsulates this:

إنّ من زاره كان كمن زار الله تعالى في عرشه

> Surely one who visits him (Imām al-Ḥusayn) is like one who visits Allāh at His throne.[29]

Tustari's own relfection on this hadith is to conclude that 'visiting Allāh' is an allusion to the intense proximity with Allāh ﷻ, in this instance achieved through the *Ziyārat.* Whereas proximity to Allāh ﷻ can only come about through a polished level of faith and cleanliness of the heart. Hence, the *Ziyārat* of the Martyr of Kerbalā assists and facilitates to complete one's level of faith, and cleanse the heart, resulting ultimately in the intense closeness with Allāh ﷻ.

پیروی رسول حق، دوستی حق آورد

---

27 J. Amoli, *Adab e Finaye Muqarraban*, Isra, Qum, 2002, p.23
28 Ibid.
29 J. Tustari, *al-Khasais al-Husayniyyah,* p.165

پیروی رسول کن، دوستی خدا طلب
شرع، سفینهٔ نجات، آل رسول، ناخداست
ساکن این سفینه شو دامن ناخدا طلب

> Following the Prophet of Truth, brings about the friendship of Truth;
>
> So follow the Prophet, thereby seek the friendship of Truth.
>
> The Shari'ah, is the ship of salvation, the Family of the Prophet, is its captain;
>
> Abide aboard the ship and seek to hold tight to the captain.[30]

Through our closeness with the Ahl al-Bayt ﷵ, we are also able to benefit from some of the grace which they are granted. In Sūra al-Aḥzāb, in one of the most well-known and oft-recited verses of the Qur'ān, Allāh ﷻ declares:

﴿إِنَّ اللّٰهَ وَمَلاَئِكَتَهُ يُصَلُّونَ عَلَى النَّبِيِّ يَاأَيُّهَا الَّذِينَ آمَنُوا صَلُّوا عَلَيْهِ وَسَلِّمُوا تَسْلِيماً﴾

> Indeed Allāh and Angels bless the Prophet; O you who believe! Invoke blessings upon him and and invoke salutations upon him with a worthy salutation.[31]

Perhaps we miss too easily our own potential in reaching such a stage, where Allāh ﷻ and His angels can bless us:

﴿يَاأَيُّهَا الَّذِينَ آمَنُوا اذْكُرُوا اللّٰهَ ذِكْراً كَثِيراً

30 M. F. Kashani, *Diwan e Fayz Kashani*, p.32. The word 'dāman' in Farsi has not been translated literally but rather its contextual meaning (au)
31 Holy Qur'ān, 33:56

وَسَبِّحُوهُ بُكْرَةً وَأَصِيلاً هُوَ الَّذِى يُصَلِّى عَلَيْكُمْ
وَمَلَائِكَتُهُ لِيُخْرِجَكُمْ مِّنَ الظُّلُمَاتِ إِلَى النُّورِ
وَكَانَ بِالْمُؤْمِنِينَ رَحِيماً تَحِيَّتُهُمْ يَوْمَ يَلْقَوْنَهُ سَلَامٌ
وَأَعَدَّ لَهُمْ أَجْراً كَرِيماً﴾

O you who believe! Remember Allāh with frequent remembrance, and glorify Him morning and evening. It is He who sends His blessings to you and so do His angels, that He may bring you out of the darkness into light, and He is Most Merciful to the believers. The day they encounter Him their greeting will be 'Peace', and He holds in store for them a noble reward.[32]

Thus Allāh ﷻ and His angels also bless certain fallible beings – those that have inculcated within themselves a plentiful remembrance. The result of this blessing is that Allāh ﷻ is able to empower them to come forth from darkness into light. As we have seen, the very same effect is true when visiting the Infallibles, who assist in our spiritual migration towards Allāh ﷻ and away from the material world. Because their source is ultimate purity, the Absolute Truth, in calling upon them to provide us with our spiritual guidance we are confident of the veracity and accuracy of the offerings we can obtain from them. Again this points towards *Tabarrī and Tawallī:* ensuring that our hosts are true hosts and truly able to offer us munificence:

﴿فَلْيَنْظُرِ الإِنْسَانُ إِلَى طَعَامِهِ﴾

So let man consider his food.[33]

---

32 Ibid. 33:41-44
33 Ibid. 80:24

Regarding the verse above, Imām al-Ṣadiq عليه السلام has declared that the allegorical meaning of the word food is 'knowledge'. He states:

عِلْمُهُ الَّذي يَأْخُذُهُ عَمَّنْ يَأْخُذُهُ

> It is his knowledge that he acquires – from whom does he acquire it?[34]

By ensuring our source of information and spiritual nourishment is pure, we will be able to avoid spiritual stagnation and prove to be a true instance of leaving the darkness and entering the light.

Ziyārat: The Return Journey from Truth (al-Ḥaq) to Creation (al-Khalq)

According to the commandments from the Holy Threshold (الناحية المقدّسة) of the Ahl al-Bayt عليهم السلام, once this enlightenment is achieved, the journey of the new possessors of light continues onwards towards their fellow human beings. As a recipient and now a guardian of this light, the true servant of the Holy Threshold discharges the duties placed upon him by helping others to emerge from darkness. He becomes the true manifestation as described in Sūra al-Anʿām:

﴿أَوَ مَنْ كَانَ مَيْتاً فَأَحْيَيْنَاهُ وَجَعَلْنَا لَهُ نُوراً يَمْشِي بِهِ فِي النَّاسِ كَمَنْ مَثَلُهُ فِي الظُّلُمَاتِ لَيْسَ بِخَارِجٍ مِنْهَا﴾

> Is he who was lifeless, then we granted him life, and granted him a light by which he walks among people, like one whose likeness is that of one who dwells in manifold darkness which he cannot escape?[35]

34 J. Amoli, *Sahbaye Safa,* Mashar, 2001, p.230 quoted from Safinah al-Bihar
35 Holy Qur'ān, 6:122

Hence the truly enlightened one seeks to offer the light and bounties he receives to others, to help them in their quest for enlightenment, and in this way may become worthy of the epithet of being a servant at the courtyard of the Holy Threshold.

Ziyārat: At the Master's Service

Thus far we have indulged ourselves in seeking from the Infallibles of the Holy Family. There is however a level of servitude and obligation expected of us, which demonstrates the comprehensiveness of Islām – a religion of faith, belief, spirituality **and** action. The Master of the believers describes this relationship in sermon 34 of the Nahj al-Balāgha. He begins by outlining the rights that we enjoy over him which include:

1. He should advise us with sincerity

2. He should collect the monies for the public treasury and spend them according to our needs

3. He should ensure our education so we do not remain ignorant

4. He should nurture us into truly scholarly people

The Imām then mentions the rights he enjoys over us:

1. Loyalty to his allegiance

2. To do *Naṣīḥah* to him in both his presence and absence

3. To answer his call when he calls us

4. To be obedient to his command

The second item in this list is worthy of some deeper contemplation. The word *Naṣīḥah* in this context should not be confused with the common usage of the word which translates to 'advice'. In this instance we are considering the choicest Imām and the truest leader, an Infallible, and the epitome of perfection; so how could advice be given from us to he who is guided by Allāh ﷻ, himself being the Straight Path of salvation?

A closer consideration of the term *al-Naṣīḥah* will reveal that its true meaning is the opposite meaning of غِشّ, a term used to denote any type of dilutedness or taintedness. For example milk that has been mixed with water is referred to as *Maghshush (مغشوش),* from the same root as غشّ. According to this analysis, this would render the meaning of *Naṣīḥah* in this context to its root: freedom from any type of dilutedness or taintedness. This meaning has also been used in the Qur'ān where Allāh ﷻ commands the believers to repent with sincerity. The word used, *Nuṣūḥan,* stems from the same root as *Naṣīḥah:*

﴿يَا أَيُّهَا الَّذِينَ آمَنُوا تُوبُوا إِلَى اللَّهِ تَوْبَةً نَصُوحاً﴾

> O you who believe! Repent to Allāh with sincere repentance![36]

The scholars of ethics have also elaborated the meaning of *Naṣīḥah* to be the opposite of jealousy *(Ḥasad).* This would add a further dimension to the meaning of *Naṣīḥah* to be that someone who truly possesses the trait of *Naṣīḥah* will wish a bounty for his brother believer that will be in his brother's benefit and something that he would wish for himself; and naturally such an act would also need to be free from any form of taintedness.[37] Therefore, offering sincere advice that is open, honest and in the benefit of the one being advised, is only one manifestation of the trait of *Naṣīḥah* and not the entire meaning of the term.

Thus the Imām in this context, by using the word *Naṣīḥah,* regards one of his rights over us as complete sincerity without any form of taintedness. This will apply both in his presence, and equally in his absence. Our conduct in thought, belief and action, should be such that the master whom we are visiting attains confidence that we are truly his, sincerely for him, and utterly devoted to his cause. The following narration may clarify this further:

---

36 Ibid. 66:8

37 J. Amoli, *Adab e Finaye Muqarraban*, Isra, Qum, 2002, p.52

قال رسول الله ﷺ : من يضمن لي خمساً أضمن له الجنّة ... النصيحة لله عز و جل والنصيحة لرسوله والنصيحة لكتاب الله والنصيحة لدين الله والنصيحة لجماعة المسلمين

> The Holy Prophet ﷺ has said, "He who can guarantee me five things, I will guarantee for him Paradise ... *Naṣīḥah* for Allāh The Mighty and The Glorious, and *Naṣīḥah* for His Prophet, and *Naṣīḥah* for the book of Allāh, and *Naṣīḥah* for the religion of Allāh, and *Naṣīḥah* to the Muslim nation."[38]

In the words of the Prophet, Paradise may be earned by someone who is pure, sincere and untainted in his conduct towards Allāh ﷻ, His Prophet, His Book, His Religion and to the Muslim Ummah.

Ziyārat: A Structured Approach to the Meeting Place at the Two Seas[39]

Marḥūm Tustari[40] has elaborated on a series of special timings at which the benefits and rewards of the *Ziyārat* of Imām al-Ḥusayn عليه السلام is particularly enhanced:

1. Every Friday
2. Every Month[41]
3. Twice per year in person for those able to afford
4. Thrice per year, to guarantee freedom from poverty
5. On the happy occasions of Nowruz, Mabʿath, Ghadir and others

38 M. Majlisi, *Bihar al-Anwar,* volume 2

39 An allusion to Holy Qur'ān, 18:60

40 J. Tustari, *al-Khasais al-Husayniyyah,* pp.166-168

41 Tustari quotes Imām al-Sadiq عليه السلام, *"Whosoever performs his Ziyarah (at least) one time per month, will earn the reward of one hundred thousand martyrs like those slain in Badr."*

6. In Rajab:
    a. On the night preceding the first day of Rajab
    b. On the first day of Rajab
    c. On the night preceding the fifteenth day of Rajab
    d. On the fifteenth day of Rajab
7. In Shaʿbān:
    a. On the third day of Shaʿbān
    b. On the night preceding the fifteenth day of Shaʿbān
    c. On the fifteenth day of Shaʿbān
8. In Ramaḍān:
    a. At any time
    b. On the night preceding the first day of Ramaḍān
    c. On the night preceding the fifteenth day of Ramaḍān
    d. On the last night of Ramaḍān
    e. On each of the nights of Qadr and the subsequent days
9. In Dhu al-Ḥijjah:
    a. On the night preceding the day of ʿArafa
    b. On the day of ʿArafa
    c. On the night preceding ʿEid al-Adhā
    d. On the day of ʿEid al-Adhā
    e. On the eleventh, twelfth and thirteenth days of Dhu al-Ḥijjah
    f. On the day of ʿEid al-Ghadīr
10. In Muḥarram:
    a. On the night preceding ʿĀshūrā and on the day of ʿĀshūrā
    b. On the thirteenth day of Muharram
11. In Safar:
    a. On the twentieth day of Safar

These are some of the meritorious times mentioned for the *Ziyārat* of

Imām al-Ḥusayn عليه السلام. However, such an action is praiseworthy and would yield benefits to an attentive and sincere heart at any time.

We beseech the master of martyrs to allow us his visitation and remembrance as long as Allāh سبحانه وتعالى grants us life and as long as time subsists.

Abbas Mohamed Husein Ismail
London
3 December 2008
4 Dhu al-Hijjah 1429

The Source of Ziyārat ʿĀshūrāʾ and Its Authenticity

Ziyārat ʿĀshūrāʾ is a sacred tradition (ḥadīth qudsī) which is authentic and veracious. Its main references are two fundamental works of authority:

1. Miṣbāh al-Mutahajjid by Shaykh al-Ṭūsī
2. Kāmil al-Ziyārāt by Ibn Qūlawayh

All the traditions that narrate this ziyārā are proven by scholars of ḥadīth to be sound and veracious. In order to establish their authenticity, they have discussed all the chains of narration at length and proven the reliability of every narrator. Those interested in understanding the intricacies of the traditions may refer to works written in this regard.[42]

The contemporary venerated jurisconsult, Āyatullāh Sayyid al-Shubayrī al-Zanjānī (may Allah protect his noble spirit) was asked about the authenticity of Ziyārat ʿĀshūrāʾ and he responded saying:

بغض النظر عن التأييدات الغيبية الواردة بطرق معتبرة حول زيارة عاشوراء والتي برأسها دليل على اعتبار هذه الزيارة الشريفة، فإنّ السند المذكور في مصباح المتهجد في ذيل هذه الزيارة سند صحيح.

Disregarding what has been narrated from reliable

42 The contemporary scholar Āyatullāh Jaʿfar Subḥānī has written a separate treatise on establishing the veracity of Ziyārat ʿĀshūrāʾ [http://www.Imāmsadeq.org/book/sub3/rasaeel-va-maghalat-j3/]

> sources about its endorsement from the unseen realm (*al-taʾyīdāt al-ghaybiyya*), which in itself suffices as a proof of the authenticity of this sacred *Ziyārat*, the chain of narration mentioned in *Miṣbāh al-Mutahajjid* after this *Ziyārat* is veracious.[43]

Other Ways of Establishing Authenticity

Apart from the aforesaid, the authenticity of this radiant *Ziyārat* can be established through other methods considered in the science of *ḥadīth*. For example, there are many other *ziyārāt* where expressions similar to those contained in Ziyārat ʿĀshūrāʾ appear. This indirectly endorses the veracity of the *Ziyārat*. Furthermore, much of the information contained in the *Ziyārat* has come in so many of our traditions, some of which are copiously narrated and even rank among the traditions that are successively narrated (*mutawātir*) in terms of meaning at least.

Shaykh Muḥammad al-Sanad, one of the contemporary Shīʿa scholars, when asked about the veracity of the different supplications and *ziyārāt*, including Ziyārat ʿĀshūrāʾ, says:

> ان مضأمين الزيارات والأدعية المدرجة في السؤال لا يقتصر ورود مضمونها على تلك الزيارات والأدعية فهناك العديد من الزيارات الأخرى والأدعية الأخرى بأسانيد أُخرى قريبة المضمون معنىً ولفظاً لقطعات من الأولى، كما أن هذه الزيارات والأدعية قد ورد كثير من مضامينها في الروايات الواردة في المعارف، وهي في كثير من طوائفها مستفيضة بل بعضها متواتر معنوي أو إجمالي، وعلى هذا

43 http://www.alhodacenter.com/ashora/details.php?id=2996

فالدغدغة في أسانيد هذه الزيارة أو تلك أو هذا الدعاء وذاك تنطوي على عدم المام بهذه الحقيقة العلمية المرتبطة بعلم الحديث والرواية

Indeed the contents of the ziyārāt and supplications under question do not only appear in their respective places, but there are a number of other ziyārāt and supplications with other chains of narration, that have similar contents both in word and meaning. Furthermore most of their contents have been narrated in other traditions on Divine Teachings, many of which have been copiously narrated. Rather some of them are also successively narrated (mutawātir) in their meaning and gist. Therefore being worried about the chains of narration of this Ziyārat or that or this supplication or that, is because of disregarding this intellectual reality that pertains to the science of traditions and narrations.[44]

Those, therefore, who persist in doubting the authenticity of the *Ziyārat* overlook the other factors that strongly endorse the *Ziyārat*. The great Shīʿa scholars have always lived with this *Ziyārat* and many of them incessantly recite it with great zeal and humility. Some ignorant people, due to the expression of imprecation contained in the *Ziyārat* try to doubt its authenticity. Such people feel that Islām is a religion of peace and hence such words must not be uttered. In response to them, we say that curse is not any kind of abusive expression. Its reality, as we shall come to learn in the commentary of the *Ziyārat* is to seek the remoteness of the accursed. Such prayer for remoteness, considering its Qur'ānic origin, is nothing but harmony with Allāh's Volition. We shall also learn that cursing those who established the foundation of

44 http://www.rafed.net/research/05/06.html

oppression and evil is also a kind of expression of one's stance against evil. If one tries to reflect carefully, one would understand that the spirit of cursing evil and its epitomes it to flee from imperfection. It is important for us therefore to tear off the veils of the periphery of the *Ziyārat* and touch the center and appreciate the universal message that it confers.

Laʿn and invoking curse is not merely an emotional state of anger that is evanescent. It is a translation of the reality. Therefore whether we invoke curse on them, or not they will always be distanced from the mercy of Allāh ﷻ, due to the seeds of mischief that they had sown in this world.

Seeking the kernel of the curses, we would come to realize that we have parables of Yazīd and Muʿāwiya in our time and age too. If we cursed the Yazīd of a thousand years ago, it was not because of himself per se, but his ideology and actions. The Yazīd of today must be repelled the same way. This is the message of curse.

May the Almighty enable us understand the spirit of the *Ziyārat*, so that we avoid discussing trivial issues that distance us from a sacred effusion that rains down perpetually and requires receptive containers.

The Holy Qurʾān says:

﴿أَنْزَلَ مِنَ السَّمَاءِ مَاءً فَسَالَتْ أَوْدِيَةٌ بِقَدَرِهَا﴾

> He sends down water from the sky whereat the valleys are flooded to [the extent of] their capacity...(13:17)

All Praises Belong to Allāh, the Lord of the Worlds

CHAPTER 1

أَلسَّلَامُ عَلَيْكَ يَا أَبَا عَبْدِ اللهِ

Peace be on you, O entirely obedient
servant of Allāh

أَلسَّلاَمُ عَلَيْكَ يَا أَبَا عَبْدِ اللّٰهِ

Peace be on You, O entirely obedient servant of Allāh

COMMENTARY

أَلسَّلاَمُ عَلَيْكَ

Peace be unto You

Salām is an infinitive noun commonly translated as "peace". Its literal import, however, is:

التَّعَرِّي مِنَ الآفَاتِ الظَّاهِرَةِ وَالْبَاطِنَةِ

> "to be free from calamities, whether apparent or hidden."[1]

Therefore by saying "*Al-salāmu 'alayka*" in its invocative sense, we are seeking the state of freedom from every kind of calamity, whether apparent or hidden, for Imām al-Ḥusayn عليه السلام.

It is clear that the Imām عليه السلام already enjoys the state of *salām* and is in fact one of the manifestations of Allāh's attribute *al-Salām.* In one of the *ziyārāt* when addressing him we say:

﴿أَلسَّلاَمُ عَلَيْكَ يَوْمَ وُلِدْتَ وَيَوْمَ تَمُوتُ وَيَوْمَ تُبْعَثُ حَيًّا، اَشْهَدُ اَنَّكَ حَيٌّ شَهِيدٌ تُرْزَقُ عِنْدَ رَبِّكَ. . . ﴾

---

1 Rāghib al-Iṣfahānī, *al-Mufradāt*, p. 421.

> You were at peace the day you were born, and will be at peace the day you die, and the day you will be raised alive. Surely I bear witness that you are a living martyr receiving sustenance near Your Lord...[3]

Here the phrase '*Al-salāmu 'alayka*' is taken as a declarative statement, and thus the difference of translation. Therefore we bear witness that Imām al-Ḥusayn عليه السلام was and will always remain in the state of *salām*.

In a tradition about the nocturnal ascent (*al-mi'rāj*) of the Holy Prophet ﷺ it is reported that when the Holy Prophet ﷺ encountered a group of Angels, Divine Apostles and Prophets, it was said to him:

يَا مُحَمَّدُ سَلِّمْ عَلَيْهِمْ

> O Muḥammad, convey your salutations to them.

So he ﷺ said:

أَلسَّلامُ عَلَيْكُمْ وَرَحْمَةُ اللَّهِ وَبَرَكَاتُهُ

> May the peace of Allāh, His mercy and His blessings be upon you

Thereupon Allāh revealed unto him:

أَلسَّلامُ وَالتَّحِيَّةُ وَالرَّحْمَةُ وَالْبَرَكَاتُ أَنْتَ وَذُرِّيَّتُكَ

> "Peace, benedictions, mercy and blessings, are you and your progeny.[4]

Here the Holy Prophet ﷺ and his progeny (*dhurriyya*) are introduced as *"al-salām"*. Hence, seeking *salām* for Imām al-Ḥusayn عليه السلام, would mean seeking higher degrees of the state of *salām* for him, since the

---

3 Ibn Qūlawayh, *Kāmil al-Ziyārāt*, p. 391

4 Shaykh al-Kulaynī, *al-Kāfī*, v.3, p. 486

levels of *salām* in the plane of contingent existence have no end. The level of *salām* in which there is no kind of imperfection whatsoever is that of *al-Salām al-Muṭlaq (the Absolute Peace)*, which solely belongs to Almighty Allāh. The Holy Qur'ān says:

﴿هُوَ اللَّهُ الَّذِي لا إِلهَ إِلا هُوَ الْمَلِكُ الْقُدُّوسُ السَّلامُ الْمُؤْمِنُ الْمُهَيْمِنُ. . .﴾

He is Allāh, other than Whom there is no God, the Sovereign Lord, the Holy One, the Peace [Free from every kind of imperfection], the Securer, the Guardian...(59:23)

Commenting on the Divine Name *al-Salām*, 'Allāma al-Ṭabāṭabā'ī in his *Tafsīr al-Mīzān* says:

وَالسَّلاَمُ مِنْ أَسْمَائِه تَعَالَى لأَنَّ ذَاتَهُ الْمُتَعَالِيَةَ نَفْسُ الْخَيْرِ الَّذِيْ لاَ شَرَّ فِيْه. . .

And *al-Salām* is among His Names, for His Exalted Essence is sheer goodness wherein there is no evil...[5]

And in a tradition, Ḥaḍrat Fāṭima al-Zahrā' ﷺ referring to this kind of *salām* says:

إِنَّ اللهَ هُوَ السَّلاَمُ، وَمِنْهُ السَّلاَمُ، وَإِلَيْهِ السَّلاَمُ .

Surely only Allāh is *the Absolute Peace* and from Him alone comes peace and unto Him alone returns peace[6]

The Holy Prophet ﷺ is reported to have once informed Ḥaḍrat

5 'Allāma al-Ṭabāṭabā'ī, *al-Mizān*, v.10, p.39

6 Shaykh al-Ṭūsī, *al-Amālī*, p. 175

Khadīja عليها السلام that Gabriel was nearby and he sent his *salāms* to her. Thereupon she said:

اَللهُ السَّلاَمُ وَلِلّٰهِ السَّلاَمُ وَعَلىَ جِبْرَائِيلَ السَّلاَمُ .

> Allāh is the Absolute Peace, and to Him alone belongs peace and upon Gabriel be peace.[7]

And since the Absolute Peace loves us, He always invites us to His abode of peace:

﴿وَاللَّهُ يَدْعُو إِلَى دَارِ السَّلاَمِ﴾

And Allāh invites to the abode of peace...(10:24)

The indefinite verb *yad'ū* in the above verse confers the sense of continuity, which means that Allāh constantly invites us towards His abode of peace, which is Paradise. Some commentators however confer a subtler interpretation, and say that Allāh is *al-Salām*, which means that He is free from every kind of imperfection whatsoever. And when He invites us to *Dār al-Salām*, He calls us to the state of freedom from every kind of imperfection whatsoever. His call will remain constant, for the stages of *salām* have no end. In his commentary on the above verse, *al-Baḥrāni* narrates the following tradition:

عَنِ الْعَلاَءِ ابْنِ عَبْدِ الْكَرِيمِ، قَالَ: سَمِعْتُ أَبَا جَعْفَرٍ عليه السلام يَقُولُ فِي قَوْلِ اللهِ عَزَّ وَجَلَّ: وَاللَّهُ يَدْعُوا إِلَى دَارِ السَّلاَمِ، فَقَالَ: إِنَّ السَّلاَمَ، هُوَ اللهُ عَزَّ وَجَلَّ، وَدَارُهُ الَّتِي خَلَقَهَا لأَوْلِيَائِهِ الْجَنَّةُ.

> Al-ʿAlā' bin ʿAbd al-Karīm reports: I heard Abū Jaʿfar al-Bāqir عليه السلام saying about the verse 'And Allāh

7 Al-Maghribī, *Sharḥ al-Akhbār*, v.3, p.21

> calls towards the abode of peace': Indeed *al-Salām* is Allāh, the Invincible and Magnificent, and His abode that He created for His near ones is Paradise.[8]

Al-janna in the above tradition is prefixed with the definite article *'al'* which also confers the connotation of a specific kind of paradise. And since Allāh ﷻ principally always calls towards the best, for his grace pours out infinitely, the loftiest paradise one can ever achieve is *jannat al-liqā'* (the paradise of meeting Allāh). Here the aspirant of paradise yearns for nothing but the proximity and vision of the All-Beloved. And scholars of insight have said that the journey to perfection never ends. Therefore it is very apt to constantly call every one to the abode of the Absolute Peace.

أَلسَّلَامُ عَلَيْكَ

Peace be unto You

The definite article *'al'* in the abovementioned phrase conveys different meanings. It can be taken to allude to something known both to the adressor as well as his addressee.[9] And because it is clear to all that no kind of perfection comes from anyone save Allāh, for He alone is the Principal Cause of the universe, we are only permitted to seek perfection from Him in the independent sense. Therefore if we employ the phrase *al-salāmu 'alayka* in the invocative sense, we can translate it as '*the peace from Allāh be upon you*'. This is when we take the article *al* to refer to the specific peace that comes from Allāh, which is a Divine bestowal and creation. However if we translate *al-salām* in the phrase *al-salāmu 'alayka* as "the specific peace that Allāh possesses", then we are

8 Al-Bāḥrānī, *Al-Burhān fī Tafsīr al-Qur'ān*, v.3, p. 24

9 In Arabic grammar terminology this kind of *al* is known as *al li al-'ahd al-dhihnī*

seeking Absolute Peace for Imām al-Ḥusayn عليه السلام. In other words, we are seeking the ultimate state for the Imām عليه السلام. Seeking such kind of peace is not unprecedented. In the well-known supplication of *al-Saḥar* of the Holy month of Ramaḍān we seek the Divine Names in their perfect form. In fact the innate nature of every human being has been faishioned to aspire for the Infinite.

أَلسَّلاَمُ عَلَيْكَ

You are at peace from my side

If the *zā'ir* however were to consider *'al'* to refer to himself, the above phrase can be taken as declarative. In other words, he is trying to say: سلاَمِيْ عَلَيْكَ *Salāmī 'alayka* (You are at peace from my side)[10]. Consequently, the *zā'ir* is trying to assure the *mazūr* (the visted one) that he is at peace with him and he would not do anything that would cause harm or disturb him. Instead, he would manifest in himself things that would be geared to seek the *mazūr's* protective physical as well as spiritual life. This is one of the very important stations of the *zā'ir*, since he is in fact reasserting his covenant with Almighty Allāh, by informing his beloved Imām عليه السلام that besides avoiding any thing that would cause harm to him عليه السلام, he would do those things that would manifest the spirit of peace as well.

One of the things that does not concur with the spirit of *salām* is to sin. If one utters the above statement and then engages in sin, he will not have maintained the spirit of the *salām* that he uttered. This is because the fourteen infallibles عليهم السلام have the ability to witness the actions of

10 In order to understand this particular kind of usage better, consider verse 19:47 where Prophet Ibrāhīm عليه السلام assures Āzar that he would not harm him. He employs the phrase '*Salāmun 'alaikum....*' Exegetes of Qur'ān well-grounded in the Arabic language, like Qāḍī al-Bayḍāwī in his *Anwār al-Tanzīl wa Asrār al-Ta'wīl* take this view into consideration.

their followers. And when they find them sinning, they get disturbed.

Following are narrations that establish the infallible Imām's ability to vision the deeds of his followers:

1. We humbly express in the well-known *Ziyārat al-Jāmi'a al-Kābīra*:

أَنْتُمُ الصِّرَاطُ الأَقْوَمُ وَشُهَدَاءُ دَارِ الْفَنَاءِ

> ...You are the upright path and **the witnesses of the abode of extinction** [i.e. the world...][11]

2. Imām al-Ṣādiq عليه السلام is reported to have said:

عَنْ أَبِي عَبْدِ اللَّهِ عليه السلام فِي قَوْلِهِ ﴿وَقُلِ اعْمَلُوا فَسَيَرَى اللَّهُ عَمَلَكُمْ وَرَسُولُهُ وَالْمُؤْمِنُونَ﴾ الْمُؤْمِنُونَ هَاهُنَا الأَئِمَّةُ الطَّاهِرَةُ عليهم السلام

> Believers referred to in the verse "And say, go on working: Allāh will see your conduct, and His Apostle *and the believers [as well]*" (9:105) are the Immaculate Imāms عليهم السلام.[12]

Hence the Imāms عليهم السلام can behold our mistakes and wrong deeds, and when they do so, they get upset:

1. Thiqat al-Islām al-Kulaynī narrates the following tradition in his al-Kāfī:

عَنْ سَمَاعَةَ عَنْ أَبِي عَبْدِ اللَّهِ عليه السلام قَالَ سَمِعْتُهُ يَقُولُ

---

11 Shaykh 'Abbās al-Qummī, *Mafātīḥ al-Jinān*, p. 622

12 Allāma al-Majlisi, *Biḥār al-Anwār*, v.23, p. 339. It should be noted that Imām al-Ṣādiq عليه السلام mentions the most perfect extensions (*atamm al-maṣādīq*) of the believers as the Imāms عليهم السلام. Otherwise the verse clearly tells us that one who has really achieved the expected state of belief can enjoy a station which would enable him to see the actions of others.

مَا لَكُمْ تَسُوءُونَ رَسُولَ اللَّهِ ﷺ فَقَالَ رَجُلٌ كَيْفَ نَسُوؤُهُ فَقَالَ أَمَا تَعْلَمُونَ أَنَّ أَعْمَالَكُمْ تُعْرَضُ عَلَيْهِ فَإِذَا رَأَى فِيهَا مَعْصِيَةً سَاءَهُ ذَلِكَ فَلَا تَسُوءُوا رَسُولَ اللَّهِ وَ سُرُّوهُ

Sumā'a reports: I heard him (i.e. Imām al-Ṣādiq عليه السلام) say: What is the matter with you? Why do you displease the Messenger of Allāh ﷺ? Thereupon a man asked him: And how do we displease him? The Imām عليه السلام said: Don't you know that your actions are presented before him; and when he finds a sin in them, he is displeased; therefore do not displease the Messenger of Allāh ﷺ but (rather) make him happy.[13]

2. Al-Kulaynī also narrates the following tradition:

عَنْ عَبْدِ اللَّهِ بْنِ أَبَانٍ الزَّيَّاتِ وَكَانَ مَكِيناً عِنْدَ الرِّضَا عليه السلام قَالَ: قُلْتُ لِلرِّضَا عليه السلام: ادْعُ اللَّهَ لِي وَلِأَهْلِ بَيْتِي فَقَالَ أَ وَلَسْتُ أَفْعَلُ وَاللَّهِ إِنَّ أَعْمَالَكُمْ لَتُعْرَضُ عَلَيَّ فِي كُلِّ يَوْمٍ وَلَيْلَةٍ قَالَ فَاسْتَعْظَمْتُ ذَلِكَ فَقَالَ لِي أَ مَا تَقْرَأُ كِتَابَ اللَّهِ عَزَّ وَجَلَّ وَ قُلِ اعْمَلُوا فَسَيَرَى اللَّهُ عَمَلَكُمْ وَرَسُولُهُ وَالْمُؤْمِنُونَ قَالَ هُوَ وَاللَّهِ عَلِيُّ بْنُ أَبِي طَالِبٍ عليه السلام

'Abdullāh bin Abān al-Zayyāt, a distinguished personality near Imām al-Riḍā عليه السلام, reports: I said to

13 Shaykh al-Kulaynī, *Al-Kāfī*, v.1, p. 219

> al-Riḍā عليه السلام: Pray to Allāh for me and my family, and he said: Don't I do that? I swear by Allāh surely your actions are presented to me every day and night. "I was extremely amazed at that," says al-Zayyāt. Then the Imām عليه السلام said: Do you not read the Book of Allāh, the Invincible and Exalted, who says: ﴾*And say, Go on working: Allāh will see your conduct, and His Apostle and the faithful [as well]*﴿(9:105) I swear by Allāh '*the faithful*' mentioned in this verse is 'Alī bin Abī Ṭālib.[14]

Hence engaging in sin, and being inconsistent with the spirit of *salām,* makes us violate our covenant with the Imām عليه السلام. Those, therefore who recite their *ziyārāt* without considering this vital point, are either hypocrites or weaklings who like to utter lies infront of the Imām عليه السلام. There is a group of sinful reciters, however, whom the self that excessively invites one to evil (*al-nafs al-ammāra*) has weakened, but are nevetheless hopeful for change. Whenever such people recite the *Ziyārat,* they should experience utter humiliation, and always seek change. They must realize that in order for one to prosper and change, one should perpetually seek Divine Succor and make a firm resolve to leave all those things that are forbidden, however minute they may seem to appear.

أَلسَّلاَمُ عَلَيْكَ

May peace from Allāh be upon you

Sometimes the article *'al'* is employed as a substitute for the second particle (*muḍāfun ilayhi*) of a genetive construction. For example, when

---

14 *Ibid.*

referring to a book whose owner is known to be a certain Zayd, we can say *al-kitābu* (the book) instead of saying كِتَابُ زَيْدٍ *kitābu Zaydin* (Book of Zayd). Here the article '*al*' is a substitute for Zayd. Likewise '*al*' in '*al-salāmu*' can be a substitute for a particular person. And bearing in mind that there is no perfection whatsoever but that it originates from Allāh, and that the preposition عَلَى '*alā*' indicates that the origin of s*alām* is from a higher plane of existence and we know that there is no Absolutely High save Allāh, '*al*' can be said to refer to Allāh. In this case the statement *al-salāmu 'alayka* either means peace from Allāh be upon you, or 'peace of Allāh' be upon you.

أَلسَّلَامُ عَلَيْكَ

I surrender all my affairs to you

Another meaning of *salām* documented by lexicographers is '*al-taslīm*' (to surrender). Therefore the statement '*Al-salāmu 'alayka*' would mean 'I surrender myself to you'. In other words, we are trying to tell Imām al-Ḥusayn عليه السلام that "I am your slave. Whatever you say, I shall obey. Your desire is mine. If you want me to reform myself and others, I shall do so." If we look at the matter from an ontological (*takwīnī*) point of view, we come to realize that whether we declare our slavehood or not, the Imām's light, which according to different traditions, is an intermediary of grace (*wāsiṭat al-fayḍ*), dominates us. Nevertheless the Divine law has facilitated volitional action, and thus nothing is forced on anyone. When surrending ourself to the Imām عليه السلام let us secretly ask the Imām عليه السلام to assist us and make us serious and keep us steadfast in our commitment.

أَلسَّلاَمُ عَلَيْكَ

Peace be unto You

Sometimes, the article *'al'* in *al-salām* conveys either of the following meanings: (1) All kinds of peace, (2) The most perfect kind of peace, or (3) The absolute peace. This is when the definite article *'al'* denotes 'genus' (*al-jins*) or 'species'. Grammatically, whenever the definite article *'al'* is taken to denote genus, one of the following three implications can be gotten:

- All the extensions (*maṣādīq*) of the genus (*jins*) are taken into consideration. For example, in chapter *al-ʿAṣr* we say: *Inna al-insāna lafī khusr*, we mean '**every human being** is in loss' (103:2) because *al* in '*al-insān*' denotes genus and all the extensions of genus are taken into consideration. In our case, when we say *'al-salāmu ʿalayka'* in the invocative sense, we mean "*all kinds of peace be upon you*"
- All the extensions of the perfect attributes of the genus are taken into consideration. For example, when we say *hādha huwa al-rajul*, we mean, '*this is a perfect man*' because '*al-rajul*' denotes '*the man who has all the perfections of a man*'. In our case, when we say *al-salāmu ʿalayka* in the invocative sense, we mean '*perfect peace be upon you*'.
- The genus (*jins*) in its absolute sense. In other words no limitation is attributed to the genus. It denotes an *absolute form.* Therefore when we say*: al-salāmu ʿalayka*, we can mean *Absolute Peace without any limitations, be upon you.* In this case, therefore, we are seeking the highest level of peace for Imām al-Ḥusayn عليه السلام.

أَلسَّلاَمُ عَلَيْكَ

May peace from Allāh **envelop You**

A grammatical intricacy worthy of consideration is that the preposition عَلَى *'alā* in اَلسَّلاَمُ عَلَيْكَ *Al-salāmu 'alayka* denotes the sense of envelopment[15]. In other words we are asking Almighty Allāh to envelop and cover Imām al-Ḥusayn عليه السلام with the state of peace and freedom from every apparent and hidden calamity that is according to his noble essence. Therefore *al-salāmu 'alayka* would mean: "May Allāh **envelop** you with the state of peace."

أَلسَّلاَمُ عَلَيْكَ

Peace from Allāh envelop **you**

Another important point to bear in mind is that the second person masculine pronoun كَ '*ka*' in عَلَيْكَ *'alayka* presupposes the presence of the *zā'ir's* addressee, and this obliges him to attain receptivity to comprehend and appreciate the same. We do not use the third person pronoun هُ *hū* to indicate that our invocation of *salām* is for an absent *mazūr* (the visted one). Some of the great saints, due to their spiritual struggle, would attain levels of receptivity that would enable them to see the Imām عليه السلام or listen to the response that our Imām عليه السلام would give. It is narrated that the late Rajab 'Alī al-Khayyāṭ, who was a tailor by occupation, due to his strict observation of Islamic laws and harmony with the teachings of the Ahl al-Bayt عليهم السلام, was endowed with a

15. Mīrzā Ṭehrānī, *Shifā al-Ṣudūr*, p. 98; *Tadhkirat al-Zā'irīn* [Ref: Persian collection '*Nigāhī be Ziyārat-e 'Āshūrā*', p. 142]

penetrating vision and could appreciate what others cannot. Shaykh Muḥammadī Rayshahrī in his collection of the memoirs of this late saint narrates the following interesting account about him:

> One of Shaykh Rajab ʿAlī Khayyāṭ's devotees said that the Shaykh had once held a session in the house of one of his friends. Before starting his talk, he felt somehow weak due to hunger and asked for some bread. Half a loaf of bread was brought for him to eat, and thereafter he began the meeting. The following night he said: "Last night I made salutations to the holy Imāms عليهم السلام but I did not see them. I pleaded to find the reason. I was told intuitively: 'You had half of that food and the hunger alleviated. Why then did you eat the other half?! Having some food that is enough for the body's need is all right, but extra to that would cause veil and darkness.'"[16]

Another interesting account is narrated by Āyatullāh Mūḥammad Taqī Bahjat, a well-known contemporary saint, who is quoted by one of his disciples to have said:

> One day Shaykh Bahjat (may Allāh elevate his status) said to us: In the past people would travel to the city of Mashhad on camels and mules. Once some farmers of Jāsib, a region of Qum, travelled to Mashhad for the *Ziyārat* of Imām al-Riḍā عليه السلام. On their return they saw a man from their village carrying a lot of fodder. So they reproved him saying: 'O Shaykh, leave struggle for the world, for that would not benefit you and go to Mashhad at

---

16 Muḥammad al-Rayshahrī, *Kīmyāye Maḥabbat* (Elixir of Love), p. 94

> least once, and they started reproving and reprehending him. The old man said to them: 'Surely you went to the *ziyara* of the Imām عليه السلام, but did the Imām عليه السلام respond to your salutation (*salām*)? They said: What is this that you are saying? Is it possible for an Imām who has died to respond to a salutation? The old man said: what do you mean by saying alive or dead? Indeed the Imām عليه السلام sees us and listens to our speech, and what is the benefit of *Ziyārat* if it is one sided? They said: Is it possible for you to enable this to happen? He said: Yes; then he stood facing Mashhad and said: *"Al-salāmu 'alayka ayyuha al-Imām al-Thāmin"* (Peace be unto you, O the Eight Leader of Guidance), and he heard a call that said: *'Wa 'alaika al-Salām..'* (And upon you [too] be peace...'). Hearing this the farmers regretted about what they had said to the old man and felt ashamed of themselves.[17]

Dear readers, these were occasions encountered by men who are not reported to have apparently immersed themselves in intellectual occupations throughout the day as is the case with Islamic scholars. But yet we see that they were able to attain receptivity that would qualify them to see or listen to the call of the Imām عليه السلام. Our endeavor therefore should be to eradicate the darkness that we have accumulated in our hearts and lift the veils, so that when we convey our humble salutations, we are privileged to listen to the sacred response of our Imām عليه السلام.

17 Maḥmūd al-Badrī, *Uswat al-'Ārifīn*, p. 215

أَلسَّلاَمُ عَلَيْكَ

May Allāh always envelop you with peace

Another important allusion worthy of consideration is hidden in the kind of sentence we employ when seeking peace for the Imām عليه السلام or declaring the same. Observe that the above sentence is a nominal sentence (*jumla ismiyya*). It starts with a noun and not a verb. Therefore it signifies continuity and permanence. Hence we can either translate it as "*May Allāh always envelop you with peace*" or "*You will always be enveloped with peace from my side*"[18].

أَلسَّلاَمُ عَلَيْكَ

I am at peace with you

Some authoritative lexicographers define s*alām* as extreme coherence (*al-muwāfaqa al-shadīda*).[19] Considering this definition, if we take the phrase '*Al-salāmu 'alayka* as declarative then we are expressing our extreme harmony and unity with Imām al-Ḥusayn عليه السلام. It is the fear of such state of *salām* expressed by the revolutionary *zā'ir* that led tyrants like the the *Abbasid al-Manṣūr al-Dawāniqī, Hārūn al-Rashīd* and *al-Mutawakkil* among other oppressors to hamper and even kill anyone who visited the shrine of Imām al-Ḥusayn عليه السلام.

In his *Maqātil al-Ṭālibiyyīn*, Abu al-Faraj al-Isfahānī says:

> Al-Mutawakkil was very hostile towards the descendants of Abū Ṭālib, cruel towards their group

---

18 Jār Allah al-Zamakhsharī, *Tafsīr al-Kashshāf*, v.4, p. 401

19 Al-Muṣṭafawī, *al-Taḥqīq*, v.5, p. 188.

> and suspicious of their activities...It occurred to him that ʿUbayd Allāh ibn Yaḥyā ibn Khāqān, his vizir, also used to think badly of them and the denunciation of their activity seemed good to him. He carried out actions against them that none of the ʿAbbasids before him had carried out. Among these, he ploughed up the grave of al-Husayn عليه السلام and removed all trace of it. He put armed garrisons on the rest of the roads. Anyone they found making a pilgrimage to it, they brought to him. He killed or punished them severely.[20]

Despite all these threats, the aspirants of al-Ḥusayn عليه السلام flocked like love birds yearning to express their love before their beloved whose love had soaked their hearts and gave them no respite. Abū al-Faraj narrates:

> Muḥammad ibn al-Ḥusayn al-Ashnanī reported to me: My promise to perform the pilgrimage seemed impossible in those days because of the terror. Then I decided to risk my life to do it. A perfume merchant helped me to do that. We set out to perform the pilgrimage, hiding by day and travelling by night until we came to the area of al-Ghāḍiriyyah. From there we departed in the middle of the night and went into between two garrisons so that we came to the grave of al-Ḥusayn عليه السلام. It was hidden from us. We began to sniff for signs of it and search for some aspect of it until we came upon it. The structure, which had been around it, had been torn down and burnt. Water had been made to flow over it and the place where bricks had been sunk down so

---

20 Shaykh Shams al-Dīn, *The Revolution of al-Ḥusayn* عليه السلام, http://www.al-islam.org/revolution/2.htm

> that it had become like a ditch. We performed the rituals of the pilgrimage to him. We threw ourselves down on the ground and smelled a fragrance from it which I have never smelled anything like. It was like some kind of perfume. I asked the perfume merchant, who was with me, 'What fragrance is this?' 'By God, I have never smelled any kind of perfume like it,' he replied. We made our farewells and put marks around the grave in a number of places. When al-Mutawakkil was killed, we gathered with a group of the descendants of Abū Ṭālib and the Shīʿah to go to the grave. We removed the marks and restored it to the state which it had been before.[21]

In their astute and accurate directions, the Imāms عليهم السلام would also encourage their followers to go to visit the shrine of Imām al-Ḥusayn عليه السلام even at the cost of death and martyrdom. They would inform them that the more the fear of being attacked the more the reward for visiting al-Ḥusayn عليه السلام. ʿAllāma Majlisī quotes Muḥammad bin Muslim saying:

> قَالَ لِيْ اَبُو جَعْفَرٍ مُحَمَّدُ بْنِ عَلِيّ عليه السلام : هَلْ تَأْتِيْ قَبْرَ الْحُسَيْنِ عليه السلام ؟ قُلْتُ: نَعَمْ عَلى خَوْفٍ وَوَجِلٍ. فَقَالَ لَهُ: مَا كَانَ مِنْ هَذاَ اَشَدّ **فَالثَّوَابُ فِيْهِ عَلى قَدَرِ الْخَوْفِ** وَمَنْ خَافَ فِيْ إِتْيَانِهِ آمَنَ اللّهُ رُوْعَتَهُ يَوْمَ يَقُوْمُ النَّاسُ لِرَبِّ الْعَالَمِيْنَ وَانْصَرَفَ بِالْمَغْفِرَةِ وَسَلَّمَتْ عَلَيْهِ الْمَلآئِكَةُ، وَزَارَهُ النَّبِي صلى الله عليه وآله وسلم وَدَعَا لَهُ...

21 Shaykh Shams al-Dīn, *The Revolution of al-Ḥusayn* عليه السلام, http://www.al-islam.org/revolution/2.htm

> Imām Abū Jaʿfar Muḥammad bin ʿAlī (al-Bāqir) عليه السلام said to me: Do you come to the grave of al-Ḥusayn عليه السلام? I said: Yes, but in dread and fear. The Imām عليه السلام said: 'If the situation is severe, its reward would be in proportion to the fear; and whosoever visits him in fear, Allāh would protect his heart on the Day when the people would stand for the Lord of the Universe; and he would leave in the state of being forgiven, and the angels would send their salutations to him, and the Holy Prophet ﷺ would visit him and pray for him...[22]

The Imāms عليهم السلام likewise expressed their extreme attachment to Imām al-Ḥusayn عليه السلام. Rather they would encourage others to pray for them near the radiant dome of Imām al-Ḥusayn عليه السلام. Consider the following traditions:

1. ʿAllāma Majlisī in vol. 101 of his *Biḥār al-Anwār* quotes Ibn Abī Yaʿfūr to have said:

قُلْتُ لِأَبِي عَبْدِ اللهِ عليه السلام : دَعَانِي الشَّوْقُ إِلَيْكَ أَنْ
تَجَشَّمْتُ إِلَيْكَ عَلَى مَشَقَّةٍ فَقَالَ لِي: لَا تَشْكُ رَبَّكَ
فَهَلَّا أَتَيْتَ مَنْ كَانَ أَعْظَمُ حَقًّا" عَلَيْكَ مِنِّي؟
فَكَانَ مِنْ قَوْلِهِ: "فَهَلَّا أَتَيْتَ مَنْ كَانَ أَعْظَمُ حَقًّا
عَلَيْكَ مِنِّي أَشَدُّ عَلَيَّ مِنْ قَوْلِهِ "لَا تَشْكُ رَبَّكَ" .
قُلْتُ: وَمَنْ أَعْظَمُ عَلَيَّ حَقًّا مِنْكَ ؟ قَالَ: اَلْحُسَيْنِ
بْنِ عَلِيٍّ أَلَا أَتَيْتَ الْحُسَيْنَ فَدَعَوْتَ اللهَ عِنْدَهُ
وَشَكَوْتَ إِلَيْهِ حَوَائِجَكَ؟

22 ʿAllāma al-Majlisī, *Biḥār al-Anwār*, v. 101, p.11

I said to Abū ʿAbdillāh [al-Ṣādiq عليه السلام]: My fervent desire to meet you called me to bear the difficulties to come to you. The Imām عليه السلام said: 'Do not complain to your Lord; and why didn't you come to one who has a greater right over you than me?' Ibn Abī Yaʿfūr says: His statement 'Why didn't you go to one who has a greater right over you than me?' made me feel more uneasy than his statement "Do not complain to your Lord". So I said: 'And who has a greater right over me than yourself?" The Imām عليه السلام said: "Al-Ḥusayn bin ʿAlī عليه السلام; why didn't you come to al-Ḥusayn عليه السلام and pray to Allāh near him, and raise your complaint to Him about your needs?[23]

2. Ibn Qūlawayh reports in his *Kāmil al-Ziyārāt* that Abū Hāshim al-Jaʿfarī, one of the companions of Imām al-Hādī عليه السلام is reported to have said:

دَخَلْتُ عَلى اَبِي الْحَسَنِ عَلِيّ بْنِ مُحَمّد عليهما السلام وَهُوَ مَحْمُوْمٌ عَلِيْلٌ، فَقَالَ لِيْ: يَا اَبَا هَاشِمِ ابْعَثْ رَجُلاً مِنْ مَوَالِيْنَا اِلى الْحَائِرِ يَدْعُو اللّٰهَ لِيْ، فَخَرَجْتُ مِنْ عِنْدِهِ، فَاسْتَقْبَلَنِيْ عَلِيّ بْنِ بِلاَل فَاَعْلَمْتُهُ مَا قَالَ لِيْ، وَسَاَلْتُهُ اَنْ يَكُوْنَ الرَّجُلُ الَّذِيْ يَخْرُجُ فَقَالَ: اَلسَّمْعُ وَالطَاعَةُ، وَلَكِنَّنِيْ اَقُوْلُ: اِنَّهُ اَفْضَلَ مِنَ الْحَائِرِ إِذْ كَانَ بِمَنْزِلَةِ مَنْ فِي الْحَائِرِ، وَدُعَاؤُهُ لِنَفْسِهِ أَفْضَلَ مِنْ دُعَائِيْ لَهُ بِالْحَائِرِ، فَاَعْلَمْتُهُ عليه السلام

23 ʿAllāma al-Majlisī, *Biḥār al-Anwār*, v. 101, p. 46; Ibn Qūlawayh, *Kāmil al-Ziyārāt*, p. 315

مَا قَالَ، فَقَالَ لِيْ: قُلْ لَهُ: كَانَ رَسُوْلُ اللهِ ﷺ
أَفْضَلَ مِنَ الْبَيْتِ وَالْحَجَرِ، وَكَانَ يَطُوْفُ بِالْبَيْتِ
وَيَسْتَلِمُ الْحَجَرَ، وَاِنَّ اللهَ تَعَالى بِقَاعًا يُحِبُّ اَنْ
يُدْعى فِيْهَا فَيَسْتَجِيْبُ لِمَنْ دَعَاهُ، وَالْحَائِرُ مِنْهَا

I came to Abū al-Ḥasan (Imām ʿAlī al-Naqī ؑ) while he had fever and was unwell. He said to me: 'O Abā Hishām, send one of our followers to the Ḥā'ir (the dome of Imām al-Ḥusayn ؑ) to pray to Allāh for me. So I left him and met ʿAlī bin Bilāl. I told him what the Imām ؑ had said and requested him to carry out the duty, and he was at his service. 'However,' said he, 'indeed the Imām ؑ is greater than the Ḥā'ir, for he equals the station of the one who is buried in the Ḥā'ir, and his supplication for himself is better than my supplication for him in the Ḥā'ir.' Abū Hishām says: I informed the Imām ؑ about what ʿAlī bin Bilāl said, whereupon he said: Tell him that the Apostle of Allāh was better than the *Bayt al-Ḥarām* and the *Ḥajar al-Aswad*, whereas he would circumambulate round the Kaʿbah and touch the Ḥajar; and indeed Allāh has places where He loves to be called, so that he may respond to the call of the caller, and the Hā'ir is one among them.[24]

24 Jaʿfar bin Muḥammad bin Qūlawayh, *Kāmil al-Ziyārāt*, p. 460

أَلسَّلاَمُ عَلَيْكَ

Peace be unto You

Al-Salām, as we came to learn earlier, is one of the attributes of Almighty Allāh, which some of his noble servants, like the infallible Imāms of the Ahl al-Bayt عليهم السلام, due to their utter submission exemplify. The path for others too is left open. Every human being is invited to the abode of peace, and therefore he must strive to attain the same. But a true beliver has an all-embracing heart, and thus yearns for the betterment of others too. Perhaps that is why we are encouraged to greet others with *al-salām*. The Holy Prophet ﷺ is reported to have said:

السَّلاَمُ اِسْمٌ مِنْ أَسْمَاءِ اللّٰهِ تَعَالَى فَافْشُوهُ بَيْنَكُمْ

> *Al-Salām* is a name from among the names of Almighty Allāh. Therefore, spread the same between yourselves...[25]

In fact the word *muslim* has originally been derived from Allāh's Name *al-Salām*. The Holy Prophet ﷺ is reported to have said:

تَسَمَّى اللّٰهُ بِاسْمَيْنِ سَمَّى بِهِمَا أُمَّتِي هُوَ السَّلاَمُ وَسَمَّى أُمَّتِي الْمُسْلِمِينَ، وَهُوَ الْمُؤْمِنُ وَسَمَّى أُمَّتِي الْمُؤْمِنِينَ

> Allāh named Himself with two names with which he [also] named my nation: He is *al-Salām* and He named my nation *muslims*, and He is *al-Mu'min*

25 Shaykh al-Ṭabrasī, *Mishkāt al-Anwār*, p.349

and He named my nation *mu'mins.*[26]

Perhaps due to this reason, scholars like Sayyid al-Shubbar in his *al-Anwār al-Lāmi'a* and ʿAllāma Majlisī in his *Biḥār al-Anwār* believe that one of the meanings of *al-salāmū ʿalayka* is[27]:

اِسْمُ السَّلاَمِ عَلَيْكَ

May Allāh always envelop you with His Name *al-Salām.*

Therefore, Almighty Allāh not only requires each of us to be at peace, but teaches us to ask for our Muslim brothers and sisters to be availed of the same. It should be understood however that the levels of peace are infinite. Therefore invoking peace for others while we greet them should never cease.

أَلسَّلاَمُ عَلَيْكَ

I declare that Absolute Peace envelops you

Scholars of insight mention one of the meanings of the phrase *al-salamu ʿalayka* as "the Divine Name *al-Salām* envelops you, and you are his manifestation". In this case the phrase is taken as declarative and *al-Salām* is taken to mean the Divine Name *al-Salām.* In his *Sharḥ al-Asmā',* Mullā Hādī Sabzawsāri when discussing about the Divine Name *al-Salām* says:

. . . أَحَدُ مَعَانِي قَوْلِنَا: سلام عليك، أَنَّ السَّلاَمَ

26 Jalāl al-Dīn al-Suyūṭī, *Tafsīr al-Durr al-Manthūr,* v.4, p. 373

27 This meaning has been narrated by both the Shī'a as well as the Sunnī scholars in their commentaries of Qur'ān and lexicons as well.

الْمُؤْمِنَ الْمُهَيْمِنَ مُحِيطٌ عَلَيْكَ وَأَنْتَ مَظْهَرُهُ.

...one of the meanings of our statement '*salamun 'alayk*" is that the Peace, the Securer, the Guardian envelops you and you are His manifestation.[28]

أَلسَّلَامُ عَلَيْكَ

Peace be unto you

It is important to understand the remote distance between the sincerity of one who merely declares or verbally seeks peace for the *mazūr* ('the visited one') and one who personifies peace in every dimension of his being and actively struggles to ensure the same for the *mazūr*. In fact some of our traditions clearly emphasize the vital role of the practical application of *al-salām*. Look at the following traditions:

1. 'Allāma Majlisī narrates the following in his *Biḥār al-Anwār*:

جَاءَتْ جَارِيَةٌ لِلْحَسَنِ عليه السلام بِطَاقِ رَيْحَانٍ فَقَالَ لَهَا أَنْتَ حُرٌّ لِوَجْهِ اللَّهِ فَقِيلَ لَهُ فِي ذَلِكَ فَقَالَ أَدَّبَنَا اللَّهُ تَعَالَى فَقَالَ ﴿إِذَا حُيِّيتُمْ الْآيَةَ﴾ وَكَانَ أَحْسَنُ مِنْهَا إِعْتَاقَهَا

One of the slave women of Imām al-Ḥasan عليه السلام came to him with a boquet of aromatic plants, whereupon the Imām عليه السلام said to her: You are free for the sake of Allāh. So the Imām عليه السلام was asked as to why did he free her, and he said: 'Almighty Allāh trained us and said: *'And When you are greeted with a greeting,*

28 Mullā Hādī al-Sabzawārī, *Sharḥ al-Asmā'*, p. 324

> *greet with a better one than it, or return it...* '(4:86). And to let her free is better return than her gift.[29]

Therefore the *taḥiyya* (lit. seeking another's life & well-being (*ṭalab al-ḥayāt*)) referred to in the above verse conventionally translated as 'greeting' is not limited to a verbal expression of peace, but embraces other examples of its etymological definition too such as 'doing virtue to another'.

2. Imām al-Ṣādiq ﵇ is reported to have said:

> اَلْمُرَادُ بِالتَّحِيَّةِ فِيْ قَوْلِه تعالى: ﴿وَإِذَا حُيِّيْتُمْ بِتَحِيَّةٍ﴾ السَّلاَمُ وَغَيْرُهُ مِنَ الْبِرِّ وَالاحْسَانِ.
>
> *Al-taḥiyyah* (greeting) in the verse '*And when you are greeted with a greeting...*' is to greet and perform other acts of virtue and good.[30]

These are traditions that show how practical s*alām* can be. Many of us do not realize this and conjecture that we have earned ample blessings and reward for our *salāms* as the holy Qur'ān and the sacred traditions of the Holy Prophet ﷺ and his infallible progeny clearly exemplify.

The Holy Qur'ān says:

> ﴿فَإِذَا دَخَلْتُم بُيُوتًا فَسَلِّمُوا عَلَى أَنفُسِكُمْ تَحِيَّةً مِّنْ عِندِ اللَّهِ مُبَارَكَةً طَيِّبَةً كَذَلِكَ يُبَيِّنُ اللَّهُ لَكُمُ الْآيَاتِ لَعَلَّكُمْ تَعْقِلُونَ﴾
>
> So when you enter houses, greet yourselves with a salutation from God, blessed and pleasant. Thus does God clarify His signs for you so that you may

29 Allāma al-Majlisī, *Biḥār al-Anwār*, v.81, p. 273

30 Shaykh al-Huwayzī, *Tafsīr Nūr al-Thaqalayn*, v.1, p. 524

apply reason. (24:61)

The Holy Prophet ﷺ is reported to have said:

إِذَا دَخَلَ أَحَدُكُمْ بَيْتَهُ فَلْيُسَلِّمْ، فَإِنَّهُ يَنْزِلُهُ الْبَرَكَةُ، وَتُؤْنِسُهُ الْمَلاَئِكَةُ

> When one enters his house, he must say *salām*, for that makes blessings descend on the house and the angels become fond of it.[31]

Should we restrict these luminant words of guidance to the realm of speech or do they portray the loftier aspects of the reality of *al-salām*? In fact if there is no coherence between what the tongue utters and what the heart and mind feel and what the actions portray, then how can we claim the honesty of the *musallim* (greeter)?

يَا أَبَا عَبْدِ اللهِ

O Abā ʿAbdillāh

The word '*yā*' is a vocative particle *(ḥarfu nidā')* employed to call the *munādā* (vocative). In simple terms it is a word used to *call* someone. However, grammarians hold that يَا '*yā*' is specifically employed for that vocative who is at a far distance[32]. For example, if we would like to call ʿAlī who is at a far distance, we say يَاعَلِيّ '*Yā ʿAlī!*'. The distance considered here was physical and spatial. Rhetoricians however employ the same when they would like to praise an exalted personality even if

31 Muḥammadī al-Rayshahrī, *al-Khayr wa al-Baraka fī al-Kitāb wa al-Sunna*, p. 206

32 Al-Ṣabbān in his glosses over Sham'ūnī's commentary over the *Alfiyya of Ibn Mālik*, says: 'Indeed a far object is only called with particles that contain letters of protraction (*ḥarf al-madd*), because when a far object is called it requires one to prolong his voice, so that the vocative can hear. *(Al-Ṣabbān, Ḥāshiyat al-Ṣabbān*, v.3, p. 1145.)

he was very near. We address Almighty Allāh, for example, who is closer to us than our jugular veins as يَاالله *Yā Allāh*, because the Essence of Allāh is Exalted. In the well-known verse of the Throne (*Āyat al-Kursī*) we declare this reality of Allāh's Exalted Essence as:

﴿وَهُوَ الْعَلِيُّ الْعَظِيمُ﴾

> And He Alone is always the Extremely High & Great (2:255)[33]

In our present situation our vocative and addressee is Imām al-Ḥusayn عليه السلام who due to his freedom from the limitations of the material world and comprehensive being is intensely close to us and can see and listen to us too. Hence the reason we employ the vocative particle *'yā* and say '*Yā Abā 'Abdillāh'* is to express his exaltedness and confess our lowliness. The people of heart, however, can well appreciate the implication manifested when the 'the lover calls the beloved'. The implication is to get near to the Beloved. Hence when we call Abā 'Abdillāh (whose import, as we shall soon expound means 'the utterly submissive slave of Allāh') we are seeking his closeness, or in other words 'the attributes that personifies his exalted being'.

أَبَاعَبْدِاللهِ

O Father of 'Abdullāh

33 This is one phrase where the comprehensive beauty of the Qur'an can well be appreciated for all those who can appreciate the subtle issues of Arabic grammar and syntax. This small verse describes so many things at the same time: (1) It is a nominal sentence (*al-jumla al-ismiyya*) and thus it signifies permanence (2) the pronoun *huwā* denotes 'specificity' and thus these two attributes that follow it are originally reserved for Allāh. (3) The form *'ali* similar to فعيل '*fa'īl*' is known as '*al-ṣifa al-mushbiha*' in the Arabic, which denotes intensity and permanence.

The words *Abā 'Abdillāh* literally mean 'the father of the obedient slave of Allāh'. Arabs honorify their fellow brothers by calling them with a teknonym (*kunya*) a name that mostly mentions the first or one of the offsprings of the 'named one'.) Hence if a person had a son named 'Abdullāh, he is called *Abū 'Abdillāh*, which means 'father of 'Abdullāh'. One of the reasons behind the Imām عليه السلام being called Abū 'Abdillāh is that he had an offspring called 'Abdullāh, famously known as الرَّضِيْعُ *al-raḍī'* (one who is still breastfeeding). He was mercilessly martyred by the enemies after Imām al-Ḥusayn عليه السلام read *adhān* in his ear following his birth. In the well-known *Ziyārat al-Nāḥiya al-Muqaddasa* Imām al-Zamān عليه السلام addresses this new born as:

أَلسَّلاَمُ عَلَى عَبْدِ اللهِ بنِ الحُسَيْنِ الطِّفْلِ الرَّضِيْعِ . . .

Perpetual peace be unto 'Abdillāh, the one who was still breastfeeding...[34]

أَبَا عَبْدِ اللَّهِ
Obedient Slave of Allāh

Sometimes however, someone is attributed with a teknonym (*kunya*) not because he is the father of so and so, but because he enjoys a certain quality. For example, one who is well known for his open-handedness and generosity is called Abū Jawād. In our case, a number of commentators of this exalted *Ziyārat*, opine that one of the reasons the holy Imām عليه السلام was given the *kunya* Abū 'Abdillāh was his extreme submissiveness to Allāh. In other words, he was the true slave of Allāh.

Traditions indicate that Imām al-Ḥusayn عليه السلام was given the teknonym

34 al-Shahīd al-Awwal, *al-Mazār*, p. 149

after his birth which subtly alludes to the submissive state of Imām ﷺ ever since his childhood. In a tradition narrated in *Biḥār al-Anwār*, Asmā' is quoted to have said:

فَلَمَّا كَانَ فِي يَوْمِ سَابِعِهِ جَاءَنِي النَّبِيّ فَقَالَ: هَلُمِّي ابْنِي فَأَتَيْتُ بِهِ... ثُمَّ وَضَعَهُ فِي حِجْرِهِ ثُمَّ قَالَ: **يَا أَبَا عَبْدِ اللهِ** عَزِيزٌ عَلَيَّ ثُمَّ بَكَى...

> 'On the seventh day after his birth, the Prophet ﷺ came to me and said: 'Bring me my son.' So I brought Husayn to him...Then he kept him on his bossom and said: **'O Abā 'Abdillāh,** it is indeed difficult for me...then he burst into tears...'[35]

This tradition indicates that the Imām ﷺ got the teknonym since his very early childhood and thus enjoyed an exalted status since then.

يَا أَبَا عَبْدِ اللهِ

O Utterly Submissive Servant of Allāh

It may be argued that if the *zā'ir* himself, due to his submissiveness to Almighty Allāh is also an *'abd* of Allāh, why should he still call the Imām with the vocative particle '*yā*'? The answer to this is very simple: *'ubūdiyya* and submissiveness are of different levels. The distance between the stage of *'ubūdiyya* that the infallible Imāms of the Ahl al-Bayt ﷺ occupy and the stage their true followers enjoy is extremely vast. Consider the following narrations:

1. 'Ibād bin Ṣuhayb is reported to have said:

35 'Allāma al-Majlisī, *Biḥār al-Anwār*, v.44, pp. 250-251

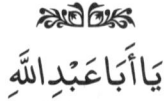

قُلْتُ لِلصَّادِقِ جَعْفَرِ بْنِ مُحَمَّدٍ عليه السلام: اَخْبِرْنِي عَنْ اَبِي ذَرٍّ، اَهُوَ اَفْضَلُ اَمْ اَنْتُمْ اَهْلُ الْبَيْتِ؟ فَقَالَ: يَا ابْنَ صُهَيْبٍ كَمْ شُهُورُ السَّنَةِ فَقُلْتُ: اِثْنَا عَشَرَ شَهْرًا، فَقَالَ: وَكَمِ الْحُرُمِ مِنْهَا؟ قُلْتُ: اَرْبَعَةُ اَشْهُرٍ، قَالَ: فَشَهْرُ رَمَضَانَ مِنْهَا؟ قُلْتُ: لاَ، قَالَ: فَشَهْرُ رَمَضَانَ اَفْضَلُ اَمِ الاَشْهُرِ الْحُرُمِ؟ فَقُلْتُ: بَلْ شَهْرُ رَمَضَانَ، قَالَ: فَكَذَلِكَ نَحْنُ اَهْلُ الْبَيْتِ لاَ يُقَاسُ بِنَا اَحَدٌ.

I asked al-Ṣādiq عليه السلام, Jaʿfar bin Muḥammad (upon whom be peace): Inform me whether Abu Dharr is better than you the Ahl al-Bayt عليهم السلام? The Imām عليه السلام said: 'O son of Ṣuhayb, how many months are there in one year'? I said: 'twelve months.' Thereupon he عليه السلام said: 'And how many among them are sacred (*ḥurum*)?' I said 'Four months.' He عليه السلام said: 'And is the month of Ramaḍān among them?' I said: 'No.' He عليه السلام said: 'Then is the month of Ramadān greater or the four sacred months?' I said: 'Rather the Holy month of Ramaḍān is greater.' The Imām عليه السلام then said: 'So is the case with us, the Ahl al-Bayt; none can be compared to us.'[36]

2. Jābir al-Ju'fī, a companion of Imām al-Bāqir is reported to have narrated that Imām al-Bāqir عليه السلام once said to him:

اِنَّا مِنَ اللّٰهِ بِمَكَانٍ وَمَنْزِلَةٍ رَفِيعَةٍ ! فَلَوْلاَ نَحْنُ مَا

36 ʿAllāma al-Majlisī, *Biḥār al-Anwār*, v.22, p. 406

خَلَقَ اللّٰهُ تعَالى سَمَاءًا وَلاَ اَرْضًا، وَلاَجَنَّةً وَلاَنَارًا، وَلاَ شَمْسًا وَلاَقَمَرًا، وَلاَجِنِّيًّا وَلاَ إِنْسِيًّا. **يَا جَابِر، إِنَّا اَهْلُ الْبَيْتِ لاَ يُقَاسُ بِنَا اَحَدٌ، مَنْ قَاسَ بِنَا احدًا مِنَ الْبَشَرِ فَقَدْ كَفَرَ** . يَا جَابِرُ، بِنَا اللّٰه أنْقَذَكُمْ، وَبِنَا هَدَاكُمْ، وَنَحْنُ وَاللّٰهِ دَلّلْنَاكُمْ عَلى رَبِّكُمْ...

Surely we have an exalted status near Allāh! Were we not there, Allāh would not have created any heaven nor earth, nor any Paradise nor Hell Fire, nor any sun or moon, or any Jinnī or human being. O Jābir! **We are the Ahl al-Bayt; none can be compared to us; whosoever compares any human being with us, has disbelieved (or covered (the truth)).** O Jābir! Through us Allāh emancipated you, and through us He guided you; and, I swear by Allāh we have guided you to your Lord...[37]

3. Imām ʿAlī عليه السلام is reported to have said to Abu Dharr:

اِعْلَمْ يَا اَبَاذَرّ اَنَا عَبْدُ اللّٰهِ عَزَّوَجَلَّ وَخَلِيفَتُهُ عَلى عِبَادِهِ لاَ تَجْعَلُوْنَا اَرْبَابًا وَقُوْلُوْا فِيْ فَضْلنَا مَا شِئْتُمْ **فَاِنَّكُمْ لاَ تَبْلُغُوْنَ كُنْهَ مَا فِينَا وَلاَ نِهَايَتَهُ**، فَاِنَّ اللّٰهَ عَزَّوَجَلَّ قَدْ اَعْطانَا اَكْبَرُ وَاَعْظَمُ مِمَّا يَصِفُهُ وَاصِفُكُمْ اَوْ يَخْطُرُ عَلى قَلْبِ اَحَدِكُمْ فَإِذَا

37 Muḥammad bin Jurayr al-Ṭabarī al-Shīʿī, *Nawādir al-Muʿjizāt*, p. 124

عَرَفْتُمُوْنَا هَكَذَا فَأَنْتُمُ الْمُؤْمِنُوْنَ .

Know, O Abū Dharr, that I am an utterly submissive servant of Allāh on the earth and His vicegerent over His other servants; do not consider us (the Ahl al-Bayt عليهم السلام) to be Lords, and then say about our merits whatever you want, ***for certainly you would not comprehend the essence of our station, nor its zenith***, for verily Allāh bestowed on us better and greater than what describers among you describe or what has penetrated in the imagination of anyone; so when you know us in this way, you surely are the believers.[38]

أَلسَّلَامُ عَلَيْكَ يَا أَبَا عَبْدِ اللهِ

Peace be unto you O Abā ʿAbdillāh

One of the areas where it is recommended for one to call his fellow Muslim brother with a teknonym is when he is present before him. In our case, therefore, because we know that Imām al-Ḥusayn عليه السلام is present before us, and we address him using the second person pronoun "*kāf*", it is apt to begin our address with his teknonym. Imām al-Riḍā عليه السلام is reported to have said:

إِذَا ذَكَرْتَ الرَّجُلَ وَهُوَ حَاضِرٌ فَكَنِّهِ وَإِذَا كَانَ غَائِباً فَسَمِّهِ

If you mention a man in his presence, then do so using his teknonym (*kunya*), and if he were to be

38 ʿAllāma al-Majlisī, *Biḥār al-Anwār*, v.26, p.2

absent, then call him by his name.[39]

أَبَا عَبْدِ اللهِ

O father of 'Abdullāh

It is important to look at the root meaning of the word '*ab*' in *Abā 'Abdillāh* which we normally translate as 'father'. In the Arabic language the word اب '*ab*' literally means:

هُوَ كُلُّ مَنْ كَانَ سَبَبًا فِي إِيْجَادِ شَيْءٍ أَوْ إِصْلَاحِهِ أَوْ ظُهُوْرِهِ

Whosoever is a cause in the existence of a thing or its reform or its manifestation is known as '*ab*'.[40]

And since Imām al-Ḥusayn عليه السلام converges with the Muḥammadan Light (al-Nūr al-Muḥammadī) which is the intermediary of Divine Grace, he is a *sabab* (cause) in the existence, reform and manifestation of the caravan of human beings. Therefore he is Abū 'Abdillāh. Whatever grace any servant of Allāh receives is through the Muḥammadan Light.

أَبَا عَبْدِ اللهِ

O father of 'Abdullāh

In a well-known tradition, we read:

---

39 'Allāma al-Majlisī, *Biḥār al-Anwār*, v.75, p. 335

40 *Sharḥ Kalimāt Amīr al-Mu'minīn* عليه السلام, p.15

إِنَّمَا الآبَاءُ ثَلاَثَةٌ: أَبٌ وَلَّدَكَ وَأَبٌ عَلَّمَكَ وَأَبٌ زَوَّجَكَ

> Indeed there are only **three fathers**: the father who was the reason for your birth, the father who taught you, and the father who married you (to his daughter).[41]

And because Imām al-Ḥusayn عليه السلام was from among the infallible Imāms عليهم السلام responsible to guide humanity and teach them the path of salvation, he is known as Abū ʿAbdillāh meaning 'father or tutor of a true servant of Allāh'. In this case every human being enjoys from al-Ḥusayn's banquet of practical submission. The previous Prophets of Allāh are no exception. Imām al-Ḥusayn عليه السلام also serves as a father to the Prophets of Allāh before the Seal of the Prophets عليه السلام, since they drew inspiration from him even before his birth. Consider the following narratives from ʿAllāma Majlisi's *Biḥār al-Anwār* and Baḥrāni's *al-ʿAwālim*:

عَنْ أَبِي عَبْدِ اللهِ عليه السلام، قَالَ: إِنَّ إِسْمَاعِيلَ الَّذِي قَالَ اللهُ تَعَالَى: ﴿**وَاذْكُرْ فِي الْكِتَابِ إِسْمَاعِيلَ إِنَّهُ كَانَ صَادِقَ الْوَعْدِ وَكَانَ رَسُولاً نَبِيًّا**﴾ لَمْ يَكُنْ إِسْمَاعِيلَ بْنَ إِبْرَاهِيمَ بَلْ كَانَ نَبِيًّا مِنَ الأَنْبِيَاءِ، بَعَثَهُ اللهُ عَزَّ وَجَلَّ إِلَى قَوْمِهِ فَأَخَذُوهُ فَسَلَخُوا فَرْوَةَ رَأْسِهِ وَوَجْهِهِ، فَأَتَاهُ مَلَكٌ، فَقَالَ: إِنَّ اللهَ جَلَّ جَلاَلُهُ بَعَثَنِي إِلَيْكَ فَمُرْنِي بِمَا شِئْتَ، فَقَالَ: لِي أُسْوَةٌ بِمَا

---

41 ʿAbd al-Wahhāb, *Sharḥ Kalimāt Amīr al-Muʾminīn* عليه السلام, p. 15

يُصْنَعُ بِالْحُسَيْنِ عليه السلام . . .

It is reported from Abī ʻAbdillāh (al-Ṣādiq عليه السلام) who said: ʻIndeed the Ismāʼīl that Almighty Allāh talks about in the verse **ʻAnd mention in the Book Ismāʼīl. Indeed he was true to his promise, and an apostle and a prophet.ʼ(19:54)** was not Ismāʼīl عليه السلام the son of Ibrāhīm عليه السلام, but was a prophet among prophets whom Allāh, the Invincible and Sublime, sent to his people; and they killed him, and skinned his scalp and face; so an angel came to him, and said: ʻSurely Allāh sent me to you; so order me to do what you want.ʼ He said: ʻI have model of emulation of what will happen to al-Ḥusayn (upon whom be peace)...[42]

وَرُوِيَ اَنَّ نُوْحًا لَمَّا رَكِبَ فِي السَّفِيْنَةِ طَافَتْ بِهِ جَمِيْعَ الدُّنْيَا، فَلَمَّا مَرَّتْ بِكَرْبَلاَ اَخَذَتْهُ الاَرْضُ وَخَافَ نُوْح اَلْغَرْقَ، فَدَعَا رَبَّهُ، وَقَالَ: إِلَهِيْ طُفْتُ جَمِيْعَ الدُّنْيَا وَمَا اَصَابَنِيْ فَزَعٌ مِثْلَ مَا اَصَابَنِيْ فِي هَذِهِ الاَرْضِ، فَنَزَلَ جِبْرَئِيْلُ عليه السلام ، وَقَالَ يَا نُوْحُ فِي هَذَا الْمَوْضِعِ يُقْتَلُ الْحُسَيْنُ عليه السلام سِبْط مُحَمَّدٍ خَاتَمِ الاَنْبِيَاءِ، وَابْنِ خَاتَمِ الاَوْصِيَاءِ، فَقَالَ: وَمَنِ الْقَاتِلُ لَهُ يَا جِبْرَئِيْلُ؟ قَالَ: قَاتِلُهُ لَعِيْنُ اَهْلِ سَبْعِ سَمَاوَاتٍ وَسَبْعِ اَرَضِيْنَ، فَلَعَنَهُ نُوْح اَرْبَعَ مَرَّاتٍ . . .

It is narrated that when Nūḥ عليه السلام boarded the Ark, it

42 Shaykh ʻAbdullāh al-Baḥrānī, *al-ʻAwālim- al-Imām al-Ḥusayn* عليه السلام, p. 108

transported him throughout the world; and when he passed by Karbalā, the earth forced the ark towards itself, and Nūḥ عليه السلام feared of drowning; so he prayed to his Lord: O my God, I went round the entire world, and nowhere was I afraid as I have been in this place; Thereupon Gabriel عليه السلام descends, and tells Nūḥ عليه السلام: "O Nūḥ this is the place where Ḥusayn عليه السلام, the grandson of the Muḥammad, the Seal of the Prophets and the son of the Seal of the Divine Trustees would be killed. Nūh asked him: And who would kill him, O Gabriel? Gabiriel said: His killer is one whom the inhabitants of seven heavens and the seven earths curse; so Nūḥ عليه السلام curses him four times...[43]

وَرُوِيَ اَنَّ اِبْرَاهِيْمَ عليه السلام مَرَّ فِيْ اَرْضِ كَرْبَلاَ وَهُوَ رَاكِبٌ فَرَسًا فَعَثَرَ بِهِ وَسَقَطَ إِبْرَاهِيْمُ وَشَجَّ رَأْسُهُ وَسَالَ دَمُهُ، فَاَخَذَ فِيْ الاِسْتِغْفَارِ، وَقَالَ: إِلِهِيْ اَيُّ شَيْءٍ حَدَثَ مِنِّيْ؟ فَنَزَلَ إِلَيْهِ جَبْرَئِيْلُ عليه السلام وَقَالَ: يَا إِبْرَاهِيْمُ مَا حَدَثَ مِنْكَ ذَنْبٌ، وَلَكِن يُقْتَلُ هُنَا سِبْطُ خَاتَمِ الاَنْبِيَاءِ، وَابْنُ خَاتَمِ الاَوْصِيَاءِ، فَسَالَ دَمُكَ مُوَافَقَةً لِدَمِهِ. قَالَ: يَا جَبْرَئِيْلُ وَمَنْ يَكُوْنُ قَاتِلُهُ؟ لَعِينُ أَهْلِ السَّمَاوَاتِ وَالأَرَضِينَ... فَرَفَعَ إِبْرَاهِيْمُ عليه السلام يَدَيْهِ وَلَعَنَ يَزِيْدَ لَعْنًا كَثِيْرًا ...

It is narrated that [Prophet] Ibrāhīm عليه السلام passed by the land of Karbalā while he was riding his horse.

43 Shaykh ʿAbdullāh al-Baḥrānī, *al-ʿAwālim- al-Imām al-Ḥusayn* عليه السلام, p. 102

> The horse made him stumble and Ibrāhīm عليه السلام fell off and his head got wounded and blood started flowing out of him. Thereupon, he began seeking Allāh's forgiveness, and said: 'O my God, what [wrong] have I done?' Thereupon Gabriel descends on him and says: 'O Ibrāhīm, you have not committed any sin; but this is the place where the grandson of the Seal of Prophets عليه السلام and the son of the Seal of the Divine Trustees would be killed; thus your blood flowed in accordance with his blood. He asked Gabriel: 'And who would be his killer?' Gabriel said: 'The one cursed by the inhabitants of the heavens and the earths...Ibrāhīm raised his hands and excessively sends curses on Yazīd...[44]

These narratives as well others which we have ommitted for the sake of brevity, clearly indicate that Imām al-Ḥusayn عليه السلام was an example for his predecessors too. In simpler words, 'he serves as a timeless model'. The curses from the Prophets in all their particularity depict the universal stance against oppression. Hence, Imām al-Ḥusayn عليه السلام educated, educates and will always educate the human beings with the lesson of utter submission, even at the cost of sacrificing everything. Consequently, we rightfully address him as Abū ʿAbdillāh (the father or tutor of a truly submissive servant of Allāh.)

عَبْدِ اللهِ
Servant of Allāh

The name ʿAbdullāh is of very great significance since it also implies

44 *Ibid.*

that 'the named' is a manifestation of all the attributes of Almighty Allāh. This is because the name Allāh which is sometimes referred to as *al-ism al-aʿẓam* (the greatest name of God) is also a name that comprehends in itself all the sublime attributes of the Divine Essence. Hence one who is a servant of such a Being, necessarily is submissive to His orders, all of which manifest His sublime attributes. Thus whatever a submissive servant of Allāh does, he would do it according to what Allāh wants, and what Allāh wants clearly depicts His sublime attributes. In simple terms: If the king of a certain town possesses excellent traits, his totally obedient servants would carry the same traits, because whatever they do accord with what the king wants.

All the prophets of Allāh as well as the Imāms of the Ahl al-Bayt عليهم السلام are *ʿIbād Allāh* (totally submissive servants of Allāh) and consequently manifestations of His Most Beautiful Attributes as well. It is for this reason perhaps that Imām ʿAlī عليه السلام is reported to have said:

نَحْنُ الاَسْمَآءُ الْحُسْنى

We are the Most Beautiful Names of Allāh[45]

أَلسَّلامُ عَلَيْكَ يا أَبا عَبْدِ اللهِ

Peace be unto you, O obedient servant of Allāh

In the Arabic rhetoric there is a rule that says:

تَعْليقُ الْحُكْمِ بِالْوَصْفِ مُشْعِرٌ بِالْعِلِّيَّةِ

When a statement is qualified with a certain attribute the quality denotes the reason behind the statement.

---

45 Al-Sayyid Hāshim al-Baḥrānī, *Madīnat al-Maʿājiz*, v.1, p. 556

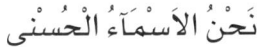

Bearing this in mind, if we consider the above verse to be a declarative statement, it would be clear for us that the reason why we declare that Imām al-Ḥusayn عليه السلام enjoys the state of s*alām* (freedom from calamities) is that he is an 'utterly submissive servant of Allāh'. In other words the reason for "*Assalāmu ʿalayka*" is "*Yā Abā ʿAbdillāh*". In simpler words, 'I declare that you are in the state of Salām, O utterly submissive servant of Allāh' [and the reason for you to be in that state is your characteristic of being utterly submissive to Allāh].

Anecdotes of Reflection

1. Ḥāj Sayyid Ahmad Bahā al-Dīnī, an employee of the Office of the late Imām Khumayni is reported to have said:

> Imām Khumaynī would pay his respects to Sayyid al-Shuhadā (Imām al-Ḥusayn عليه السلام) before and after every canonical prayer: he would for example pay his respects before the morning prayer, and then after the morning prayer, before the *maghrib* prayer, before the 'īshā' prayer, and then after the 'īshā' prayer, before the *ẓuhr* prayer, before the 'aṣr prayer and then after the 'asr prayer. In this way he would altogether pay his respects eight times a day to Sayyid al-Shuhadā'[46].

2. A friend of the late saint, Shaykh Rajab ʿAlī al-Khayyāṭ, narrates:

> 'Together with the Shaykh we went to Kāshān. The Shaykh had the habit that wherever he traveled, he would visit the cemetery of that place. As we entered the cemetery in Kāshān, he said: "*Al-Salāmu ʿalayka yā Abā ʿAbd Allāh* عليه السلام" ("Salutations be on you O

46 It is Imām al-Ḥusayn who established prayer and ensured its perpetuity. In the well-known *ziyārat al-wārith* we address the martyred Imām عليه السلام as follows: اشهد انك قد اقمت الصلاة...I bear witness that you established prayer. (Author)

Imām Husayn عليه السلام") We walked a few steps further on, and then he said: "Do you not smell anything?" 'No, what smell?' We asked. Then he asked: "Don't you feel the smell (scent) of red apples?" Our answer was 'no' again. We went further on and met the man in charge of the cemetery. The Shaykh asked him: "Has anyone been **buried** here today?" The man answered: "Just before you arrived someone was buried', and then he took us to a newly covered tomb. There it was! We all smelled the scent of red apples. We asked the Shaykh about the scent, to which he answered: "When this person was buried here, the sacred person of Sayyid al- Shuhadā' [Imām Ḥusayn عليه السلام] came here and for the sake of this person (and by the blessed visit of Sayyid al-Shuhadā' عليه السلام) the punishment was removed from those buried in this cemetery."[47]

47 Muḥammad al-Rayshahrī, *Kīmyāye Maḥabbat*, p. 115

CHAPTER 2

أَلسَّلَامُ عَلَيْكَ يَا بْنَ رَسُولِ اللهِ

Peace be on you, O son of the Messenger of Allāh

أَلسَّلَامُ عَلَيْكَ يَابْنَ رَسُولِ اللهِ

Peace be on You, O son of the Messenger of of Allāh

COMMENTARY

يَابْنَ رَسُولِ اللهِ

O son of the Messenger of Allāh

Ibnu Rasūlillāh is a patronym[1]. Imām al-Ḥusayn عليه السلام in this verse is introduced as the son of the Holy Prophet صلى الله عليه وآله. There has been a controversy in the past about this bond and relationship. The enemies of the Ahl al-Bayt عليهم السلام throughout history would try to denounce it and declare that the Imāms of the Ahl al-Bayt عليهم السلام are not from the progeny of the Holy Prophet صلى الله عليه وآله but rather only from the progeny of Amīr al-Mu'minīn ʿAlī عليه السلام. The Ahl al-Bayt عليهم السلام, however, would cogently prove to them the veracity of their relationship with the Holy Prophet صلى الله عليه وآله. In fact the most cogent of all proofs is the well-known verse of *mubāhala* (imprecation), where Almighty Allāh says to His Apostle صلى الله عليه وآله:

﴿فَمَنْ حَاجَّكَ فِيهِ مِنْ بَعْدِ مَا جَاءَكَ مِنَ الْعِلْمِ فَقُلْ
تَعَالَوْا نَدْعُ أَبْنَاءَنَا وَأَبْنَاءَكُمْ وَنِسَاءَنَا وَنِسَاءَكُمْ
وَأَنْفُسَنَا وَأَنْفُسَكُمْ ثُمَّ نَبْتَهِلْ فَنَجْعَلْ لَعْنَتَ اللَّهِ عَلَى
الْكَاذِبِينَ﴾

Should anyone argue with you concerning him, after

---

1 A patronymic, or patronym, is a component of a personal name based on the name of one's father.

the knowledge that has come to you, say, "Come! Let us call our sons and your sons, our women and your women, our souls and your souls, then let us pray earnestly and call down Allāh's curse upon the liars." (3:61)

This verse speaks of the Holy Prophet ﷺ's confrontation with the Christians of Najrān in the well-known incident of *mubāhala* (imprecation), when just beholding the brilliant faces of the *Ahl al-Kisā* عليهم السلام overwhelmend the Christians and made their bishop say:

إِنِّيْ لأَرَى وُجُوْهًا لَوْ سَأَلُوا اللّهَ أَنْ يُزِيْلَ جَبَلاً مِنْ مَكَانِهِ لأَزَالَهُ بِهَا فَلاَ تُبَاهِلُوْا فَتَهْلِكُوْا وَلاَ يَبْقَى عَلَى وَجْهِ الأَرْضِ نَصْرَانِيٌّ إِلى يَوْمِ الْقِيامَةِ.

Indeed I am seeing faces, who if ask Allāh to uproot a mountain from its place, He would surely do so. Therefore do not imprecate, for if you do so you will perish, and there would remain no Christian on the face of the earth until the Judgment Day.[2]

In the aforementioned verse we clearly find the phrase "*Let us call our sons (abnā'ana) and your sons (abnā'akum)...* ". Muslim historians have unanimously narrated that the Holy Prophet ﷺ had brought Imām al-Ḥasan عليه السلام and Imām al-Ḥusayn عليه السلام as his sons for this event[3].

Ḥaḍrat Fāṭima al-Zahrā' عليها السلام narrates from the Holy Prophet ﷺ that:

كُلُّ بَنِي أُمٍّ يَنْتَمُونَ إِلَى عَصَبَتِهِمْ إِلاَّ وُلْدَ فَاطِمَةَ فَإِنِّي أَنَا أَبُوهُمْ وَعَصَبَتُهُمْ

2 Fakhr al-Dīn al-Rāzī, *Mafātīḥ al-Ghayb*, v.8, p. 247

3 Jār Allāh al-Zamakhsharī, *Al-Kashhāf 'an Ḥaqā'iqi Ghawāmiḍ al-Tanzīl*, v.1, p. 368

> The son of every mother is [solely] attributed to his paternal relations, save the sons of Fāṭima, for surely I am their father and paternal relation.[4]

This tradition, which is found with slight variations in so many works of traditions, is vocal enough to specify the exceptional relationship between the Holy Prophet ﷺ and the sons of Ḥaḍrat Fāṭima عليها السلام.

Throughout the dark pages of history, however, the illegitimate rulers of the Muslim world, due to their jealousy and hatred, always debated this relationship but did not suceed. Following are some examples worthy of consideration:

1. Al-Arbilī in his *Kashf al-Ghumma* narrates:

عَنْ ذَكْوَان مَوْلَى مُعَاوِيَة قَال قَالَ مُعَاوِيَة: لاَ أعْلَمَنَّ أحَداً سَمَّى هَذَيْنِ الْغُلاَمَيْنِ إبْنَيْ رَسُوْلِ اللّه ﷺ. وَلَكِنْ قُوْلُوا: ابْنَيْ عَلِيٍّ عليه السلام. قَالَ ذَكْوَان: فَلَمَّا كَانَ بَعْدَ ذَلِك، أمَرَنِيْ أنْ أكْتُبَ بَنِيْهِ فِي الشَّرَفِ. قَالَ: فَكَتَبْتُ بَنِيهِ وَبَنِي بَنِيهِ، وَتَرَكْتُ بَنِيْ بَنَاتِه.. ثُمَّ أتَيْتُهُ بِالْكِتَابِ، فَنَظَرَ فِيْه، فَقَالَ: وَيْحَك، لَقَدْ أغْفَلْتَ كُبر بَنِيّ! فَقُلْتُ: مَنْ؟ فَقَالَ: أما بَنُوْ فُلاَنَة - لابْنَتِه - بَنِيَّ؟ أمَا بَنُوْ فُلاَنَة - لابْنَتِه - بَنِيّ؟. قَالَ: قُلْتُ: اَللّه!! أيَكُوْنُ بَنُوْ بَنَاتِكَ بَنِيكَ، وَلاَ يَكُوْنُ بَنُوْ فَاطِمَة بَنِي رَسُوْلِ اللّه ﷺ؟! قَالَ: مَالَكَ؟ قَاتَلَكَ اللّهُ! لاَ يَسْمَعَنَّ

---

4 ʿAllāma Majlis*ī*, *Biḥār al-Anwār*, v. 43, p. 228

هَذاَ أَحَدٌ مِنْكَ ؟!

Dhakwān, a slave of Muʿāwiya, reports: Muʿāwiya [once] said [to me]: Surely I do not know anyone call these two boys (Imām al-Ḥasan and Imām al-Ḥusayn عليهما السلام) the two sons of the Messenger of Allāh صلى الله عليه وآله. Therefore say: "They are the sons of ʿAli عليه السلام". Later, Muʿāwiya ordered me to write down the names of his sons in sequence of nobility. I wrote the names of his sons and the names of the sons of his sons, but did not write the names of the sons of his daughters. Then I came to him with the written script. He looked at it, and retorted: Woe be unto you! You have forgotten the elders from among my children! I said: Who are they? He said: Aren't the sons of that daughter [of mine] my sons? Aren't the sons of such and such daughter of mine my sons? Dhakwān said: I remarked [in amazement]: God!! Are the sons of your daughters your sons, whereas the sons of Fāṭima عليها السلام not the sons of the Messenger of Allāh صلى الله عليه وآله? He said: What is the matter with you? May Allāh kill you! No one should hear this from you![5]

2. Fakhr al-Dīn al-Rāzī in his *Tafsīr Mafātīḥ al-Ghayb* narrates the following from Shuʿbī:

كُنْتُ عِنْدَ الْحَجَّاجِ، فَأُتِيَ بِيَحْيَى بْنِ يَعْمَرَ، فَقِيهُ
خُرَاسَانَ، مِنْ بَلْخٍ، مُكَبَّلاً بِالْحَدِيدِ فَقَالَ لَهُ
الْحَجَّاجُ: أَنْتَ زَعَمْتَ: أَنَّ الْحَسَنَ وَالْحُسَيْنَ مِنْ

---

5 Arbilī, *Kashf al-Ghumma*, v.2, p. 176

ذُرِّيَّةِ رَسُوْلِ اللهِ ﷺ؟ فَقَالَ: بَلَى. فَقَالَ الْحَجَّاجُ:
لَتَأْتِيْنِي بِهَا وَاضِحَةً بَيِّنَةً مِـنْ كِـتَـابِ اللهِ، أوْ
لَأَقْطَعَنَّكَ عُضْواً عُضْواً. فَقَالَ: آتِيْكَ بِهَا بَيِّنَةً
وَاضِحَةً مِنْ كِتَابِ اللهِ يَا حَجَّاجُ. قَالَ. فَتَعَجَّبْتُ
مِنْ جُرْأَتِهِ بِقَوْلِهِ: يَا حَجَّاجُ. فَقَالَ لَهُ: وَلَا تَأْتِّي
بِهَذِهِ الآيَةِ: ﴿نَدْعُ أَبْنَاءَنَا وَأَبْنَاءَكُمْ﴾. فَقَالَ: آتِيْكَ
بِهَا بَيِّنَةً وَاضِحَةً مِـنْ كِـتَـابِ اللهِ، وَهُـوَ قَوْلُـهُ:
﴿وَنُوْحـاً هَـدَيْنَاهُ مِـنْ قَبْـلُ، وَمِـنْ ذُرِّيَّتِـهِ دَاوُد
وَسُـلَيْمَانَ﴾ . . إلَى قَوْلِـهِ: ﴿وَزَكَرِيَّـا، وَيَحْيَـى،
وَعِيسَى﴾. فَمَنْ كَانَ أَبُو عِيسَى، وَقَدْ أُلْحِقَ بِذُرِّيَّةِ
نُوحٍ!؟. قَالَ: فَأَطْرَقَ الْحَجَّاجُ مَلِيّاً، ثُمَّ رَفَعَ رَأْسَهُ
فَقَـالَ: كَـأَنِّي لَـمْ أَقْرَأْ هَـذِهِ الآيَـةَ مِنْ كِـتَابِ اللهِ
حُلُّوا وِثَاقَهُ . . إلخ

I was with Ḥajjāj [bin Yūsuf al-Thaqafī] and Yāḥyā
bin Ya'mar, the jurisprudent of Khurāsān, was
brought from Balkh shackled with iron. Ḥajjāj said
to him: You think that Ḥasan and Ḥusayn are from
the progeny of the Holy Prophet ﷺ? He said:
Ofcourse yes. Thereupon Ḥajjāj said: You must
bring me a clear exposition for that from the Book
of Allāh or I surely will cut your body into parts. He
said: I will bring for you a clear exposition from the
Book of Allāh, O Ḥajjāj. Shu'bī says: I was surprised
at his audacity in responding with the [concluding]
words, "O Ḥajjāj!" Thereupon Ḥajjāj said to him:

But do not bring for me the verse "*let us call our sons...*" (3:61) He said: I will bring you a clear exposition from the Book of Allāh, and that is Allāh's speech *"...And Noah We had guided before, and from his offspring, David and Solomon up to the phrase [in the next verse] "...and Zechariah, John, Jesus...(84-85)* Who then was the father of Jesus, while he is attached to the progeny of Noah? Shuʿbi says: Thereupon Hajjaj lowered his head for some time, and then raised it and said: It is as if I have not read this verse from the Book of Allāh. Release him![6]

3. Thiqat al-Islām Muḥammad bin Yaʿqūb al-Kulaynī narrates in his Al-Kāfī:

عَنْ أَبِي الْجَارُودِ عَنْ أَبِي جَعْفَرٍ عليه السلام قَالَ قَالَ لِي أَبُو جَعْفَرٍ عليه السلام يَا أَبَا الْجَارُودِ مَا يَقُولُونَ لَكُمْ فِي الْحَسَنِ وَالْحُسَيْنِ عليه السلام قُلْتُ يُنْكِرُونَ عَلَيْنَا أَنَّهُمَا ابْنَا رَسُولِ اللَّهِ صلى الله عليه وآله وسلم قَالَ فَأَيَّ شَيْءٍ احْتَجَجْتُمْ عَلَيْهِمْ قُلْتُ احْتَجَجْنَا عَلَيْهِمْ بِقَوْلِ اللَّهِ عَزَّ وَجَلَّ فِي عِيسَى ابْنِ مَرْيَمَ عليه السلام ﴿وَمِنْ ذُرِّيَّتِهِ دَاوُدَ وَسُلَيْمَانَ وَأَيُّوبَ وَيُوسُفَ وَمُوسَى وَهَارُونَ وَكَذَلِكَ نَجْزِي الْمُحْسِنِينَ وَزَكَرِيَّا وَيَحْيَى وَعِيسَى﴾ فَجَعَلَ عِيسَى ابْنَ مَرْيَمَ مِنْ ذُرِّيَّةِ نُوحٍ عليه السلام قَالَ فَأَيَّ شَيْءٍ قَالُوا لَكُمْ قُلْتُ قَالُوا قَدْ يَكُونُ وَلَدُ الابْنَةِ مِنَ

6 Fakhr al-Dīn al-Rāzī, *Mafātīḥ al-Ghayb*, V.2, p. 412

الْوَلَدِ وَلاَ يَكُونُ مِنَ الصُّلْبِ قَالَ فَأَيَّ شَيْءٍ
احْتَجَجْتُمْ عَلَيْهِمْ قُلْتُ احْتَجَجْنَا عَلَيْهِمْ بِقَوْلِ اللَّهِ
تَعَالَى لِرَسُولِهِ ﷺ ﴿فَقُلْ تَعَالَوْا نَدْعُ أَبْنَاءَنَا
وَأَبْنَاءَكُمْ وَنِسَاءَنَا وَنِسَاءَكُمْ وَأَنْفُسَنَا
وَأَنْفُسَكُمْ﴾ قَالَ فَأَيَّ شَيْءٍ قَالُوا قُلْتُ قَالُوا قَدْ
يَكُونُ فِي كَلاَمِ الْعَرَبِ أَبْنَاءُ رَجُلٍ وَآخَرُ يَقُولُ
أَبْنَاؤُنَا قَالَ فَقَالَ أَبُو جَعْفَرٍ عليه السلام يَا أَبَا الْجَارُودِ
لَأُعْطِيَنَّكَهَا مِنْ كِتَابِ اللَّهِ جَلَّ وَ تَعَالَى أَنَّهُمَا مِنْ
صُلْبِ رَسُولِ اللَّهِ ﷺ لاَ يَرُدُّهَا إِلاَّ الْكَافِرُ قُلْتُ وَ
أَيْنَ ذَلِكَ جُعِلْتُ فِدَاكَ قَالَ مِنْ حَيْثُ قَالَ اللَّهُ تَعَالَى
﴿حُرِّمَتْ عَلَيْكُمْ أُمَّهَاتُكُمْ وَبَنَاتُكُمْ
وَأَخَوَاتُكُمْ﴾ الْآيَةَ إِلَى أَنِ انْتَهَى إِلَى قَوْلِهِ تَبَارَكَ
وَتَعَالَى وَحَلاَئِلُ أَبْنَائِكُمُ الَّذِينَ مِنْ أَصْلاَبِكُمْ
فَسَلْهُمْ يَا أَبَا الْجَارُودِ هَلْ كَانَ يَحِلُّ لِرَسُولِ اللَّهِ
ﷺ نِكَاحُ حَلِيلَتَيْهِمَا فَإِنْ قَالُوا نَعَمْ كَذَبُوا وَ
فَجَرُوا وَ إِنْ قَالُوا لاَ فَهُمَا ابْنَاهُ لِصُلْبِهِ.

It is narrated from Abū al-Jārūd: Abū Jaʿfar [al-Bāqir عليه السلام] said to me: O Aba al-Jārūd, what do they say about al-Ḥasan عليه السلام and al-Ḥusayn عليه السلام? I said: They are against our belief that they are the two sons of the Holy Prophet ﷺ. He عليه السلام said: Then with what [proof] did you argue with them? I said: With the word of Allāh about ʿIsā bin Maryam "...*And from his [Noah's] offspring, David and Solomon, Job, Joseph, Moses and Aaron thus do We reward the virtuous; and Zechariah, John, 'Isā..."* (6:84-85) Therefore He placed *'Isā* in the progeny of Noah عليه السلام. Imām عليه السلام said: So what did they say to you? I said: They said: It is possible for a son of a female to be a son, but he would not be from the loin. He عليه السلام said: So with what [other proof] did you argue against them? I said: We argued against them with the word of Allāh, *"... Come! Let us call our sons and your sons..."* (3:61) He عليه السلام said: And what did they say to you? I said: They said that sometimes in Arabic rhetoric a person may call the sons of another man as "our sons". Thereupon Abū Jaʿfar عليه السلام said: O Aba al-Jārūd indeed I will give you a verse from the Book of Allāh, the Sublime and Exalted [proving] that they (Imām al-Ḥasan and Imām al-Ḥusayn عليه السلام) are from the loin of the Holy Prophet صلى الله عليه وآله, and none save the disbeliever would negate it. I said: And where is it, may I be made your ranson? He عليه السلام said: From where Allāh, the Exalted, says "*Forbidden to you are your mothers, your daughters and your sisters, your paternal aunts and your maternal aunts, your brother's daughters and your sister's daughters, your] foster- who have suckled you and your sisters through fosterage, your wives" mothers, and your stepdaughters who are under your care] born [of the wives whom you have gone into but if you have not gone into them there is no sin upon you and the wives of your sons who are from your own loins.."* (4:23) Ask them, O Aba al-Jārūd, was it permitted for the Messenger of Allāh صلى الله عليه وآله to marry with the wives of al-Ḥasan and al-Ḥusayn عليه السلام? If they say 'yes', then surely they have

lied and voilated the bounds. And if they say "no",
then they [surely] are his two sons from his loin.[7]

We wish to suffice with the aforesaid incidents. Otherwise there are so
many other traditions where this relationship is clearly and explicitly
mentioned.

⁂

يَا ٱبْنَ رَسُوْلِ اللهِ

O product of the Messenger of Allāh

The word ٱبن *'ibn'* etymologically means *'the edifice of* or the *'product
of'*. Al-Iṣfahānī in his *al-Mufradāt* says:

انَّ الْإِبن سُمّي ابْنًا لِكَوْنِه بِنَاءً لِلْأَبَ ، فَإِنَّ الْأَبَ
هُوَ الَّذيْ بَنَّاهُ وَجَعَلَهُ اللهُ بِنَّاءً فِيْ ايْجَاده ، وَيُقَالُ
لِكُلّ مَا يَحْصُلُ مِنْ جِهَة شَيْء أوْ مِنْ تَرْبِيَته أوْ
بِتَفَقُّده أوْ كَثْرَة خِدْمَته لَهُ أوْ قِيَامِه بِأَمْرِه: هُوَ
ابْنُهُ . . .

Surely الإبن *al-ibn* was known to be so because it is a
building (*binā*) of the father, for it is the father who
built him and Allāh made him to be the builder in
his existence; and *ibn* is known to be anything that
is attained because of another thing or training or
guardianship or a lot of service or doing something
on one's behalf...[8]

---

7 Al-Kulaynī, *Al-Kāfī*, v.8, p. 217

8 Al-Iṣfahānī, *al-Mufradāt*, p. 147

Therefore it is right to say that Imām al-Ḥusayn ﵇ is the product or fruit of the Holy Prophet ﷺ in terms of spiritual upbringing. It is in the environment of the Holy Prophet ﷺ that Imām al-Ḥusayn ﵇ grew and learnt so many important things. In some traditions the Holy Prophet ﷺ also addresses Imām al-Ḥusayn ﵇ as *thamarata fu'ādī* (the fruit of my heart). For example, once 'Ā'isha seeing the cordial encounter of the Prophet ﷺ with al-Ḥusayn ﵇ who was then a small baby on the laps of the Prophet ﷺ, asked him:

يَا رَسُوْلَ اللّٰهِ مَا اَشَدَّ اِعْجَابِكَ بِهَذَا الصَّبِيِّ

> O Apostle of Allāh, how attached are you to this child!

And the Prophet ﷺ said:

وَيْلَكِ وَكَيْفَ لاَ أُحِبُّهُ وَلاَ اَعْجَبُ بِهِ، وَهُوَ ثَمَرَةُ فُؤَادِيْ وَقُرَّةُ عَيْنِيْ. . .

> Woe be to you, and how should I not love him and not get attracted to him, while ***he is the fruit of my heart*** and the apple of my eyes?[9]

يَاابْنَ رَسُوْلِ اللهِ

O product of **the Messenger of Allāh**

The genitive construction '*Rasūlullāh*' alludes to a particular identity of the Holy Prophet ﷺ which is his apostleship (*al-risāla*). Therefore *Ibnu Rasūlillāh* would mean the product of the Messenger of Allāh. Specifying this patronym alludes to the reality that Imām al-Ḥusayn

9 Ibnu Qūlawayh, *Kāmil al-Ziyārāt*, p. 144

عليه السلام was built to exemplify the attributes that a Divine Messenger must have. Obviously this does not mean that he عليه السلام was a Divinely proclaimed Messenger, for the Holy Prophet ﷺ was the Seal of all the Apostles (*khātam al-rusul*), but alludes to the fact that he manifested the qualities of a Divine Messenger. In fact the word '*rasūl*' when employed in the general sense refers to any kind of Allāh's messenger, such as the Angels. When Angel Jibra'īl عليه السلام appears before Ḥaḍrat Maryam عليها السلام in the form of a handsome young man, and the latter seeks refuge in Allāh and advises him to observe piety, Jibra'īl عليه السلام responds saying:

﴿إِنَّمَا أَنَا رَسُولُ رَبِّكِ لِأَهَبَ لَكِ غُلَامًا زَكِيًّا﴾

> Surely I am only **a messenger of your Lord**, so that I may gift you a pure male offspring. (19:19)

And Imām 'Alī عليه السلام is reported to have said:

اَلْمَلَائِكَةُ هُمْ رُسُلُ اللّٰهِ كَسَايِرِ أَنْبِيَاءِ اللّٰهِ إِلَى اَلْخَلْقِ

> ...The angels are the messengers of Allāh to the creatures like the rest of the prophets of Allāh...[10]

Sometimes the word '*rasūl*' is also used for a destitute who is extremely poor. If he seeks help, then he is in reality spreading the message of being openhanded. Those therefore who shun such people are in reality shunning a messenger of Allāh. Imām 'Alī عليه السلام is reported to have said:

اَلْمِسْكِينُ رَسُولُ اللّٰهِ إِلَيْكُمْ فَمَنْ مَنَعَهُ فَقَدْ مَنَعَ اللّٰهَ، وَمَنْ أَعْطَاهُ فَقَدْ أَعْطَى اللّٰهَ.

> The extremely poor is a messenger of Allāh unto

---

10 Al-Shaykh al-Ṭabrasī, *al-Iḥtijāj*, v.2, p. 266

> you; so whosoever refuses to help him, surely he has refused Allāh, and whosoever gives him, then surely he has given to Allāh.[11]

يَابْنَ رَسُوْلِ اللهِ

O product of the Messenger **of Allāh**

The word 'Allāh' here specifies the kind of message that the Holy Prophet ﷺ bears. As explained earlier, the name *Allāh* exemplifies all the perfect attributes of God, and therefore the Holy Prophet is the bearer of the message of all the perfect attributes. The Holy Qur'ān in fact is a written document that calls the human beings to embellish themselves with the attributes of Almighty Allāh. And Imām al-Ḥusayn عليه السلام being the fruit and edifice of a messenger of *Allāh*, qualifies as a caller to all the perfect Divine Attributes. In fact one of the characteristics of the Infallible Imāms of the Ahl al-Bayt عليهم السلام is that they are الدعاة إلى الله *'al-du'āt ilā Allāh'* (callers to Allāh). This call is not only in the realm of words. Their deeds and actions portray the Divine Atrributes. In the well-known *Ziyārat al-Jāmi'a* we read:

اَلسَّلاَمُ عَلَى الدُّعَاةِ إِلى اللّٰهِ

> Peace be on you callers unto Allāh.[12]

In another *Ziyārat* of Imām al-Ḥusayn عليه السلام declaring our total commitment and harmony with his noble spirit, we repeat the following seven times:

---

11 Imām 'Alī ('a), *Nahj al-Balāghah*, v.4, p. 74

12 Al-Mashhadī, *Al-Mazār*, p. 525

لَبَّيْكَ دَاعِيَ اللّٰهِ إِنْ كَانَ لَمْ يُجِبْكَ بَدَنِي فَقَدْ أَجَابَكَ قَلْبِي وَشَعْرِي وَ بَشَرِي وَرَأْيِي وَ هَوَايَ عَلَى التَّسْلِيمِ لِخَلَفِ النَّبِيِّ الْمُرْسَلِ وَالسِّبْطِ الْمُنْتَجَبِ

Here I am, O caller to Allāh; if my body did not respond to your call [due to its absence during the tragedy of Karbalā], then surely my heart, hair, skin, opinion, and desire have responded in submission to the call of the successor of the Divinely sent Prophet ﷺ and his chosen gradson.[13]

Here there is another allusion worthy of contemplation: notice the words "*khalaf al-nabī al-mursal*" which brilliantly manifest the kind of relationship we are trying to declare. In the Arabic, a *khalaf* is "a successor". And when the adjective *al-mursal* follows *al-nabī*, there is a particular implication we are trying to convey. In short, we are delcaring that Imām al-Ḥusayn عليه السلام succeeds the role of shouldering the mission of the Apostle of Almighty Allāh.

There are other clear indications also that show that the Infallible Imāms of the Ahl al-Bayt عليهم السلام possessed attributes that qualified them to be bearers of Allāh's message and inviters of the same. In *Ziyārat al-Jāmi'a* we read:

فَبَلَغَ اللّٰهُ بِكُمْ اَفْضَلَ شَرَفِ مَحَلِّ الْمُكَرَّمِينَ،وَاَعْلَى مَنَازِلِ الْمُقَرَّبِينَ، وَاَرْفَعَ دَرَجَاتِ الْمُرْسَلِينَ، حَيْثُ لاَ يَلْحَقُهُ لاَحِقٌ، وَلاَ يَفُوقُهُ فَائِقٌ. . .

And Allāh made you attain the best sanctimonious

13 'Allāma Majlisī, *Biḥār al-Anwār*, v.98, p. 168

> station of the ennobled ones, and the highest stations of the near ones, and **the most exalted stations of the *mursalīn* (apostles)**, where none can join or transcend...[14]

This clearly tells us that the Imāms ﷺ had qualities to carry out the duty of passing on the message of Allāh to the people. And by the phrase *"arfa'a darajāt al-mursalīn"* we should appreciate the fact that they even transcended messengers of Allāh preceding the Holy Prophet ﷺ. This is because they bore the message of *Khātam al-Rusul* (the Seal of the Messengers).

In another *Ziyārat* of Imām al-Ḥusayn ﷺ we address him as:

السَّلَامُ عَلَيْكَ يَا وَارِثَ مُحَمَّدٍ رَسُوْلِ اللهِ

> Peace be on you, O Inheritor of Muḥammad, the Messenger of Allāh.[15]

Those who can appreciate the subtle implications of the above statement, understand how vocal it is in revealing the distinction of Imām al-Ḥusayn ﷺ. We confess that he inherited the Holy Prophet ﷺ's duty of conveying the message of Allāh. All the components of the above expression such as "*al-salāmu*", "*alayka*", "*yā*", "*wāritha Muḥammad*", "*wāritha Muḥammadin Rāsūlillāh*", "*Rāsūl*", *"Rasūlillāh"*, *"Allāh"*, etc. are worthy of reflection. Therefore, read and ascend!

The Relation between ʿAbd and Rasūl

An important point to bear in mind is that in order for Imām al-Ḥusayn ﷺ to really be a *rasūl* and a conveyer of Allāh's message to the people, it is incumbent on him to be an ʿ*abd* (an utterly submissive servant of Allāh). Hence it was apt to address him with the teknonym

---

14 ʿAllāma Majlisī, *Biḥār al-Anwār*, v.99, p. 130

15 Sayyid Raḍī al-Dīn bin Ṭāwūs, *Iqbāl al-A'māl*, v.3, p.70

Abū 'Abdillāh in the first verse and thereafter with the patronym *ibnu Rasūlillāh*. We find a similar case when we recite our *tashahhud* in the cananonical prayer. We say:

اَشْهَدُ اَنْ لاَ إِلَهَ إِلاَّ اللهُ وَحْدَهُ لاَ شَرِيْكَ لَهُ وَاَشْهَدُ اَنَّ مُحَمَّدًا عَبْدُهُ وَرَسُوْلُهُ

> I bear witness that other than Allāh there is no god, and I bear witness that Muḥammad is **His utterly obedient servant and Apostle**.

Notice that the phrase *"'abduhū"* precedes "*wa rasūluh*", which alludes to the sequence we are talking about.

However, this station is even higher than being the servant of "Allāh". Here the third person pronoun "hu" affixed to ʿabd and rasūl refer to the Divine Essence. Discussing this intricacy here is beyond the scope of this commentary.

CHAPTER 3

أَلسَّلَامُ عَلَيْكَ يَا بْنَ أَمِيرِ الْمُؤْمِنِينَ

وَابْنَ سَيِّدِ الْوَصِيِّينَ

Peace be on you, O son of the Commander of the Faithful and the son of the leader of the successors

السَّلامُ عَلَيْكَ يَا بْنَ أَمِيرِ الْمُؤْمِنِينَ وَابْنَ سَيِّدِ الْوَصِيِّينَ

Peace be on You, O son of the the Commander of the Faithful and the son of the Leader of the Successors

---

COMMENTARY

يَا بْنَ أَمِيرِ الْمُؤْمِنِينَ

O *son of* the Commander of the Faithful

The apparent import of this verse signifies that Imām al-Ḥusayn عليه السلام is the son and offspring of Amīr al-Mu'minīn عليه السلام. This is a historical fact and we would not like to go into details about the same. However to reveal how brilliant is the origin of Imām al-Ḥusayn عليه السلام verses 19-20 of Sūrat al-Raḥmān come to mind:

﴿مَرَجَ الْبَحْرَيْنِ يَلْتَقِيانِ . بَيْنَهُما بَرْزَخٌ لا يَبْغِيانِ﴾

He merged the two seas, meeting each other. There is a barrier between them which they do not overstep. (55:19-20)

Yaḥyā bin Sa'īd narrates:

سَمِعْتُ أَبَا عَبْدِ اللهِ عليه السلام يَقُولُ فِي قَوْلِهِ عَزَّ وَجَلَّ: مَرَجَ الْبَحْرَيْنِ يَلْتَقِيانِ بَيْنَهُما بَرْزَخٌ لا يَبْغِيانِ قَالَ: عَلِيٌّ وَفَاطِمَةُ عليهما السلام ، بَحْرَانُ مِنَ الْعِلْمِ عَمِيقَانِ لا

يَبْغِي أَحَدُهُمَا عَلَى صَاحِبِهِ يَخْرُجُ مِنْهُمَا اللُّؤْلُؤُ وَالْمَرْجَانُ، اَلْحَسَنُ وَالْحُسَيْنُ عليهما السلام.

I heard Abā ʿAbdillāh [al-Ṣādiq] عليه السلام saying the following about the verse of Allāh "He merged the two seas, meeting each other. There is a barrier between them which they do not overstep.": ***ʿAlī and Fāṭima are two deep seas of knowledge***, none of who oversteps the other. From them emerge the pearl and the coral, who are al-Ḥasan and al-Ḥūsayn عليهما السلام.[1]

The appellation Amīr al-Mu'minīn was conferred to Imām ʿAlī عليه السلام by Allāh Himself in the higher levels of existence prior to this material world. Consider the following traditions:

1. Shaykh Ṣadūq narrates in his *Al-Khiṣāl*:

عَنِ النَّبِيِّ صلى الله عليه وآله قَالَ: فِي اللَّوْحِ الْمَحْفُوظِ تَحْتَ الْعَرْشِ عَلِيُّ بْنُ أَبِي طَالِبٍ أَمِيرُ الْمُؤْمِنِينَ

The Holy Prophet صلى الله عليه وآله is reported to have said: In the Guarded Tablet under the Divine Throne is [written] ʿAlī bin Abī Ṭālib is Amīr al-mu'minīn (Commander of the faithful) عليه السلام.[2]

2. Al-Kulaynī in his *Al-Kāfī* narrates with his chain of narrators:

عَنْ جَابِرٍ عَنْ أَبِي جَعْفَرٍ عليه السلام قَالَ قُلْتُ لَهُ لِمَ سُمِّيَ أَمِيرَ الْمُؤْمِنِينَ قَالَ اللَّهُ سَمَّاهُ وَهَكَذَا أَنْزَلَ فِي كِتَابِهِ وَإِذْ أَخَذَ رَبُّكَ مِنْ بَنِي آدَمَ مِنْ ظُهُورِهِمْ

1 Shaykh Ṣadūq, *Al-Khiṣāl*, v.1, p. 65

2 Sayyid Raḍī al-Dīn bin Ṭāwūs, *Al-Yaqīn*, p. 152

ذُرِّيَّتَهُمْ وَأَشْهَدَهُمْ عَلَى أَنْفُسِهِمْ أَلَسْتُ بِرَبِّكُمْ وَأَنَّ مُحَمَّداً رَسُولِي وَأَنَّ عَلِيّاً أَمِيرُ الْمُؤْمِنِينَ.

Jābir reports[3]: I said to Abū Jaʿfar [al-Bāqir عليه السلام]: Why was Imām ʿAlī عليه السلام named Amīr al-Mu'minīn? He عليه السلام said: Allāh is the One who named him, and this is how He revealed it in His Book: "When your Lord took from the children of Adam, from their loins, their descendants and made them bear witness over themselves, [He said to them,] Am I not your Lord (7:172) and isn't Muḥammad My Messenger and ***ʿAlī Amīr al-mu'minīn (the commander of the faithful)?***[4]

3. Fūrāt bin Ibrāhīm in his *Tafsīr Furāt al-Kūfī* narrates the following tradition:

عَنْ أَبِي جَعْفَرٍ عليه السلام قَالَ: لَوْ أَنَّ الْجُهَّالَ مِنْ هَذِهِ الْأُمَّةِ يَعْلَمُونَ مَتَى سُمِّيَ عَلِيٌّ أَمِيرَ الْمُؤْمِنِينَ لَمْ يُنْكِرُوا وِلَايَتَهُ وَطَاعَتَهُ قَالَ فَسَأَلْتُهُ وَمَتَى سُمِّيَ عَلِيٌّ أَمِيرَ الْمُؤْمِنِينَ؟ **قَالَ حَيْثُ أَخَذَ اللَّهُ مِيثَاقَ ذُرِّيَّةِ آدَمَ...**

Imām al-Bāqir عليه السلام is reported to have said: If the ignorant of this nation would know when Imām ʿAlī عليه السلام was named Amīr al-mu'minīn, they would

---

3 Al-Kulaynī, *Al-Kāfī*, v.1, p. 412

4 It should be noted that Imām al-Bāqir عليه السلام wanted to inform Jābir about what is not apparently indicated in the verse, but is a reality that exists in the higher realm. Therefore one should not misconstrue and conjecture that the exposition of the Imām عليه السلام is a physical part of the Qur'ān.

> not reject his guardianship and obedience. The reporter said: I asked him عليه السلام: And when was Imām ʿAlī عليه السلام named Amīr al-mu'minīn? He replied: ***It was when Allāh took the covenant with the progeny of Adam...***[5]

Some traditions clearly tell us that the Holy Prophet صلى الله عليه وآله called Imām ʿAlī عليه السلام Amīr al-mu'minīn عليه السلام on different occasions during his life time. Consider the following:

1. When Ḥaḍrat Fāṭima bint al-Asad, the noble mother of Imām ʿAlī عليه السلام, comes out of the Ka'ba with her exalted offspring ʿAlī عليه السلام, the following is reported to have transpired:

> قَالَ عَلِيٌّ عليه السلام أَلسَّلَامُ عَلَيْكَ يَا أَبَهْ وَرَحْمَةُ اللّٰهِ وَبَرَكَاتُهُ ثُمَّ تَنَحْنَحَ وَقَالَ ﴿بِسْمِ اللّٰهِ الرَّحْمٰنِ الرَّحِيمِ قَدْ أَفْلَحَ الْمُؤْمِنُونَ﴾ . . . فَقَالَ رَسُولُ اللّٰهِ صلى الله عليه وآله قَدْ أَفْلَحُوا بِكَ أَنْتَ وَاللّٰهِ أَمِيرُهُمْ تَمِيرُهُمْ مِنْ عِلْمِكَ فَيَمْتَارُونَ وَأَنْتَ وَاللّٰهِ دَلِيلُهُمْ وَبِكَ وَاللّٰهِ يَهْتَدُونَ

> Imām ʿAlī عليه السلام said: Peace be unto you, O father and may Allāh's mercy and blessings be upon you. Thereafter he coughed a little and recited [the following verses of Sūrat al-Mu'minūn]: ***In the name of Allāh, the All-Beneficent, the All-Merciful. Indeed the believers have become victorious (23:1)***... Thereupon the Messenger of Allāh said: Surely they have gained victory by you; ***You are, by Allāh, their Amīr (commander)***, you provide them from your

5 Furāt bin Ibrāhīm al-Kūfī, *Tafsīr Fūrāt al-Kūfī*, p. 147

> knowledge, and hence they gain knowledge; and I swear by Allāh you are their Guide, and I swear by Allāh they attain guidance through you.[6]

This tradition has so many allusions worthy of contemplation. Not only does the Holy Prophet ﷺ call Imām ʿAlī عليه السلام as the commander of the faithful, but also informs us the close relationship between one's commandership of the faithful and one's vast knowledge. In clearer words, since Imām ʿAlī عليه السلام is the commander of the faithful he practically serves as the source and treasure trove of their knowledge. And that is why he provides them with the knowledge they require. Another allusion worthy of consideration is that Imām عليه السلام upon birth already manifested an ocean of knowledge. Perhaps it alludes to the Muḥammadan Light (*al-Nūr al-Muḥammadī*) where he unites with the Holy Prophet ﷺ. For, any kind of grace, whether knowledge or otherwise, is conferred to the creation through this very reality. This truth is elicited from a tradition narrated from Jābir bin Abdillāh al-Anṣārī:

> قُلْتُ لِرَسُوْلِ اللهِ ﷺ: أَوَّلُ شَيْءٍ خَلَقَ اللهُ تَعَالَى مَا هُوَ؟ فَقَالَ ﷺ: نُوْرُ نَبِيِّكَ يَا جَابِرُ، خَلَقَهُ اللهُ، ثُمَّ خَلَقَ مِنْهُ كُلَّ خَيْرٍ
>
> I asked the Messenger of Allāh ﷺ: What is the first thing that Allāh created? He ﷺ said: The light of your prophet O Jābir. Allāh created it; ***thereafter He created from it every good.***[7]

2. ʿAmr bin Ḥuṣayb, the brother of Burayda bin Ḥuṣayb is reported to have said:

---

6 ʿAllāma Majlisī, *Biḥār al-Anwār*, v.35, p.17

7 ʿAllāma Majlisī, *Biḥār al-Anwār*, v.25, p.21

بَيْنَا أَنَا وَأَخِي بُرَيْدَةُ عِنْدَ النَّبِيِّ ﷺ إِذْ دَخَلَ أَبُو بَكْرٍ فَسَلَّمَ عَلَى رَسُولِ اللَّهِ ﷺ فَقَالَ لَهُ انْطَلِقْ فَسَلِّمْ عَلَى أَمِيرِ الْمُؤْمِنِينَ فَقَالَ يَا رَسُولَ اللَّهِ وَمَنْ **أَمِيرُ الْمُؤْمِنِينَ؟ قَالَ: عَلِيُّ بْنُ أَبِي طَالِبٍ.** قَالَ عَنْ أَمْرِ اللَّهِ وَأَمْرِ رَسُولِهِ؟ قَالَ: نَعَمْ. ثُمَّ دَخَلَ عُمَرُ فَسَلَّمَ فَقَالَ انْطَلِقْ فَسَلِّمْ عَلَى أَمِيرِ الْمُؤْمِنِينَ فَقَالَ: يَا رَسُولَ اللَّهِ وَمَنْ أَمِيرُ الْمُؤْمِنِينَ؟ قَالَ ﷺ: عَلِيُّ بْنُ أَبِي طَالِبٍ. قَالَ: عَنْ أَمْرِ اللَّهِ وَأَمْرِ رَسُولِهِ؟ قَالَ: نَعَمْ.

While I and my brother Burayda were in the presence of the Prophet ﷺ, Abū Bakr entered and greeted the Messenger of Allāh ﷺ, and he ﷺ said: Go and greet Amīr al-mu'minīn. *Abū Bakr asked: O Messenger of Allāh, and who is Amīr al-mu'minīn? The Prophet ﷺ said: ʿAlī bin Abī Ṭālib* عليه السلام. Abu Bakr asked: Is this by the command of Allāh and the Apostle of Allāh? The Prophet ﷺ said: yes. Thereafter 'Umar entered and greeted, and the Prophet ﷺ said to him: Go and greet Amīr al-Mu'minīn عليه السلام. 'Umar said: O Messenger of Allāh, and who is Amīr al-mu'minīn? The Prophet ﷺ said: ʿAlī bin Abī Ṭālib عليه السلام. Umar asked: Is this by the command of Allāh and the Apostle of Allāh? The Prophet ﷺ said: yes.[8]

3. Imām al-Riḍā عليه السلام is reported to have narrated from his fathers from

8 Shaykh al-Ṭūsī, *Al-Amālī*, p. 289

Imām al-Ḥusayn bin ʿAlī عليه السلام:

قَالَ لِي بُرَيْدَةُ: أَمَرَنَا رَسُولُ اللَّهِ ﷺ أَنْ نُسَلِّمَ عَلَى أَبِيكَ بِإِمْرَةِ الْمُؤْمِنِينَ.

Burāydā said to me: The Messenger of Allāh commanded us to greet your father ***with the name Amīr al-mu'minīn***.[9]

يَابْنَ أَمِيرِ الْمُؤْمِنِينَ

O son of the **Commander of the Faithful**

The appellation Amīr al-mu'minīn, according to different traditions, has different meanings, all of which aptly befit the exalted personality of Imām ʿAlī عليه السلام. Therefore in reality there is no contradiction. The most well-known meaning of this appellation is 'commander of the faithful'. The word *amīr* comes from the word *amr* (order, command). Imām ʿAlī عليه السلام manifesting faith in its utmost purity in all the dimensions of his being qualified to be the *amīr* of the faithful. One of the milestomes of history that brilliantly manifested this reality is the battle of Khandaq, when after having permitted Imām ʿAlī عليه السلام to fight against *'Amr bin 'Abd Wudd*, the Holy Prophet ﷺ said:

بَرَزَ الإِيْمَانُ كُلُّهُ إِلى الشِّرْكِ كُلِّهِ

Faith in its totality has come out to fight with polytheism in its totality...[10]

The Holy Prophet ﷺ in calling Imām ʿAlī عليه السلام *al-īmān kulluh (faith in*

9 Shaykh al-Ṣadūq, *'Uyūn Akhbār al-Riḍā* عليه السلام, v.1, p. 73

10 Sayyid Raḍī al-Dīn bin Ṭāwūs, *Al-Ṭarāʾif fī Maʿrifati Madhāhib al-Ṭawāʾif*, p. 60

its totality) resonated a wealth of information, which only the comprehending ears (*al-udhun al-wāʿiyah*) were able to appreciate. It is such epitomization of faith that makes the entity of ʿAlī emanate nothing but instructions of faith and makes him worthy of being the commander of the faithful. Unfortunately those who later branded themselves with this title were oblivious of the simple reality that '*fāqid al-shay' lā yu'tīh*" (one who lacks something cannot confer the same). One who clearly disobeys Allāh and usurps the right of others becomes a laughing stock when he names himself Amīr al-mu'minīn. This is because only one who totally submits to Allāh ﷻ and personifies faith can confer injunctions and directions of faith. In an interesting tradition narrated from 'Umar bin al-Khaṭṭāb we are told:

سَمِعْتُ رَسُولَ اللَّهِ ﷺ يَقُولُ إِنَّ السَّمَاوَاتِ السَّبْعَ وَالأَرَضِينَ السَّبْعَ لَوْ وُضِعَتْ فِي كِفَّةٍ وَوُضِعَ إِيمَانُ عَلِيٍّ عليه السلام فِي كِفَّةٍ لَرَجَحَ إِيمَانُ عَلِيٍّ عليه السلام

I heard the Messenger of Allāh ﷺ say: Surely if the seven heavens and the seven earths were placed in one of the palms of the scale, and the faith of ʿAlī bin Abī Ṭālib placed on the other, the faith of ʿAlī would be heavier.[11]

In another tradition the Holy Prophet ﷺ vocally informs us that the yardstick of the belief of the believers is the radiant being of ʿAlī. In one of his conversations with Imām ʿAlī عليه السلام, the Holy Prophet ﷺ says:

لَوْ لاَ أَنْتَ لَمْ يُعْرَفِ الْمُؤْمِنُونَ مِنْ بَعْدِي . . .

If you were not there, the believers would not be

11 Hāji al-Nūrī, *Mustadrak al-Wasā'il*, V.15, p. 337

known after me...[12]

Therefore Imām ʿAlī عليه السلام serves as the scale of faith (*mīzān al-īmān*).

يَابْنَ اَمِيرِ الْمُؤْمِنِينَ

O ***the edifice of*** the Commander of the Faithful

As explained in the previous verse, the word اِبْن *ibn* can either refer to the meaning 'the son of' or 'the product of'. Hence, Imām al-Ḥusayn عليه السلام is both the physical edifice[13] of his noble father as well as his spiritual artifact. And if we consider the genitive construction *Amīr al-mu'minīn* to mean 'commander of the faithful' then he becomes an edifice of one who deserves to command the faithful, and consequently inherits and acquires the same qualities.

Due to his infallibility in thought, speech, and action, and ability to bear the Divine Leadership (*imāma*), Imām al-Ḥusayn عليه السلام is qualified to command the faithful. In the radiant salutational recital *Ziyārat al-Jāmiʿa* narrated from Imām al-Hādī عليه السلام, we address the Imāms of the Ahl al-Bayt عليهم السلام as follows:

﴿. . . وَعِبَادِهِ الْمُكْرَمِينَ لاَ يَسْبِقُونَهُ بِالْقَوْلِ وَهُمْ بِأَمْرِهِ يَعْمَلُونَ . . .﴾

And His ennobled servants who do not advance

12 ʿAllāma Majlisī, *Biḥār al-Anwār*, v.37, p. 272

13 In his well-known Treatise of Rights, Imām Zayn al-ʿĀbidīn عليه السلام specifying the rights of the father alludes to his fundamental mediation of the existence of his offpring. He says: And as for the right(s) of your father, you should know that he is your source (*faʿlam annahu aṣluk*), and that was it not for him you would not have existed; so whatever you find in yourself that pleases you, then know that your father is the source of the blessing (*faʿlam anna abāka aṣl al-niʿma*), then praise and thank Allāh. (Shaykh al-Ṣadūq, al-Amālī, pp. 453-454)

> Him in speech, and **act according to His Command**...[14]

And in another place of the same *Ziyārat* we say:

> فَـانّي لَـكُـمْ مُطيـعٌ، ﴿مَـنْ اَطـاعَـكُمْ فقَـدْ اَطـاعَ اللّهَ﴾، وَمَنْ عَصاكُمْ فقَدْ عَصَى اللّهَ...
>
> So indeed I am obedient to you; **whosoever obeys you has obeyed Allāh**, and whosoever disobeys you has indeed disobeyed Allāh...[15]

There are other traditions too that clearly depict that the Imāms of the Ahl al-Bayt ﻉ are the *ulū al-amr* (those worthy to command) mentioned in the following verse:

> ﴿يَا أَيُّهَا الَّذِينَ آمَنُوا أَطِيعُوا اللَّهَ وَأَطِيعُوا الرَّسُولَ وَأُولِي الأَمْرِ مِنْكُمْ فَإِنْ تَنَازَعْتُمْ فِي شَيْءٍ فَرُدُّوهُ إِلَى اللَّهِ وَالرَّسُولِ إِنْ كُنْتُمْ تُؤْمِنُونَ بِاللَّهِ وَالْيَوْمِ الآخِرِ ذَلِكَ خَيْرٌ وَأَحْسَنُ تَأْوِيلاً﴾
>
> O you who have faith! Obey Allāh and obey the Apostle ***and those among you who hold command.*** And if you dispute concerning anything, refer it to Allāh and the Apostle, if you have faith in Allāh and the Last Day. That is better and more favourable in outcome. (4:59)

Jābir al-Juʿfī narrates: I heard Jābir bin ʿAbdillāh al-Anṣārī say:

---

14 Shaykh al-Kafʿamī, *Miṣbāḥ*, p. 505

15 ʿAllāma Majlisī, *Biḥār al-Anwār*, v.99, p. 133

لَمَّا أَنْزَلَ اللّٰهُ عَزَّ وَجَلَّ عَلَى نَبِيِّهِ مُحَمَّدٍ ﷺ : ﴿**يَا أَيُّهَا الَّذِينَ آمَنُوا أَطِيعُوا اللَّهَ وَأَطِيعُوا الرَّسُولَ وَأُولِي الأَمْرِ مِنْكُمْ**﴾ قُلْتُ: يَا رَسُولَ اللّٰه، عَرَفْنَا اللّٰه وَرَسُولَهُ، فَمَنْ أُولُو الأَمْرِ الَّذِيْنَ قَرَنَ اللّٰهُ طَاعَتَهُمْ بِطَاعَتِكَ؟ فَقَالَ ﷺ : «**هُمْ خُلَفَائِي** - يَا جَابِرُ - وَأَئِمَّةُ الْمُسْلِمِيْنَ مِنْ بَعْدِي، أَوَّلُهُمْ عَلِيُّ بْنُ أَبِي طَالِبٍ، ثُمَّ الْحَسَنُ، ثُمَّ الْحُسَيْنُ، ثُمَّ عَلِيُّ بْنُ الْحُسَيْنِ، ثُمَّ مُحَمَّدُ بْنُ عَلِيٍّ الْمَعْرُوفُ فِي التَّوْرَاةِ بِالْبَاقِرِ، سَتُدْرِكُهُ - يَا جَابِرُ - فَإِذَا لَقِيْتَهُ فَاقْرَأْهُ مِنِّي السَّلاَمَ، ثُمَّ الصَّادِقُ جَعْفَرُ بْنُ مُحَمَّدٍ، ثُمَّ مُوْسَى بْنُ جَعْفَرٍ، ثُمَّ عَلِيُّ بْنُ مُوْسَى، ثُمَّ مُحَمَّدُ بْنُ عَلِيٍّ، ثُمَّ عَلِيُّ بْنُ مُحَمَّدٍ، ثُمَّ الْحَسَنُ بْنُ عَلِيٍّ، ثُمَّ سَمِيِّي وَكُنْيِي حُجَّةُ اللّٰهِ فِي أَرْضِهِ، وَبَقِيَّتُهُ فِي عِبَادِهِ ابْنُ الْحَسَنِ بْنِ عَلِيٍّ، ذَاكَ الَّذِيْ يَفْتَحُ اللّٰهُ تَعَالَى ذِكْرَهُ عَلَى يَدَيْهِ مَشَارِقَ الأَرْضِ وَمَغَارِبَهَا. . .

When Allāh revealed unto His Prophet Muḥammad ﷺ the verse *"O you who have faith! Obey Allāh and obey the Apostle* ***and those among you who hold command"***(4:59). I asked [the Prophet ﷺ]: O Messenger of Allāh, we know about Allāh and His Messenger. But who are the *Ulū al-Amr* (those who hold command) whose obedience Allāh placed in

> line with your obedience? He ﷺ said: *They are my successors,* O Jābir, and the leaders of the Muslims after me. The first among them is ʿAlī bin Abī Ṭālib ؑ, then comes al-Ḥasan ؑ, and then al-Ḥusayn ؑ, then ʿAlī the son of al-Ḥusayn ؑ, then Muḥammad the son of ʿAlī ؑ who is well-known in the Torah as al-Bāqir (the cleaver). Soon you will meet him, O Jābir! And when you meet him convey to him my salāms (greetings). Then comes al-Ṣādiq Jaʿfar bin Muḥammad ؑ, then Mūsā bin Jaʿfar ؑ, then ʿAlī bin Mūsā ؑ, then Muḥammad bin ʿAlī ؑ, then ʿAlī bin Mūḥammad ؑ, then al-Ḥasan bin ʿAlī ؑ, then one whose name and teknonym (*kunya*) would be like mine, the proof of Allāh on the earth and His remnant among His servants, the son of al-Ḥasan bin ʿAlī ؑ. He is the one by whom Allāh will conquer the easts and wests of the earth...[16]

Therefore all the Imāms of the Ahl al-Bayt ؑ qualify in the universal sense to be *Amir al-mu'minīn* (commander of the faithful).

يَابْنَ اَمِيرِ الْمُؤْمِنِينَ

O edifice of the Commander of ***all the*** Faithful

A grammatical allusion worthy of consideration, can be understood by looking at the article '*al*' prefixed in the plural "*al-mu'mīnīn*" (the faithful) above. One the well-known grammatical laws is that when the article '*al*' precedes a plural, it signifies that all the extensions of the

16 Al-Baḥrānī, *Tafsīr al-Burhān*, v.2, p. 103

plural are taken into consideration. In our case, when we say *al-mu'minūn*, we mean "all the faithful". Therefore, the appellation Amīr al-mu'minīn signifies that Imām ʿAlī عليه السلام is the commander of *all the faithful*. In a tradition the Holy Prophet صلى الله عليه وآله after informing Imām ʿAlī عليه السلام how Allāh Himself named him Amīr al-mu'minīn, says:

> . . . فَأَنْتَ يَا عَلِيُّ أَمِيْرُ مَنْ فِي السَّمَاءِ وَأَمِيْرُ مَنْ فِي الأَرْضِ وَأَمِيْرُ مَنْ مَضَى وَأَمِيْرُ مَنْ بَقِي فَلاَ أَمِيْرَ قَبْلَكَ وَلاَ أَمِيْرَ بَعْدَكَ لأَنَّهُ لاَ يَجُوْزُ أَنْ يُسَمَّى بِهَذَا الاِسْمِ مَنْ لَمْ يُسَمِّهِ اللّٰهُ تَعَالَى بِهِ
>
> ...Therefore, you, ***O ʿAlī, are the commander (amīr) of those in the heavens and the commander (amīr) of those in the earth, and the commander (amīr) of those who have past, and the commander (amīr) of those who remain. Hence there is no amīr prior to you, nor is there any amīr after you.*** For it is impermissible to name someone with this name whom Allāh has not named.[17]

Consequently his edifice, Imām al-Ḥusayn عليه السلام, who is *ibnu Amīr al-mu'minīn* is also the *amīr* of all the believers.

Amīr al-Mu'minīn – An Exclusive Apellation

It should be known that the appellation '*Amīr al-mu'minīn*' although widely employed by different people in history, is exclusively for Imām ʿAlī عليه السلام. The other Imāms عليهم السلام would not allow their followers to use it for them. Observe the following narrations:

1. Imām ʿAlī عليه السلام is reported to have said:

---

17 Muḥammad bin Aḥmad al-Qummī, *Mi'at Manqaba*, pp. 52-53

قَالَ رَسُولُ اللَّهِ ﷺ لَمَّا أُسْرِيَ بِي إِلَى السَّمَاءِ
كُنْتُ مِنْ رَبِّي كَقَابِ قَوْسَيْنِ أَوْ أَدْنَى فَأَوْحَى
إِلَيَّ رَبِّي مَا أَوْحَى ثُمَّ قَالَ يَا مُحَمَّدُ اقْرأْ عَلَى عَلِيِّ
بْنِ أَبِي طَالِبٍ عليه السلام أَمِيرِ الْمُؤْمِنِينَ السلام **فَمَا
سَمَّيْتُ بِهِ أَحَداً قَبْلَهُ وَلاَ أُسَمِّي بِهَذَا أَحَداً بَعْدَهُ**

The Messenger of Allāh ﷺ said: When I was made to ascend to the Heavens, I was at a distance from my Lord that was like the length of two bows or nearer. So my Lord Revealed unto me what He Revealed. Then He said: O Muḥammad send your greetings to ʿAlī bin Abī Ṭālib, Amīr al-mu'minīn عليه السلام. *Indeed I have not named anyone with this appellation before him, and will never name anyone with it after him.*[18]

2. ʿAllāma Majlisī in his *Biḥār al-Anwār* narrates:

قَالَ رَجُلٌ لِلصَّادِقِ عليه السلام : يَا أَمِيرَ الْمُؤْمِنِينَ فَقَالَ: مَهْ
فَإِنَّهُ لاَ يَرْضَى بِهَذِهِ التَّسْمِيَةِ أَحَدٌ إِلاَّ ابْتَلاَهُ بِبَلاَءِ أَبِي
جَهْلٍ.

A man called Imām al-Ṣādiq عليه السلام 'O Commander of the faithful! whereupon the Imām عليه السلام said: Stop! For surely no one approves being named so, save that he is tried with the trial of Abū Jahl.[19]

3. Shaykh al-Kulaynī in his al-Kāfī narrates the following tradition:

---

18 Shaykh al-Ṭūsī, *Al-Amālī*, p. 295

19 ʿAllāma Majlisī, *Biḥār al-Anwār*, v. 37, p. 334

سَأَلَهُ رَجُلٌ عَنِ الْقَائِمِ يُسَلَّمُ عَلَيْهِ بِإِمْرَةِ الْمُؤْمِنِينَ قَالَ لاَ ذَاكَ اسْمٌ سَمَّى اللَّهُ بِهِ أَمِيرَ الْمُؤْمِنِينَ عليه السلام لَمْ يُسَمَّ بِهِ أَحَدٌ قَبْلَهُ وَ لاَ يَتَسَمَّى بِهِ بَعْدَهُ إِلاَّ كَافِرٌ قُلْتُ جُعِلْتُ فِدَاكَ كَيْفَ يُسَلَّمُ عَلَيْهِ قَالَ يَقُولُونَ السَّلاَمُ عَلَيْكَ يَا بَقِيَّةَ اللَّهِ ثُمَّ قَرَأَ بَقِيَّتُ اللَّهِ خَيْرٌ لَكُمْ إِنْ كُنْتُمْ مُؤْمِنِينَ

A person asked Imām al-Ṣādiq عليه السلام about [Imām] Al-Qā'im عليه السلام, whether it is proper to greet him with [the appellation] Amīr al-Mu'minīn, and he said: No. That is a name that Allāh named Amīr al-Mu'minīn with it, none before him was named with it, and none will name himself with it after him save a disbeliever. The person said: may I be made your ransom, how should one greet him? He عليه السلام said: They should say: Peace be unto you, O remnant of Allāh (*Baqiyyat Allāh*). Thereafter he عليه السلام read the verse of Qur'an, "*What remains of Allāh's provision is better for you...*"(11:86)[20]

يَابْنَ اَمِيرِ الْمُؤْمِنِينَ

O the Edifice of **the Provider of the Faithful**

Another meaning of '*Amīr al-mu'minīn*' is the 'one who provides knowledge to the believers'. This is when the word Amīr stems from the infinitive مِيرٌ '*mīr*' which means جَلْبُ الطعام '*jalb al-ṭa'ām*' (to draw food).

20 Al-Kulaynī, *Al-Kāfī*, v.1, p. 411

Al-Ṭurayḥī in his *Gharīb al-Qur'ān* says:

يُقَالُ : فُلاَنٌ يَمِيرُ اَهْلَهُ اذَا حَمَلَ إِلَيْهِمْ اَقْوَاتَهُمْ مِنْ غَيْرِ بَلَدِهِمْ مِنَ الْمِيْرَةِ بِكَسْرِ الْمِيْمِ وَسُكُوْنِ الْيَاءِ طَعَامٌ يَمْتَارُهُ الإِنْسَانُ اَيْ يَجْلُبُهُ مِن بَلَدٍ الى بَلَدٍ.

> It is said: *Fulān yamīru ahlahu* (So and so provides his family) when he carries to them their provisions from another town. It comes from *al-mīra* which is food that a person obtains or takes from one town to another.[21]

And food in this case does not only refer to 'physical food' that satisfies one's stomach, but fundamentally to spiritual food that elevates the human being. Under the verse of the holy Qur'ān that says '*Then let man look at his food*' (80:24). Imām al-Ṣādiq عليه السلام explains to Zayd al-Shaḥḥām[22], one of his companions that food here refers to knowledge, and that the human being is told to reflect on his knowledge and its origin. Likewise, as we shall soon see, the '*mīr*' referred to in this case is interpreted by the infallible Imāms of the Ahl al-Bayt عليهم السلام to mean knowledge. Consider the following narrations:

1. 'Allāma Majlisī in his *Biḥār al-Anwār* reports :

عَنْ جَابِرٍ عَنْ أَبِي جَعْفَرٍ عليه السلام قَالَ قُلْتُ جُعِلْتُ فِدَاكَ: لِمَ سُمِّيَ اَمِيرُ الْمُؤْمِنِيْنَ اَمِيرَ الْمُؤْمِنِيْنَ؟ قَالَ: لاَنَّهُ يَمِيْرُهُمْ اَلْعِلْمَ، اَمَا سَمِعْتَ كِتَابَ اللّٰهِ عَزَّوَجَلَّ ﴿ونمير أهلنا﴾؟

21 Al-Ṭurayḥī, *Gharīb al-Qur'ān*, p. 279. Also check his *Maj'ma' al-Baḥrayn* v.4, p. 253

22 Shaykh al-Baḥrānī, *Al-Burhān fī Tafsīr al-Qur'ān*, v.5, pp. 584-585

> Jābir is reported to have said:I asked Abī Jaʿfar (al-Bāqir عليه السلام): "May I be made your ranson; why was Amīr al-Mu'minīn (Imām ʿAlī عليه السلام) known as Amīr al-mu'minīn?" The Imām عليه السلام said: 'It is because he provides them (*yamīruhum*) with knowledge; haven't you heard the Book of Allāh '*wa namīru ahlanā*' (*...we will get provisions for our family... (12:65)*)?[23]

2. ʿAllāma Majlisī in his *Biḥār al-Anwār* reports :

> أَبَانُ بْنُ الصَّلْتِ عَنِ الصَّادِقِ عليه السلام : سَمِيُّ أَمِيرِ الْمُؤْمِنِينَ إِنَّمَا هُوَ مِنْ مِيْرَةِ الْعِلْمِ ، وَذَلِكَ أَنَّ الْعُلَمَاءَ مِنْ عِلْمِهِ امْتَارُوا وَمِنْ مِيرَتِهِ اسْتَعْمَلُوا

> Abān bin al-Ṣalt is reported to have said that Imām al-Ṣādiq عليه السلام said: Indeed naming *Amīr al-mu'minīn is* from 'the provision of knowledge'; and that is because the knowledgeable ones took knowledge from him, and took advantage of his provision.[24]

Some esteemed *muḥaddithūn* like the late ʿAllāma Majlisī give the probability that the word Amīr instead of being a common noun meaning 'commander' is an indefinite verb (*al-fi'l al-muḍāri'*) meaning 'I provide' (أَمِيْرُ) that later turned into a proper noun ('*alam*). In other words, Imām ʿAlī عليه السلام said "*Amīru* (I provide) *al-mu'minīna* (the believers)' and thereafter the whole statement turned into a noun referring to Imām ʿAlī عليه السلام. They liken this with name تَأَبَّطَ شَرّاً (lit. he put evil beneath his armpit). The well-known poet Thābit bin Jābir was called that because it is said that the sword never left him.[25] According

---

23 ʿAllāma Majlīsī, *Biḥār al-Anwār*, v.37, p.293

24 Allāma Majlisī, *Biḥār al-Anwār*, v. 37, p. 334

25 E.W.Lane, *E.W.Lane Arabic-English Lexicon*, see under the root word '*abaṭa*'

to a narration indicated in the *Biḥār al-Anwār*, he was known to be so because:

تَـأبَّط سَـيْفًا وَخَـرَجَ فقِيْلَ لأمِّـه: ايْـنَ هُـوَ؟ فقَالَـتْ:
تَأبَّط شَرًّا وَخَرَجَ.

> ...he put a sword beneath his armpit (*ta'abbaṭa sayfan*) and went out; and when his mother was asked, 'Where is he?' she said: He put evil under his armpit (*ta'abbaṭa sharran*) and left.[26]

In short, therefore, *Amīr al-mu'minīn (I provide the faithful)* could be a sentence which later turned into a proper noun.

يَابْنَ اَمِيرِ الْمُؤْمِنِينَ

O son of the **Commander of the Bestowers of Protection**

If we carefully consider the meaning of *al-mu'minūn* (plural of *al-mu'min*) in the genetive construction Amīr al-mu'minīn we may be able to unravel and draw some of the secrets of this radiant verse. Following are some narratives that define the word *mu'min*:

1. Imām al-Ṣādiq ﷺ was asked why a believer was known as *mu'min* and he said:

لِأنَّـهُ اشْـتَقَّ لِلْمُـؤْمِنِ اسْـماً مِـنْ أسْـمَائِه تَعَـالَى فَسَـمَّاهُ مُؤْمِنـا، وَإنَّمَـا سُـمِّيَ الْمُؤْمِنُ لِأنَّـهُ يُؤْمَنُ مِـنْ عَذَابِ اللّهِ تَعَالَى، وَيُـؤْمِنُ عَلَـى اللّهِ يَـوْمَ الْقِيَامَـةِ فَيُجِيْـزُ لَـهُ

26 *Ibid*,, v. 35, p. 133

ذَلِكَ.

It is because He (Allāh) derived for the believer a name from His Names, and named him *mu'min.* And he was named *mu'min* because he is protected from the punishment of Allāh, the Exalted, and gives warrant to Allāh [for others] on the Judgment Day, and Allāh would approve that for him.

2. Imām al-Sadiq عليه السلام when defining the meaning of the Divine Name *al-Mu'min* is reported to have said:

سُمِّيَ الْبَارِئُ عَزَّ وَجَلَّ مُؤْمِنًا لأَنَّهُ يُؤْمِنُ مِنْ عَذَابِهِ مَنْ أَطَاعَهُ

The Maker, Invincible and Exalted, was named *Mu'min* because He protects (*yu'minu*) whosoever obeys Him from His punishment...[27]

Notice carefully that the aforementioned traditions allude to the following important realities:

(a) The believer is a manifestation of the Divine Name *al-Mu'min.*

(b) He enjoys protection (*amān*), and

(c) He confers protection (*yu'minu*) by seeking the same for others from Allāh.

3. The Holy Prophet ﷺ is reported to have said:

أَلاَ أُنَبِّئُكُمْ لِمَ سُمِّيَ الْمُؤْمِنُ مُؤْمِنًا؟ لإِيمَانِهِ النَّاسَ عَلَى أَنْفُسِهِمْ وَأَمْوَالِهِمْ

Should I not inform you why a believer was named

27 Shaykh Saduq, *Al-Tawhid*, p. 205

mu'min? It is because he grants security to people in themselves and their wealth.

4. The Holy Prophet ﷺ is reported to have said:

وَاللَّهِ مَا سُمِّيَ الْمُؤْمِنُ مُؤْمِناً إِلاَّ كَرَامَةً لِأَمِيرِ الْمُؤْمِنِينَ

"I swear by Allāh, the believer was not named *mu'min* save in honor of Amīr al-Mu'minīn

If we study the various derivatives of the word *mu'min* as expounded in the above traditions, we would realize that all of them converge at one single attribute: protection (*amān*). The reason why a believer is called *mu'min* is because he 'enjoys protection' and 'confers the same'. The fourth tradition however requires deliberation to comprehend. Perhaps it would like to tell us that in order to bestow the honorable appellation Amir al-mu'minin to Imām 'Alī عليه السلام, Allāh named the believer as *mu'min*. For the appellation Amīr al-mu'minīn would have no meaning in the absence of people called '*mu'minun*'. Obviously this should not be considered a kind of superficial honorification. The Imām عليه السلام most brilliantly manifesting the Divine Attribute al-Mu'min, qualified to command the believers who manifest this attribute acording to their limitations. Therefore Allāh bestowing honor to Him called the believer a *mu'min* and named Him Amir al-mu'minin.

In conclusion, the genitive construction Amīr al-Mu'minīn means 'The commander of those who confer protection'. Therefore Imām 'Alī عليه السلام is the commander of one who enjoys and confers protection. Consequently, he is the professor and teacher of the lesson of protection (*amān*). He is not merely a theoretical professor, but 'a commander' and thus 'a practical mentor'. And the believers always benefit from his banquet. If we ponder over the abovementioned traditions we would realize that the protection that is spoken about is not always physical protection. A believer fundamentally seeks the spiritual protection of others.

The entire life of Amir al-mu'minin ؏ serves as a lesson for those who would like to learn how to protect themselves and others. The yardstick of such a life, as mentioned in the aforementioned tradition of Imām al-Ṣādiq ؏, is obedience to Allāh. The Imām's thoughts, words, and deeds, all reflect utter submission to Allāh's will.

The Holy Prophet ﷺ describing some of the phenomena of the Day of Judgment to Imām ʿAlī ؏ says:

$$...ثُمَّ يُنَادِيْ مُنَادٍ مِنْ قِبَلِ اللّٰهِ تَعَالى: أَلاَ إِنَّ عَلِيًّا$$
$$وَشِيْعَتَهُ الآمِنُوْنَ يَوْمَ الْقِيَامَة$$

...Thereafter a caller on behalf of Allāh would call: Look! Surely ʿAlī and his followers are the protected ones (al-āminūn) on the Judgment Day.[28]

And in another tradition, the Holy Prophet ﷺ says:

$$يَا عَلِيُّ، أَنْتَ وَشِيْعَتُكَ عَلَى الْحَوْضِ تَسْقُوْنَ مَنْ$$
$$أَحْبَبْتُمْ، وَتَمْنَعُوْنَ مَنْ كَرِهْتُمْ، وَأَنْتُمُ الآمِنُوْنَ يَوْمَ$$
$$الْفَزَعِ الأَكْبَرِ...$$

O ʿAli, you and your followers would quench the thirst of whom you love at the Fountain, and hamper those whom you abhor. *You are the protected ones (al-āminun)* on the Day of the great terror (See 21:103)...[29]

Some of the verses of the Holy Qur'ān also inform us that by maintaining pure faith and observing *taqwā*, 'protection' (*amān*) is a

---

28 ʿAllāma Majlisī, *Biḥār al-Anwār*, v. 37, p. 75

29 ʿAllāma Majlisī, *Biḥār al-Anwār*, v. 65, p. 45

guarantee:

﴿الَّذينَ آمَنُوا وَلَمْ يَلْبِسُوا إيمانَهُمْ بِظُلْمٍ أُولئِكَ لَهُمُ الأَمْنُ وَهُمْ مُهْتَدُونَ﴾

Those who have faith and do not taint their faith with wrongdoing ***for such there shall be safety***, and they are the [rightly] guided."(6:82)

﴿إِنَّ الْمُتَّقِينَ فِي مَقامٍ أَمِينٍ﴾

Indeed the God wary ***are in a secure station*** (44:51)

Imām al-Husayn عليه السلام who is *ibnu Amir al-mu'minin* is in this sense "the product of the commander of those who confer protection". Necessarily, then, he likewise enjoys the characteristics of his father. His entire life serves as a lesson of *amān* and protection from Hell Fire.

In one of the supplications of the Holy month of Sha'ban we express the following about the Ahl al-Bayt عليهم السلام:

اَللّهُمَّ صَلِّ عَلى مُحَمَّدٍ وَآلِ مُحَمَّدٍ اَلْفُلْكِ الْجارِيَةِ فِي اللُّجَجِ الْغامِرَةِ يَأْمَنُ مَنْ رَكِبَها وَيَغْرَقُ مَنْ تَرَكَها

O Allāh bless Muhammad and his progeny, the moving ark in the covering depths [of the sea], whosoever boards in it is protected and whosoever leaves it drowns.[30]

Recitation & Realization

Reciting this verse after having known its comprehensive meaning undoubtedly fills the heart of the loving *zā'ir* with awe and veneration for the *mazūr*. However, as we had mentioned in the very beginning of

30 'Allāma Majlisī, *Biḥār al-Anwār*, v. 87, p. 19

this commentary, the most important and fundamental purpose of our recitation must be unity and coherence with the *mazūr*. If we address Imām al-Ḥusayn ☙ with *ibnu Amīr al-mu'minīn*, and believe that he is fit to command the believers, then we must resolve to practically follow his commands. Believing someone to be *amīr* is practically realized when one follows him. And when we understand Amīr al-mu'minīn ☙ as the commander of those who confer *amān* and safety, then we must practically seek and follow the lesson of confering safety from Imām ☙ and apply the same in our lifetimes. And if we comprehend the appellation Amīr al-mu'minīn as the provider of knowledge to the believers, then we must practically draw our fundamental knowledge from authorities like Imām 'Alī ☙ and the Ahl al-Bayt ☙. And if we understand the meaning of Amīr al-mu'minīn ☙ as the Commander of those who have faith, then we should resolve in following his footsteps and drawing closer to him so that we are entitled to be the bearers of *īmān* and faith.

يَابْنَ اَمِيرِ الْمُؤْمِنِينَ

O Son Of The **Commander Of Those Who Confer Tranquility**

The word *mu'min* is conventionally translated as '*faithful*' or '*believer*'. Its literal import however is worthy of consideration. It comes from the word '*amn*' which according to leading lexicographers like al-Isfahani, means '*tuma'ninat al-nafs*' (tranquility and contentment of the heart). And the word *iman* which we translate as faith actually means '*to place in oneself or another [the state of] amn (tranquility)*. And when we say آمن بالله '*āmana billahi*' which we conventionally translate as 'he believed in Allāh' we literally mean 'he attained contentment and tranquility by Allāh'. Principally when we speak of *īmān billāh* we mean to agree and have tranquility that God exists, He is the overwhelming One, and to Him belong the Attributes of Beauty and Majesty. However, such tranquility which is limited to the belief in the existence of God is substantially different from the tranquility and serenity attained in Allāh. Perhaps the most apt example of tranquility one can cite in the life of the commander of the tranquil ones (Amir al-mu'minin) is what transpired on the well-known *laylat al-mabīt* when Imām 'Ali عليه السلام rests with utter peace and tranquility on the blessed bed of the Holy Prophet صلى الله عليه وآله وسلم while the Prophet صلى الله عليه وآله وسلم sets for his well-known migration to Madina. Indeed I feel it is only the Holy Qur'an that can properly narrate the nature of this historic incident. Almighty Allāh says:

﴿وَمِنَ النَّاسِ مَنْ يَشْرِي نَفْسَهُ ابْتِغَاءَ مَرْضَاتِ اللَّهِ وَاللَّهُ رَؤُوفٌ بِالْعِبَادِ﴾

And among the people is he who sells his soul seeking the pleasure of Allāh, and Allāh is most kind to [His] servants.(2:207)

Imām Zayn al-'Abidīn عليه السلام is reported to have said:

نَزَلَتْ فِيْ عَلِيٍّ عليه السلام حِيْنَ بَاتَ عَلَى فِرَاشِ رَسُوْلِ اللهِ صلى الله عليه وآله وسلم

This verse was revealed about 'Alī عليه السلام when he slept on the bed of the Messenger of Allāh صلى الله عليه وآله وسلم.[31]

In another tradition which shows the extent of *iṭmi'nān* and tranquility of 'Alī عليه السلام, we are told:

. . . فَبَاتَ عَلِيٌّ عليه السلام مُوَطِّنًا نَفْسَهُ عَلَى الْقَتْلِ

So Imām 'Ali عليه السلام slept while he stationed his soul to

31 Al-Bahrayni, *Al-Burhan fi Tafsir al-Qur'an*, v.1, p. 442

be killed...[32]

The phrase *'muwaṭṭinan nafsahu 'alā al-qatl'* reveals so much. It shows the Imām's readiness to be martyred in the way of Allāh. The word '*muwaṭṭinan*' literally connotes that Imām 'Alī (عليه السلام) had stationed his spirit in the *waṭan* (hometown) of martyrdom.

Ayatullāh al-Rayshahrī quoting *al-Ṭabaqāt al-Kubrā* among other historical texts writes in his *Mawsū'at al-Imām 'Alī bin Abī Ṭālib* (عليه السلام):

> . . . فَاقْتَرَحَ ﷺ عَلى عَلِيٍّ (عليه السلام) أَنْ يَبِيْتَ فِيْ فِرَاشِهِ تِلْكَ اللَّيْلَةَ، فَسَأَلَهُ: أَوَ تَسْلَمْ يَا رَسُوْلَ اللهِ؟ قَالَ: نَعَمْ. فَرَحَّبَ الإِمَامُ (عليه السلام) بِهَذَا الاقْتِرَاحِ مُوَطِّنًا نَفْسَهُ لِلْقَتْلِ عِنْدَ مُوَاجَهَةِ الْمُشْرِكِيْنَ صَبَاحًا، وَسَجَدَ سَجْدَةَ الشُّكْرِ عَلَى هَذِهِ الْمَوْهِبَةِ الْعَظِيْمَةِ وَالْتَحَفَ بِالْبُرْدِ الْيَمَانِي الأَخْضَرِ الَّذِيْ كَانَ يَلْتَحِفُ بِهِ النَّبِيُّ ﷺ عِنْدَ نَوْمِهِ، وَنَامَ مُطْمَئِنًّا فِيْ فِرَاشِهِ ﷺ

> ...So the Prophet ﷺ suggested to 'Alī (عليه السلام) that he sleeps that night in his bed, and 'Alī (عليه السلام) asked him: Would you be protected thereby O Messenger of Allāh? He ﷺ said: Yes. So the Imām (عليه السلام) welcomed this suggestion while stationing himself to be martyred when he confronts the polytheists in the morning, and he prostrated in thanks to Allāh for this great gift, and wrapped himself with the green Yemenite cloak that the Messenger of Allāh would cover himself with when he slept, *and he slept in the*

32 Ibid., v.1, pp. 442-443

state of tranquility...[33]

The phrase '*wa nāma muṭma'innan fī firāshihi'* (*and he slept in the state of tranquility in the Prophet's bed)* is worthy of reflection. It shows how Amīr al-mu'minīn having sold his soul to the only beloved is overwhelmed and overtaken with utmost composure and tranquility.

Bearing the aforesaid understanding of the appellation Amir al-mu'minin in mind, the meaning of *ibnu Amir al-mu'minin* confers the implication that Imām al-Husayn ﵇ who is the edifice of the commander of the tranquil spirits also exemplifies the same attribute of tranquility.

Both his words as well as his deeds reveal this reality. In his well-known supplication of 'Arafa, Imām al-Ḥusayn ﵇ is narrated to have said:

مَا ذَاوَجَدَ مَنْ فَقَدَكَ وَمَا الَّذِيْ فَقَدَ من وَجَدَكَ؟

What has he who has lost You found? And what has he who has found You lost?[34]

And Imām al-Ṣādiq ﵇ is reported to have said:

اقْرَؤُوا سُوْرَةَ الْفَجْرِ فِيْ فَرَائِضِكُمْ وَنَوافِلِكُمْ،
فَإِنها سُوْرَةُ الْحُسَيْنِ وَارْغَبوا فيْهَا رَحِمَكُمُ اللّه
فَقَالَ لَهُ أبُو أُسَامَةَ وَكَانَ حَاضِرَ الْمَجْلِس: كَيْفَ
صَارَتْ هَذه السُّوْرَةُ لِلْحُسَيْنِ ﵇ خَاصَّةً؟ فَقَالَ:
ألاَ تَسْمَعُ إِلَى قَوْلِه تَعَالَى: ﴿يَا أَيَّتُهَا النَّفْسُ
الْمُطمَئِنَّة ارْجِعِيْ إِلَى رَبِّكِ رَاضِيَةً مَرْضِيَّة فَادْخُلِيْ

33 Al-Rayshahrī, *Mawsū'at Imām 'Alī bin Abī Ṭālib*, v.1, pp. 158-159

34Al-Rayshahrī, *Mīzān al-Ḥikma*, v.1, p. 502

فِيْ عِبَادِي وَادْخُلِي جَنَّتِيْ﴾ إِنَّمَا يَعْنِي الْحُسَيْنَ بْنَ عَلِيٍّ صَلَوَاتُ اللهِ عَلَيْهِمَا، فَهُوَ ذُوْ النَّفْسِ الْمُطْمَئِنَّةِ الرَّاضِيَةِ الْمَرْضِيَّةِ. . .

> Read *Sūrat al-Fajr* in your obligatory and supererogatory prayers, for indeed it is the chapter of al-Husayn عليه السلام, and have a liking to it, may Allāh have mercy on you. Thereupon Abū Usāma, who was present in the gathering asked him عليه السلام: How did this *sūra* become specifically for al-Husayn عليه السلام? The Imām عليه السلام said: Do you not listen to Allāh's word "O contented spirit (*yā ayyatuha al-nafs al-mūtma'inna*), return to your Lord, while you are pleased with Him, and He is pleased with you, and enter the company of My servants, and enter My paradise". It refers to Imām al-Husayn bin 'Ali عليه السلام, for he is the contented spirit who is pleased with his Lord and his Lord is pleased with him...[35]

Al-Baḥrānī narrates a beautiful tradition from Imām Zayn al-ʿĀbidīn عليه السلام which describes the situation of Imām al-Ḥusayn عليه السلام and his brilliant companions before their departure from this world when the situation intensified as follows:

. . . وَكَانَ الْحُسَيْنُ عليه السلام وَبَعْضُ مَنْ مَعَهُ مِنْ خَصَائِصِهِ تُشْرِقُ أَلْوَانُهُمْ، وَتَهْدَأُ جَوَارِحُهُمْ، وَتَسْكُنُ نُفُوْسُهُمْ. . .

> ...while the situation of al-Ḥusayn عليه السلام and some of those with him, would be such that their colors

35 'Allāma Majlisī, *Biḥār al-Anwār*, v. 24, p. 93

> would shine, the parts of their bodies would be composed, and their spirits would be in the state of serenity...[36]

Having known the subtle meaning of *ibnu Amīr al-mu'minīn* as the edifice of the possessor and bestower of tranquility, our aspiration should be to uplift ourselves and realize the characteristics of a tranquil soul.

ʿAllāma Majlisī in his *Biḥār al-Anwār* narrates:

> عَنْ أَنَس بْن مَالك قَالَ: قَالَ رَسُوْلُ اللّه ﷺ: ﴿اَلَّذِيْنَ آمَنُوْا وَتَطْمَئِنُّ قُلُوْبُهُمْ بِذِكْرِ اللّه أَلاَ بِذِكْرِ اللّه تَطْمَئِنُّ الْقُلُوْب﴾: أَتَدْرِيْ مَنْ هُمْ يَا ابْنَ أُمِّ سليم؟ قُلْتُ: مَنْ هُمْ يَا رَسُوْلَ اللّه؟ قَالَ: نَحْنُ أَهْلُ الْبَيْتِ وَشِيْعَتُنَا.

> Anas bin Mālik is reported to have said: The Messenger of Allāh recited *"And those who have faith and their hearts are tranquil by the remembrance of Allāh..."* (13:28) and said: Do you know who they are, O son of Umm Sulaym? I said: Who are they, O Messenger of Allāh? He ﷺ said: They are we and our Shīʿa.[37]

---

36 Al-Baḥrānī, *Al-ʿAwālim*, pp. 350-351.

37 ʿAllāma Majlisī, *Biḥār al-Anwār*, v. 35, p. 405

...وَابْنَ سَيِّدِ الْوَصِيِّينَ

...and the son of the **Leader of the Successors**

Here, as in the previous cases, اِبْن 'ibn' bears two different messages: Imām al-Ḥusayn عليه السلام is the son of *sayyid al-waṣiyyīn*, as well as his spiritual product. And because he is the spiritual product of the master of all the past successors of the prophets of Allāh, he likewise excels them and is embellished with the attributes of his father. The word '*sayyid*' literally means 'leader'. Its correlatives are the verbs *sādā-yasūdu* (he led, he is leading). That which makes Imām ʿAlī عليه السلام to be *sayyid al-waṣiyyīn* is his capability to succeed the Leader of the Apostles (*sayyid al-rusul*), who bore the most comprehensive message of Allāh, the Qurʾān, which is introduced as *al-Muhaymin*. Consider the following verse of the Holy Qurʾān:

﴿وَأَنزَلْنَا إِلَيْكَ الْكِتَابَ بِالْحَقِّ مُصَدِّقًا لِّمَا بَيْنَ يَدَيْهِ مِنَ الْكِتَابِ وَمُهَيْمِنًا عَلَيْهِ فَاحْكُم بَيْنَهُم بِمَا أَنزَلَ اللَّهُ وَلَا تَتَّبِعْ أَهْوَاءَهُمْ عَمَّا جَاءَكَ مِنَ الْحَقِّ...﴾

> We have sent down to you the Book with the truth, confirming what was before it of the Book and as a guardian (*muhayminan*) over it. So judge between them by what God has sent down, and do not follow their desires against the truth that has come to you. (5:48)

No Divine Messenger (*rasūl*) or Successor (*waṣī*) can bear the message of the Holy Prophet ﷺ save Imām ʿAlī and his successors, for every

Prophet ﷺ enjoys the station of the Book that was revealed unto him. Therefore because the Imāms of the Ahl al-Bayt ﷷ are the bearers of the Qur᾿ān *(ḥamalat kitābilLāh)* they excel the other prophets and their successors and are rightly known as *sādat al-awṣiyā᾿*. Consider the following narrations:

قَالَ رَسُولُ اللَّه ﷺ : أَنَا سَيِّدُ النَّبِيِّينَ وَوَصِيِّي سَيِّدُ الْوَصِيِّينَ وَأَوْصِيَاؤُهُ سَادَةُ الأَوْصِيَاء

The Apostle of Allāh, upon whom and whose immaculate progeny be peace, said: 'I am the leader of the Prophets and ***my successor is the leader of all the successors, and his successors are the leaders of all the successors.***[38]

وعَنِ ابْنِ عَبَّاسٍ قَالَ قَالَ رَسُولُ اللَّه ﷺ : أَنَا سَيِّدُ الأَنْبِيَاءِ وَالْمُرْسَلِينَ وَأَفْضَلُ مِنَ الْمَلائِكَةِ الْمُقَرَّبِينَ وَأَوْصِيَائِي سَادَةُ أَوْصِيَاءِ النَّبِيِّينَ وَالْمُرْسَلِينَ وَذُرِّيَّتِي أَفْضَلُ ذُرِّيَّاتِ النَّبِيِّينَ وَالْمُرْسَلِينَ. . .

Ibn 'Abbās is reported to have said: The Holy Prophet ﷺ said: 'I am the leader of the Prophets and Apostles, and better than the angels nearmost to Allāh, **and my successors are the the leaders of the successors** of the other prophets and apostles, and my lineage is the best of the lineages of the Prophets and Apostles of Allāh.[39]

38 Shaykh al-Ṭūsī, *Man lā Yaḥḍuruhu al-Faqīh*, v.4, p. 174

39 ʿAllāma Majlisī, *Biḥār al-Anwār*, v.8, p. 22

And in the proximity of the radiant dome of Imām al-Ḥusayn عليه السلام, Imām al-Ṣādiq عليه السلام tells his companion Ṣafwān that all the Divine prophets and their sucessors visit Imām al-Ḥusayn عليه السلام, including the Imām عليه السلام himself. He عليه السلام says

> ... وَمُحَمَّدٌ اَفْضَلُ الاَنْبِيَاءِ وَنَحْنُ اَفْضَلُ الاَوْصِيَاءِ...
>
> ...[including] Muḥammad **the best of the Prophets and we, the best successors...**[40]

In the first volume of his well-known thematic exegesis of Qurʾān, the grand Āyatullāh Jawādī Āmulī (may the Almighty protect his noble self) says:

> 'Inasmuch as the Noble Qurʾān is *muhaymin (supervisor and protector)*, the Seal of the Apostles is also *muhaymin* over the prophets, for every Apostle invites his community to the station of his book, and the station of every prophet is the same as the station of his book, and the station of the Messenger of Allāh ﷺ is the same as the station of the Message that he brought.[41]

And when trying to establish how Imām al-Ḥusayn عليه السلام is the Leader of martyrs, Āyatullah Jawadī Āmulī in his *Shekūfaieye ʿAql* says:

> Ḥusayn عليه السلام is the leader and superior to all the martyrs of the universe. And this station is due to his company with the reality of the Holy Qur'an which is a guardian over all other heavenly scriptures. In other words:

---

40 *Ibid.*, v.101, p. 60

41 Āyatullāh Jawadī Āmulī, *Qurʾān dar Qurʾān*, p. 292

1- The reality of the Prophet ﷺ's progeny is at par with the Holy Qur'an.

2- The reality of Qur'an, apart from verifying the previous books has a supervisory role over them.

3- Every prophet is at par with the heavenly book given to him.

4- When the Progeny of the Holy Prophet ﷺ is equal to the noble Qur'an, they [obviously] are guardians over the great divine men of the past.

This same evidence can be employed to prove that Imām al-Ḥūsayn عليه السلام is among the leaders of all the sucessors of the previous prophets of Allāh (*sayyid al-waṣiyyīn*).

...وَابْنَ سَيِّدِ الْوَصِيِّينَ

...and the son of the **Leader of the Successors**

The word *waṣiyyīn* is the plural of *waṣī* and it literally means [the] 'trustee' to whom one entrusts his will (*waṣiyya*). In the present context, however, it refers to the Divine Trustee who is entrusted with a Divine Will, which is to govern the Islamic state and rule according to the Divine Laws. And Imām ʿAlī عليه السلام was entrusted with this Divine Will before the demise of the Holy Prophet ﷺ on several occasions, the fundamental of which was in *Ghadīr Khumm*, where he ﷺ announced Imām ʿAlī عليه السلام as his successor and sought confirmation from others too. Therefore, when we say that Imām al-Ḥusayn عليه السلام is the edifice, product, and inheritor of the Leader of the Divine successors and trustees, we are also implying that he has inherited the qualities of such successorship. And in rising against an illegal government that would ruin and demolish the material and spiritual felicity of the believers, he practically manifested his trustworthiness and successfully undertook his mission of Divine leadership.

CHAPTER 4

أَلسَّلاَمُ عَلَيْكَ يَا بْنَ فَاطِمَةَ

سَيِّدَةِ نِسَآءِ الْعَالَمِيْنَ

Peace be on you, O son of Fāṭima – the leader of the women of the worlds

أَلسَّلاَمُ عَلَيْكَ يَاابْنَ فَاطِمَةَ

سَيِّدَةِ نِسَآءِ الْعَالَمِيْنَ

Peace be on You, O son of Faṭima-
the Leader of the Women of the Worlds

COMMENTARY

أَلسَّلاَمُ عَلَيْكَ يَاابْنَ فَاطِمَةَ

Peace be unto you, O son of Fāṭima

This verse is one of the most radiant verses of *Ziyārat 'Āshūrā'*, for it reveals the pleasant origin of Imām al-Ḥusayn ﷺ and his utter purity. Not only is the Imām ﷺ a physical offspring of the sublimest example of purity and goodness, he is her spiritual artifact (*binā'*) as well. One of the appellations of Ḥaḍrat Faṭima ﷺ is *al-Ṭayyiba* (the pleasant one). In a well-known *Ziyārat* of the Holy Prophet ﷺ we supplicate as follows:

. . . اَللَّهُمَّ صَلِّ عَلَى فَاطِمَةَ الطَّيِّبَةِ الطَّاهِرَةِ الْمُطَهَّرَةِ، الَّتِي انْتَجَبْتَهَا وَطَهَّرْتَهَا وَفَضَّلْتَهَا عَلَى نِسَاءِ الْعَالَمِيْنَ. . .

...O Allāh, bless Fāṭima, *the pleasant one* (*al-Ṭayyiba*), the pure, the purified, whom You chose, purified and preferred over all the women of the worlds...[1]

Imām al-Ḥusayn عليه السلام being the offspring of a pure mother the like of *al-Ṭayyiba*, also inherits utter purity. Small wonder it is that one of his appellations is *al-Ṭayyib*: Abū Shibl narrates:

> قُلْتُ لأَبِي عَبْدِ اللَّهِ عليه السلام أَزُورُ قَبْرَ الْحُسَيْنِ عليه السلام قَالَ نَعَمْ زُرِ الطَّيِّبَ وَأَتِمَّ الصَّلاَةَ فِيهِ. . .
>
> I said to Imām al-Ṣādiq عليه السلام: I visit the grave of *al-Ḥusayn* عليه السلام He عليه السلام said: Yes, *visit al-Ṭayyib*[2] *(the pleasant one)*, and pray the complete prayer (and not *qaṣr*) near him...[3]

In another tradition, Abū Saʿīd al-Madāʾinī says: I entered in the presence of Abū ʿAbdillāh [al-Ṣādiq عليه السلام], and I said: May I be made your ransom. Should I visit the grave of al-Ḥusayn عليه السلام? He (ʿa) said:

> نَعَمْ يَا أَبَا سَعِيدٍ ائْتِ قَبْرَ الْحُسَيْنِ عليه السلام ابْنِ رَسُولِ اللَّهِ صلى الله عليه وآله أَطْيَبِ الأَطْيَبِينَ وَأَطْهَرِ الطَّاهِرِينَ وَأَبَرِّ الأَبْرَارِ فَإِنَّكَ إِذَا زُرْتَهُ كَتَبَ اللَّهُ لَكَ بِهِ خَمْساً وَ عِشْرِينَ حَجَّةً.
>
> Yes O Abā Saʿīd, visit the grave of al-Ḥusayn عليه السلام, the offspring of the Messenger of Allāh صلى الله عليه وآله, **the most**

1 ʿAllāma Majlisī, *Biḥār al-Anwār*, v.98, pp.262-263

2 The root meaning of *al-ṭayyib* is 'that which is desirable, in which there is no kind of apparent or hidden dirt...' [See *Muṣṭafawī's al-Taḥqīq*, v.7, p. 151]. Al-Iṣfahānī confers a similar definition in his *Al-Mufradāt*. He says: '*wa aṣl al-ṭayyib mā tastalidhhuhu al-ḥawās, wa mā tastalidhhuhu al-nafs*' (and the root meaning of *al-ṭayyib* is that by which the senses take pleasure, and that which the soul takes pleasure [See *Al-Mufradāt of Al-Iṣfahānī*, , p. 527.]

3 Shaykh al-Kulaynī, *al-Kāfī*, v.4, p. 587

> **pleasant of the most pleasant ones and the most pure of the pure ones**, and the most righteous of the righteous ones; for surely if you visit him, Allāh will write for you the reward of twenty five pilgrimages (*ḥajjs*).[4]

In the well-known *Ziyarat al-Jāmi'a al-Kabīra* there is a statement that alludes to the *process of the transfer* of purity. We are taught to address the Ahl al-Bayt عليهم السلام in the following way:

. . . وَأَنَّ أَرْوَاحَكُمْ وَنُورَكُمْ وَطِينَتَكُمْ وَاحِدَةٌ
طَابَتْ وَطَهُرَتْ بَعْضُهَا مِنْ بَعْضٍ . . .

> ...and that your spirits, your light, and your nature are one; they became pleasant and purified some from others...[5]

In another tradition where the *basis of transfer* is clearly depicted, the Holy Prophet ﷺ presents a Divine law:

. . . فَأَبَى أَنْ يُخْرِجَ مِنَ الطَّيِّبِ إِلاَّ الطَّيِّبَ

> ...And He [Allāh] did not allow to produce from a pleasant entity save a pleasant entity.[6]

In a beautiful conversation with Kumayl bin Ziyād al-Nakha'ī Amīr al-mu'minīn 'Alī عليه السلام narrates the Prophet ﷺ as saying:

**عَلِيٌّ مِنِّي وَابْنَايَ مِنْهُ وَالطَّيِّبُونَ مِنِّي وَأَنَا مِنْهُمْ وَهُمُ
الطَّيِّبُونَ بَعْدَ أُمِّهِمْ وَهُمْ سَفِينَةٌ مَنْ رَكِبَهَا نَجَا وَمَنْ**

---

4 'Allāma Majlisī, *Biḥār al-Anwār*, v.98, pp. 41

5 Shaykh al-Ṭūsī, *Man Lā Yaḥḍuruhu al-Faqīh*, v.2, p. 613

6 'Allāma Majlisī, *Biḥār al-Anwār*, v.65, p. 24

تَخَلَّفَ عَنْهَا هَوَى . . .

> ʿAlī is from me, and my two sons are from him, and the *ṭayyibūn* [a reference to the A'imma عليهم السلام] are from me, and I am from them, and they are the *tayyibūn* (pleasant ones) after their mother, and they are the Ark upon which whoever boards is emancipated, and whosoever lags behind, falls...[7]

Readers are requested to reflect on the phrase "*wa hum al-ṭayyibūn ba'da ummihim*" (and they are the pleasant ones after their mother) which subtly alludes to the root and transfer of their purity.

In order to understand better the transfer of purity, let us consider the following verses and narrations:

1- The Holy Qur'ān presents a parable of universal significance:

﴿أَلَمْ تَرَى كَيْفَ ضَرَبَ اللَّهُ مَثَلاً كَلِمَةً طَيِّبَةً كَشَجَرَةٍ طَيِّبَةٍ أَصْلُهَا ثَابِتٌ وَفَرْعُهَا فِي السَّمَاءِ. تُؤْتِي أُكُلَهَا كُلَّ حِينٍ بِإِذْنِ رَبِّهَا وَيَضْرِبُ اللَّهُ الأَمْثَالَ لِلنَّاسِ لَعَلَّهُمْ يَتَذَكَّرُونَ﴾

> Don't you see how Allāh sets forth a parable? **A pleasant word**[8] (*kalima ṭayyiba*) is like a goodly tree, whose root is firmly fixed, and its branches (reach) to the heavens, It brings forth its fruit at all times, by the leave of its Lord. So Allāh sets forth parables

---

7 ʿAllāma Majlisī, *Biḥār al-Anwār,* v.74, p. 278

8 Unlike the word of man which is expressed by the tongue, *kalima* with regard to Almighty Allah refers to His creation. His creation is His speech. Therefore *kalima ṭayyiba* refers to a being of purity. Prophet ʿIṣā عليه السلام in the Holy Qur'ān is referred to as "*... wa kalimatuhu alqāha ilā Maryam...*" (and His Word that He cast toward Mary) (4:171)

for men, in order that they may receive admonition. (14:24)

This verse must be understood in light of the fact that Allāh's word is different from the word of the human being. According to a radiant expression of Amīr al-mu'minīn 'Alī عليه السلام in *Nahj al-Balāgha*, Allāh's words are His very creations. He عليه السلام says: '*And surely His speech is the action that He originates...*'[9] Therefore when we speak of *kalima ṭayyiba* we refer to a pleasant and good being. And among the fundamental requisites of such an entity, as depicted in the above verse, is a firm and powerful origin. One who is born to parents of firm knowledge and action, would always inhabit the skies of spiritual elevation, and benefit others every moment by the permission of their Lord. In a tradition Imām al-Bāqir عليه السلام says the following about the aforementioned verse:

... نَحْنُ الشَّجَرَةُ الَّتِيْ قَالَ اللهُ تَعَالَى ﴿أَصْلُهَا ثَابِتٌ وَفَرْعُهَا فِي السَّمَاءِ﴾، نَحْنُ نُعْطِي شِيعَتَنَا مَا نَشَاءُ مِنْ عِلْمِنَا

We are the tree about which Almighty Allāh said "...*whose root is firmly fixed, and its branches (reach) to the heavens*" (14:24). We are the ones who give our Shī'as what we want from our knowledge...[10]

2. Imām Amīr al-mu'minīn 'Alī عليه السلام alluding to the reality that the fruit depends on the water of the plant says:

... وَاعْلَمْ أَنَّ كُلَّ عَمَلٍ نَبَاتٌ، وَكُلَّ نَبَاتٍ لاَ غِنَى بِهِ عَنِ الْمَاءِ، وَالْمِيَاهُ مُخْتَلِفَةٌ، فَمَا طَابَ سَقْيُهُ

9 Imām 'Alī عليه السلام, *Nahj al-Balāgha*, sermon 228

10 Quṭb al-Dīn al-Rāwandī, *Al-Kharā'ij wa al-Jarāyiḥ*, v.2, p. 596

طابَ غَرْسُهُ، وَحلَتْ ثَمَرَتُهُ، وَمَا خَبُثَ سَقْيُهُ خَبُثَ غَرْسُهُ، وَأَمَرَّتْ ثَمَرَتُه.

...and know that every action is a plant, and every plant is not needless of water, and waters are of different kinds. And if the water of a plant is pure and pleasant, its growth would be pleasant and its fruit sweet. And if the water of a plant is dirty and unpleasant, its growth would be unpleasant and its fruit bitter.[11]

3. Alluding to the fundamental importance of the land where the plant grows, the Holy Qur'ān says:

﴿وَالْبَلَدُ الطيِّبُ يَخْرُجُ نَبَاتُهُ بِإِذْنِ رَبِّهِ وَالَّذِي خَبُثَ لاَ يَخْرُجُ إِلاَّ نَكِدًا﴾

The good land its vegetation comes out by the permission of its Lord, and as for that which is bad, it does not come out except sparsely. (7:58)

4. In a well-known *Ziyārat* when addressing the Imāms of the Baqī' cemetery in Madina we say:

. . . طِبْتُمْ وَطابَ مَنْبِتُكُم . . .

You are pleasant and the place of your growth too is pleasant and pure...[12]

5. Alluding to the pleasant growth of Ḥaḍrat Maryam عليها السلام Almighty Allāh says:

---

11 'Allāma Majlisī, *Biḥār al-Anwār*, v.29, p. 600

12 Shaykh al-Kulaynī, *Al-Kāfī*, v.4, p. 559

﴿فَتَقَبَّلَهَا رَبُّهَا بِقَبُولٍ حَسَنٍ وَأَنْبَتَهَا نَبَاتاً حَسَناً . . .﴾

Thereupon her Lord accepted her with a beautiful acceptance, and caused her to grow as a lovely plant...(3:37)

6. Imām al-Ḥusayn ﵇ says in his well-known supplication of ʿArafa:

خَلَقْتَنِي مِنَ التُّرَابِ، ثُمَّ أَسْكَنْتَنِي الأَصْلاَبَ آمِناً لِرَيْبِ الْمَنُونِ وَإِخْتِلاَفِ الدُّهُوْرِ، **فَلَمْ أَزَلْ ظَاعِناً مِنْ صُلْبٍ إِلى رَحِمٍ فِيْ تَقَادُمِ الأَيَّامِ الْمَاضِيَةِ وَالْقُرُوْنِ الْخَالِيَةِ**

...You created me from clay, then established me in loins safe from the unpredictable turn of destiny and the difference of times; **then I have been shifting from the loin to the womb along the course of the bygone days and the past centuries.**"[13]

Here Imām al-Ḥusayn ﵇ is trying to teach us of a profound reality: the question of transfer of purity or impurity is not necessarily from the immediate parents. Generations are responsible.

7. In the well-known *Ziyārat al-Wārith* we address Imām al-Ḥusayn ﵇ in the following way:

أَشْهَدُ أَنَّكَ نُوْراً فِي **الأَصْلاَبِ الشَّامِخَةِ وَالأَرْحَامِ الْمُطَهَّرَةِ** لَمْ تُنَجِّسْكَ الْجَاهِلِيَّةُ بِأَنْجَاسِهَا . . .

Surely I bear witness that you were **a light in the great loins and the pure wombs,** the [age of]

13 Sayyid Raḍī al-Dīn bin Ṭāwūs al-Ḥasanī, *Iqbāl al-Aʿmāl*, v.2, p.74

> ignorance did not taint you with its dirt...[14]

Here again notice the words *al-aṣlāb* (loins) and *al-arḥām* (wombs) are in the plural form, which means that Imām al-Ḥusayn عليه السلام is the edifice of a whole generation, and not mere one *ṣulb* (loin) and *raḥim* (womb).

8. In his address to the disobedient Kūfans on the plains of Karbalā he alluded to his pure origin saying:

> اَلاَ اِنَّ الدَّعِيَّ بْنَ الدَّعِيِّ قَدْ رَكَزَ بَيْنَ اثْنَتَيْنِ، بَيْنَ الْقِلَّةِ وَالذِّلَّةِ، وَهَيْهَاتَ مَا آخُذُ الدَّنِيَّةَ، اَبَى اللّٰهُ ذَلِكَ وَرَسُوْلُهُ، وَجُدُوْدٌ طَابَتْ وَحُجُوْرٌ طَهُرَتْ، وَاُنُوْفٌ حَمِيَّةٌ وَنُفُوْسٌ اَبِيَّةٌ. . .
>
> Beware the illegal offsping, product of the illegal offspring, has made me to choose between the two: fighting with my few men and accepting the degradation [of paying oath of allegiance to Yazīd]; This [i.e.accepting the latter] is farfetched; I will never accept degradation; Allāh and His Messenger and ***pleasant grandparents and pure bossoms and leaders of valor and protective souls*** do not allow that...[15]

The aforementioned quotations teach us that in order for one to be bestowed with an offspring the like of Imām al-Ḥusayn عليه السلام, one is required to travel through a similar spiritual chain. Obviously a completely indentical chain is impossible to attain, but one can establish the foundation of a chain that nurtures the values of the lineage of Imām al-Ḥusayn عليه السلام. There is always time for rectification and change. The Holy Qur᾿ān says:

---

14 Sayyid Raḍī al-Dīn bin Ṭāwūs al-Ḥasanī, *al-Luhūf fī Qatlā al-Ṭufūf*, p.6

15 ʿAllāma Majlisī, *Biḥār al-Anwār*, v.45, p.9

﴿يُخْرِجُ الْحَيَّ مِنَ الْمَيِّتِ وَيُخْرِجُ الْمَيِّتَ مِنَ الْحَيِّ
وَيُحْيِي الْأَرْضَ بَعْدَ مَوْتِهَا وَكَذَلِكَ تُخْرَجُونَ﴾

He brings forth the living from the dead and brings
forth the dead from the living, and gives life to the
earth after its death, and thus shall you be brought
forth. (30:19)

Imām al-Ṣādiq ☙ explaining the phrase '*He brings forth the living
from the dead and brings forth the dead*' in a tradition says:

فَالْحَيُّ اَلْمُؤْمِنُ الَّذِي تَخْرُجُ طِينَتُهُ مِنْ طِينَةِ
الْكَافِرِ. وَالْمَيِّتُ الَّذِي يَخْرُجُ مِنَ الْحَيِّ هُوَ
اَلْكَافِرُ الَّذِي يَخْرُجُ مِنْ طِينَةِ الْمُؤْمِنِ.

The living is the believer whose clay comes out from
the clay of a disbeliever, and the dead that comes out
from the living is a disbeliever, who comes out from
the clay of a believer.[16]

Therefore if we firmly resolve to purify our beliefs and actions and
unite with the spirit of *tawḥīd*, we can serve as the foundation of a
powerful generation to come[17]. This is where determining issues such as
'the formation of the worldview of the youth', 'spouse selection and its
correct criteria', 'etiquette of spousal interaction', 'prenatal care in both
the physical as well as spiritual dimensions', 'child upbrining','the
importance of the temperament of the wetnurse during breastfeeding'
etc. come into focus. Modern science has partially contributed in

---

16 Shaykh al-Kulaynī, *Al-Kāfī*, v.2, p. 5

17 One of the interpretations given for *kalima ṭayyiba* is *kalimat Lā ilāha illa Allah*. If
the parents purify themselves and make their foundations of belief and action firm,
they would serve as origins of those human beings who truly personify *Lā ilāha illa
Allāh*.

showing how some of these factors determine the felicity and happiness of the child.

The Canadian Psychiatrist, Dr. Thomas Verny, well-known as the world's leading expert on the effects of the prenatal and the early post-natal environment on personality development in his '*The Secret Life of the Unborn Child*' has interesting information to reveal. He says:

> ... a woman is her baby's conduit to the world. Everything that affects her, affects him. And nothing affects her as deeply or hits with such lacerating impact as worries about her husband (or partner). Because of that, few things are more dangerous to a child, emotionally and physically, than a father who abuses or neglects his pregnant wife...
>
> An equally vital factor in the child's emotional well-being is his father's commitment to the marriage. Any number of things can influence a man's ability to relate to his partner, from the way he feels about his wife or his own father to his job pressures or his own insecurities. (Ideally, of course, the time to work out these problems is before conceiving, not during a pregnancy.)[18]
>
> (The mother's) thoughts and feelings are the material out of which the unborn child fashions himself. When they are positive and nurturing, the child can ... withstand shocks from almost any quarter. But the fetus cannot be misled either. If he is good at sensing what is on his mother's mind generally, he is even better at sensing her attitude towards him...[19]

---

18 Dr. Thomas Verny, *The Secret Life of the Unborn Child*, p.25

19 Ibid., p. 43

Certainly exemplifying the method of how to prepare the foundation of a powerful generation would require a separate work in itself. One of the very important secrets for the success of the future child is the perfection of the preparatory causes. If both the spouses enjoy a sound temperament and spiritual purity, and both consume the right foods before and after copulation, and both maintain an environment of serenity and Divine love, they would always serve as foundations of powerful generations to come. The Holy Qur'ān cites a beautiful parable showing that Divine Grace is abundantly showered to all. The limitations of the receptacles, however, determine the nature of their bodies and spirits. The more deficient the receptacle, the more deificient the result. This also pertains to physical beauty. Hence you may find some children with excellent physical features, but poor moral traits, and vice versa. The Holy Qur'ān says:

﴿أَنزَلَ مِنْ السَّمَاءِ مَاءً فَسَالَتْ أَوْدِيَةٌ بِقَدَرِهَا. . .﴾

He sends down water from the skies, and the channels flow, each according to its measure...(13:17)

Philosophically explaining the differences in quality of the off-springs born, the late Imām al-Khumaynī in his book *'al-Ṭalab wa al-Irāda* says:

فاعلم أنَّ واجب الوجود بالذَّات لمَّا كان واجب
الوجود من جميع الجهات والحيثيَّات يمتنع عليه
قبض الفيض عن الموضوع القابل فإنَّ قبضه بعد
تماميَّة الاستعداد وعدم نقصٍ في جانب القابل
مستلزمٌ لنقصٍ في الفاعل أو جهة امكانٍ فيه
تعالى عنه. وهذا اللزوم والوجوب كلزوم عدم
صدور القبيح وامتناع صدور الظلم عنه اختياريٌّ

اراديٌّ لا يضُرُّ بكونه مريداً مختاراً قَادِراً فَإِذَا تَمَّت الإستعدادات في القوابل أفيضت الفيوضات والوجودات من المبادي العالية. وأمّا إفَاضة الفيض الوجودي بمقدار الاستعداد وقابلية المواد للتاسب بين المادة والصورة للتركيب الطبيعي الإتحادي بينهما لا يمكن قبولها صورة الطف من مقتضى استعدادها كما لا يمكن منعها عمّا استُعِدّت له...

Then be it known to you that because the Essentially Necessary Being is necessary in every dimension, it is impossible to withhold grace from the receptacle of grace. This is because withholding it while the latter enjoys complete receptivity or does not have any deficiency, necessitates the imperfection of the Provider of grace or His contingent nature, exalted is He from such attributions. And such kind of necessity [when we say that it is impossible to withhold Divine Grace] is similar to the essential impossibility of evil and oppression issuing from God, which is something volitional and does not contradict His possession of free will and power. Hence when there exists complete receptivity in the receptacles, grace is bestowed from higher causes. And as for bestowing existential grace in proportion to the receptivity of potency of the receptacle (*al-mādda*), it is because there is a specific coherence between the potency of a receptacle (*al-mādda*) and the actuality of its form (*al-ṣūra*), due to a united

> natural composition between them, and thus the receptacle cannot accept a subtler and more perfect form than the requisite of its aptitude. Similarly it is impossible to deprive it from that which it can potentially accept.

Therefore there is no stinginess or favoritism from the All-Gracious. He bestows abundance of grace to every human being from the onset. The receptacles, however, are deficient, and thus limit or hamper the grace. The doors, however, are never closed. The temporal life of this world is an opportunity to change. The human being, from which ever land it starts developing, is in possession of an unsullied innate nature. It is the parents that blemish their attitudes and direct them to the path of spiritual destruction.

Imām al-Ṣādiq عليه السلام is reported to have said:

> مَا مِنْ مَوْلُودٍ يُولَدُ إلاَّ عَلَى الْفِطْرَةِ فَأَبَوَاهُ اللَّذَانِ يُهَوِّدَانِهِ وَ يُنَصِّرَانِهِ وَ يُمَجِّسَانِهِ
>
> No baby is born save with the sound nature (*fiṭra*). Thereafter it is his parents that change him into a Jew, a Christian, or a Magian.[20]

أَلسَّلَامُ عَلَيْكَ يَابْنَ فَاطِمَةَ

Peace be unto you, O son of **Fāṭima**

Ibnu Fāṭima is a matronym worthy of contemplation. In order to understand it well it is imperative for us to look at the origins of the name *Fāṭima*. According to traditions of the Ahl al-Bayt عليهم السلام, the name

20 Shaykh Ṣadūq, *Man lā Yaḥḍuruhu al-Faqīh*, v.2, p. 49

'*Fāṭima*' has various derivatives. Some of them are as follows:

1. Her weaning (*fiṭām*) was concurrent with Divine inspiration and she was detached from impurity (*fuṭimat ʿan al-tamth*):

Imām Abū Jaʿfar [al-Bāqir عليه السلام] is reported to have said:

> لَمَّا وُلِدَتْ فَاطِمَةُ عليها السلام أَوْحَى اللَّهُ إِلَى مَلَكٍ فَأَنْطَقَ بِهِ لِسَانَ مُحَمَّدٍ ﷺ فَسَمَّاهَا فَاطِمَةَ ثُمَّ قَالَ إِنِّي فَطَمْتُكِ بِالْعِلْمِ وَفَطَمْتُكِ مِنَ الطَّمْثِ ثُمَّ قَالَ أَبُو جَعْفَرٍ عليه السلام وَاللَّهِ لَقَدْ فَطَمَهَا اللَّهُ بِالْعِلْمِ وَعَنِ الطَّمْثِ فِي الْمِيثَاقِ
>
> When Fatima عليها السلام was born, Allāh sent down a revelation to an angel, who thereupon made the tongue of Muḥammad ﷺ speak whereupon he named her Fatima عليها السلام. Then Allāh تعالى said: Indeed I detached you [from ignorance] through knowledge (*faṭamtuki bi al-'ilm*) and detached you from menstruation (*faṭamtuki min al-tamth*). Thereafter Abu Jaʿfar عليه السلام said: I swear by Allāh, indeed Allāh detached her [from ignorance] through knowledge and detached her from menstruation during the Divine covenant (*fī al-mīthāq*).[21]

Commenting on this, ʿAllāma Majlisī in his *Biḥār al-Anwār* says:

> بيان: فطمتك بالعلم أي أرضعتك بالعلم حتى استغنيت وفطمت، أو قطعتك عن الجهل بسبب العلم أو جعلت فطامك من اللبن مقرونا بالعلم

21 Al-Kulaynī, *Al-Kāfī*, v.1, p. 460

كناية عن كونها في بدو فطرتها عالمة بالعلوم الربانية. وعلى التقادير كان الفاعل بمعنى المفعول كالدافق بمعنى المدفوق

> Exposition: *Faṭamtuki bi al-ʿilm* (I detached you through knowledge) means *arḍaʾtuki bi al-ʿilm* (I fed you with knowledge) until you were satisfied and weaned. Or it means "I detached you from ignorance by means of knowledge", or "I made your weaning from milk accompany knowledge", which alludes that from the very beginning of her inner makeup she was endowed with the Divine knowledge (*ʿulūm Rabbāniyya*). In the aforesaid possibilities, the active participle (*fāʿil*) is in the meaning of the passive participle (*mafʿūl*) such as *al-dāfiq* in the meaning of *al-madfūq* (86:6)[22]

Considering Imām al-Husayn عليه السلام as *ibnu Fāṭima*, we conclude that he is an offspring of one who was free from physical impurities and endowed with Divine knowledge even before her descent to this worldly life. Consequently he (Imām عليه السلام) also possesses similar qualities: his birth did not accompany any kind of impurity and he was endowed with Divine knowledge from the very onset. Following are traditions worthy of contemplation:

- In a tradition narrated in al-Kāfī, Imām al-Bāqir عليه السلام enumerating some of the characteristics of an infallible Imām says:

. . . يُولَدُ مُطهَّراً مَخْتُوناً وَإذا وَقَعَ عَلَى الأرْضِ وَقَعَ

---

22 ʿAllāma Majlisī, *Biḥār al-Anwār, v. 43, p. 13.* Allāma is trying to simply say that the word Fāṭima which is in the pattern of an active participle signifies the meaning of a passive participle. This is because she is "cut off from ignorance" and "cut off from impurity". So in this case she is the passive participle.

عَلَى رَاحَتِهِ رَافِعاً صَوْتَهُ بِالشَّهَادَتَيْنِ . . .

...He [the infallible Imām عليه السلام] is born pure and circumcised, and when he descends on the ground he falls on his arms, while he loudly declares the *shahādatayn*...[23]

- In another tradition narrated from Ḥaḍrat Ṣafiyya Bint ʿAbd al-Muṭṭalib, where the specific details of the pure birth of Imām al-Ḥusayn عليه السلام is mentioned we read:

لَمَّا سَقَطَ الْحُسَيْنُ بْنُ فَاطِمَةَ عليها السلام كُنْتُ بَيْنَ يَدَيْهَا فَقَالَ لِيَ النَّبِيُّ ﷺ هَلُمِّي إِلَيَّ بِابْنِيَّ فَقُلْتُ يَا رَسُولَ اللَّهِ إِنَّا لَمْ نُنَظِّفْهُ بَعْدُ فَقَالَ النَّبِيُّ ﷺ أَنْتَ تُنَظِّفِينَهُ إِنَّ اللَّهَ قَدْ نَظَّفَهُ وَطَهَّرَهُ . . .

When al-Ḥusayn عليه السلام, the son of Fāṭima عليها السلام descended to the ground, I was near Fāṭima عليها السلام. Thereupon the Prophet ﷺ said to me: Bring to me my son. I said: O Messenger of Allāh, we have not yet cleaned him. So the Prophet ﷺ said: Do you think you would clean him? Indeed Allāh has cleaned and purified him...[24]

- With regard to Imām al-Ḥusayn عليه السلام's knowledge even prior to his descent in this material world, we have ample traditions that reveal that the Ahl al-Bayt عليهم السلام possessed knowledge even prior to their birth. One of these that speak of this reality is as follows:

قَالَ رَسُولُ اللَّهِ ﷺ أَنَا وَعَلِيٌّ وَفَاطِمَةُ وَالْحَسَنُ

23 Al-Kulaynī, Al-Kāfī, v.1, p. 388

24 ʿAllāma Majlisī, *Biḥār al-Anwār*, v. 43, p. 256

وَالْحُسَيْنُ كُنَّا فِي سُرَادِقِ الْعَرْشِ نُسَبِّحُ اللَّهَ وَتُسَبِّحُ الْمَلَائِكَةُ بِتَسْبِيحِنَا قَبْلَ أَنْ خَلَقَ اللَّهُ عَزَّ وَ جَلَّ آدَمَ بِأَلْفَيْ عَامٍ . . .

The Holy Prophet ﷺ is reported to have said: I, ʿAlī, Fāṭima, Ḥasan and Ḥusayn, were in the pavilion of the Divine Throne glorifying Allāh, and the angels would glorify through our glorification. This was two thousand years before Allāh created Adam...

This tradition speaks of their light which was prior to their earthly descent. The fact that they resided in the pavilion of Divine Throne reveals their vast knowledge already. This is because in other traditions the ʿArsh is translated as Divine Knowledge:

Imām al-Ṣādiq عليه السلام is reported to have said:

. . . وَالْعَرْشُ هُوَ الْعِلْمُ الَّذِي لاَ يَقْدِرُ أَحَدٌ قَدْرَهُ

...And the throne is knowledge which none can measure...[25]

2. She and her followers are detached from the Hell Fire

The Holy Prophet ﷺ is reported to have said to Ḥaḍrat Fāṭima عليها السلام in the presence of Imām ʿAlī عليه السلام:

يَا فَاطِمَةُ أَتَدْرِينَ لِمَ سُمِّيْتِ فَاطِمَةَ؟ فَقَالَ عَلِيٌّ عليه السلام: يَا رَسُولَ اللهِ لِمَ سُمِّيَتْ؟ قَالَ: **لأَنَّهَا فُطِمَتْ هِيَ وَشِيْعَتُهَا مِنَ النَّارِ.**

O Fāṭima, do you know why you were named

25 ʿAllāma Majlisī, *Biḥār al-Anwār*, v. 4, p. 89

> Fāṭima? Imām ʿAlī said: O Messenger of Allāh, why was she named Fāṭima? He said: Because she and her Shī'as are detached from the Hell Fire.[26]

Imām al-Ḥusayn, who is the offspring and fruit of Fāṭima likewise enjoys the same characteristic: in sacrificing whatever he had for the emancipation of the entire humanity, he serves as a radiant signpost of detaching those who follow his noble footsteps from Hellfire. In fact, in visiting his grave and expressing our salutation to his noble self there is emancipation from Hellfire. Ibn Qūlawayh narrates in his masterpiece collection *Kāmil al-Ziyārāt*:

> قَالَ أَبُو عَبْدِ اللّٰهِ عليه السلام: مَنْ أَتَى قَبْرَ أَبِي عَبْدِ
> اللّٰهِ عليه السلام فَقَدْ وَصَلَ رَسُولَ اللّٰهِ صلى الله عليه وآله وَوَصَلَنَا
> وَحَرُمَتْ غِيْبَتُهُ وَحَرُمَ لَحْمُهُ عَلَى النَّارِ . . .

> Imām al-Ṣādiq said: Whosoever comes to the grave of Abū ʿAbdillāh [al-Ḥusayn], has indeed established contact with the Messenger of Allāh as well as us, and backbiting him is forbidden and his flesh ***is forbidden on the Hell-Fire***...[27]

On the day of ʿĀshurā' while addressing Imām al-Ḥusayn as our host, we request him to ask Allāh to emancipate us from Hell Fire:

> يَا أَبَا عَبْدِ اللَّهِ أَنَا ضَيْفُ اللَّهِ وَضَيْفُكَ وَجَارُ اللَّهِ
> وَجَارُكَ وَلِكُلِّ ضَيْفٍ وَجَارٍ قِرًى وَقِرَايَ فِي هَذَا
> الْوَقْتِ أَنْ تَسْأَلَ اللَّهَ سُبْحَانَهُ وَتَعَالَى أَنْ يَرْزُقَنِي

26 Ibid., v. 43, p. 14

27 Ibnu Qūlawayh, *Kāmil al-Ziyārāt*, p. 127

فَكَاكَ رَقَبَتِي مِنَ النَّارِ إِنَّهُ سَمِيعُ الدُّعَاءِ قَرِيبٌ
مُجِيب.

O Abā ʿAbdillāh, I am the guest of Allāh and your guest, and the refugee of Allāh and your refugee; and for every guest there is a hospitable reception; and the hospitable reception I need from you at this moment is that you ask Allāh, to provide me with emancipation from Hell Fire. Surely He listens to prayers and is near to us.[28]

We must try to understand this tradition carefully. What we seek from Imām al-Ḥusayn عليه‌السلام is not prayer for future safety but current emancipation. And emancipation presumes that we are already burning in Hell Fire. Scholars of gnosis tell us that due to our inner blindness, we cannot perceive our inner pathetic state. Otherwise, if the curtains of darkness were unveiled from our hearts we would comprehend the fire that is in us.

3. She was severed and detached from evil

Yūnus bin Ẓabyān is reported to have said: Abū ʿAbdillāh [al-Ṣādiq] عليه‌السلام said:

أَتَدْرِيْ أَيُّ شَيْءٍ تَفْسِيرُ فَاطِمَة؟ قُلْتُ: أَخْبِرْنِيْ يَا
سَيِّدِيْ، قَالَ: فُطِمَتْ مِنَ الشَّرِّ.

Do you know what is the meaning of the name Fāṭima? I said: Inform me, O master. He عليه‌السلام said: [It means that] she was detached from evil (sharr)....[29]

And sharr (lit. evil) is interpreted by some scholars as sin. The Holy

28 ʿAllāma Majlisī, Biḥār al-Anwār, v. 4, p. 89

29 Shaykh Ṣadūq, Al-Khiṣal, p. 414

Qur'ān sometimes also employs it for the same meaning:

﴿فَمَنْ يَعْمَلْ مِثْقَالَ ذَرَّةٍ خَيْراً يَرَهُ. وَ مَنْ يَعْمَلْ مِثْقَالَ ذَرَّةٍ شَرًّا يَرَهُ﴾

So whoever does an atom's weight of good will see it, and whoever does an atom's weight of evil will see it. (99:78)

Observe that the word "*sharr*" here is employed to denote an evil action, which is "sin" itself.

Hence Fāṭima ﷺ was *maʿṣūma* (infallible). Her offspring and the fruit of her noble being, who is Imām al-Ḥusayn ﷺ likewise was free from sin. This is because he is among the Ahl al-Bayt ﷺ whom Allāh ﷻ Himself purified from sin and indecency.
The Holy Qur'ān says in Sūrat al-Aḥzāb:

﴿. . . إِنَّمَا يُرِيدُ اللَّهُ لِيُذْهِبَ عَنْكُمُ الرِّجْسَ أَهْلَ الْبَيْتِ وَ يُطَهِّرَكُمْ تَطهِيراً﴾

...Indeed Allāh desires to repel all impurity from you, O People of the Household, and purify you with a thorough purification. (33:33)

4. Her lovers are detached from Hellfire

The Holy Prophet ﷺ is reported to have said:

إِنِّي سَمَّيْتُ ابْنَتِي فَاطمَةَ لِأَنَّ اللَّهَ عَزَّ وَجَلَّ فَطمَهَا وَفَطمَ مَنْ أَحَبَّهَا مِنَ النَّارِ

Indeed I named by daughter as Fāṭima because Allāh, the Invincible and Exalted, **detached her and**

those who love her from the Hell-Fire.[30]

According to a universal principle conveyed by the Holy Qur'ān, a true lover is a sincere follower:

﴿قُلْ إِنْ كُنْتُمْ تُحِبُّونَ اللَّهَ فَاتَّبِعُوني يُحْبِبْكُمُ اللَّهُ وَيَغْفِرْ لَكُمْ ذُنُوبَكُمْ وَ اللَّهُ غَفُورٌ رَحِيمٌ﴾

Say, "If you love Allāh, then follow me; Allāh will love you and forgive you your sins, and Allāh is all-forgiving, all-merciful." (3:31)

Therefore those who sincerely follow the footsteps of Ḥaḍrat Zahrā' ﷿ and hence enjoy true love for her, would obviously be detached from Hell Fire. In a very beautiful tradition Imām al-Bāqir ﷿ says:

وَهَلِ الدِّينُ إِلاَّ الْحُبُّ

And is religion other than love?[31]

Imām al-Ḥusayn ﷿ in this sense being *ibnu Fāṭima* ﷿ likewise is one whose love emancipates one from Hell Fire. In fact there is a narration that pertains to the true love of all the Ahl al-Bayt ﷿. The Holy Prophet ﷺ is reported to have said:

مَنْ أَحَبَّنَا أَهْلَ الْبَيْتِ حَشَرَهُ اللَّهُ آمِناً يَوْمَ الْقِيَامَة

Whosoever loves us the Ahl al-Bayt, Allāh would raise him in the state of protection on the Day of Judgment.[32]

5. She is an intermediary of Divine Grace

---

30 'Allama Majlisi, *Biḥār al-Anwār*, v. 43, p. 12

31 Shaykh al-Kulaynī, *Al-Kāfī*, v.8, p. 79

32 'Allāma Majlisī, *Biḥār al-Anwār*, v. 27, p. 79

In different traditions we are told that Allāh derived the name Fāṭima from His Name *Fāṭir al-samāwāti wa al-arḍ* (6:79) (The Cleaver of the heavens and the earth). The name *al-Fāṭiru* comes from the word *faṭr* which means to "cleave". Here it means one who cleaves and breaks non-existence and brings about existence. In conclusion, as some scholars have written in their works, it means 'The Originator'. Observe the following traditions:

- In a lengthy tradition, where the Ahl al-Kisā' were present, the Holy Prophet at one point addresses Ḥaḍrat Fāṭima saying:

. . . وَشَقَّ لَكِ يَا فَاطِمَةُ اسْماً مِنْ أَسْمَائِهِ فَهُوَ
الْفَاطِرُ وَأَنْتِ فَاطِمَةُ

...And He derived for you O Fāṭima a name from His Names, for He is *al-Fāṭiru* (the Originator), and you are *Fāṭima*.[33]

- Almighty Allāh in a conversation with prophet Adam introduces the light of Fāṭima as follows:

. . . وَهَذِهِ فَاطِمَةُ وَأَنَا فَاطِرُ السَّمَاوَاتِ وَالأَرْضِ
فَاطِمُ أَعْدَائِي عَنْ رَحْمَتِي يَوْمَ فَصْلِ قَضَائِي
وَفَاطِمُ أَوْلِيَائِي عَمَّا يَعْتَرِيهِمْ وَيَشِينُهُمْ فَشَقَقْتُ لَهَا
اسْماً مِنِ اسْمِي

...and this is *Fāṭima* while I am the *Fāṭir al-samāwāti wa al-arḍ* (Originator of the heavens and the earth), *Fāṭimu a'dā'ī min Raḥmatī yawma faṣli qaḍā'ī* (the Severer of My enemies from My mercy on the day of My judgment), and *Fāṭimu awliyā'ī 'ammā*

33 Ibid., v. 37, p. 47

ya'tarīhim wa yashīnuhum (the Relinquisher of affliction and disgrace from those near to me). So I derived for her a name from My Name.

- In a supplication taught by Angel Jibrā'īl ﷺ to Prophet Adam ﷺ we read as follows:

يَا حَمِيدُ بِحَقِّ مُحَمَّدٍ يَا عَالِي بِحَقِّ عَلِيٍّ يَا فَاطِرُ بِحَقِّ فَاطِمَةَ . . .

O praised one, I swear by the station of Muḥammad, O Exalted One, I swear by the station of 'Alī, O Originator, I swear by the station of Fāṭima ﷺ...[34]

Readers must understand that this tradition does not speak simply of the method of derivation that we commonly know. Fāṭima ﷺ plays a fundamental role in the creation and origination of the heavens and the earth. She unites with the Muḥammadan Light which is the first Divine Creation, from which proceeds every good.

Imām al-Ḥusayn ﷺ, being *ibnu Fāṭima* ﷺ, also manifests the attribute of *al-Fāṭiru*. This is also because he is united with the Muḥammadan Reality (*al-Nūr al-Muḥammadī*), which is the intermediary of Divine grace.

Other traditions also indicate that they - the Ahl al-Bayt ﷺ - are the intermediaries (*wasā'iṭ*) between Allāh and the creation. For example, in one of his brilliant messages, our 12th Holy Imām ﷺ is reported to have said:

نحنُ صَنَائِعُ رَبِّنا و الخَلقُ بَعْدُ صَنَائِعُنَا

We are the actions of our Lord, and the creation

34 Ibid., v.44, p.245

> thereafter are our actions.[35]

And in a lengthy tradition, the Holy Prophet ﷺ tells Imām ʿAlī ؑ:

> . . . يَا عَلِيُّ وَلَوْلاَ نَحْنُ مَا خَلَقَ اللّٰهُ آدَمَ وَلاَ حَوَّاءَ وَلاَ الْجَنَّةَ وَلاَ النَّارَ وَلاَ السَّمَاءَ وَلاَ الأَرْضَ . . .
>
> ...O ʿAlī, and was it not for us (the Ahl al-Bayt ؑ), Allāh would not have created Adam, nor Ḥawā', nor Paradise, nor Hell Fire, nor the sky, nor the earth...[36]

Commenting on this tradition, Imām Khumaynī in his book of gnosis, *Miṣbāḥ al-Hidāya* says:

> قوله ﷺ: ((لَوْلاَ نَحْنُ مَا خَلَقَ اللّٰهُ آدَمَ)) إلى آخره. **لأنهم وسائط بين الحق والخلق** وروابط بين الحضرة الوحدة المحضة والكثرة التفصيلية؛ وفي هذه الفقرة بيان وساطتهم بحسب أصل الوجود، وكونهم مظهر الرحمة الرحمانية التي هي مفيض أصل الوجود . . .
>
> The Holy Prophet ﷺ said: '*Was it not for us Allāh would not create Adam...*' This is because they (the Ahl al-Bayt ؑ) are intermediaries (*wasā'iṭ*) between God and the creation, and links between the Presence of Sheer Unity (*al-ḥaḍra al-waḥda al-maḥḍa*) and separative plurality (*al-kathra al-tafṣīliyya*); and this part of the tradition explains their intermediary

35 Ibid., v.53, p. 178

36 Ibid., v.18, p. 345

> role in terms of existence, and that they are manifestations of the All-comprehensive Mercy of Allāh, which confers existence itself...[37]

6. The creation cannot comprehend her reality

In the well-known Qur'ānic commentary of *Furāt al-Kūfī* we read the following tradition narrated from Imām al-Sādiq عليه السلام about the chapter al-Qadr:

عَنْ أَبِي عَبْدِ اللَّهِ عليه السلام أَنَّهُ قَالَ ﴿إِنَّا أَنْزَلْنَاهُ فِي لَيْلَةِ
الْقَدْرِ﴾ اللَّيْلَةُ فَاطِمَةُ وَالْقَدْرُ اللَّهُ فَمَنْ عَرَفَ فَاطِمَةَ
حَقَّ مَعْرِفَتِهَا فَقَدْ أَدْرَكَ لَيْلَةَ الْقَدْرِ وَإِنَّمَا سُمِّيَتْ
فَاطِمَةَ لِأَنَّ الْخَلْقَ فُطِمُوا عَنْ مَعْرِفَتِهَا

> Imām Abū 'Abdillāh al-Sādiq عليه السلام is reported to have said that in the verse 'Indeed we sent it on the *laylat al-qadr*' the word *al-layla* refers to Fāṭima عليها السلام and the word *al-qadr* refers to Allāh. Therefore whosoever knows Fāṭima عليها السلام the way she must be known, then indeed he has comprehended the *laylat al-qadr*. And surely she was named *Fāṭima* because the creation was detached from comprehending her reality (*li anna al-khalqa fuṭimū 'an ma'rifatihā*).

Readers should understand that the Imām عليه السلام is referring to the esoteric and inner meaning of this verse.[38]

Expounding on this tradition[39], the saintly scholar, Āyatullāh 'Alī Sa'ādat Parwar (may Allāh elevate his noble spirit) in his brilliant

---

37 Imām Khumaynī, *Miṣbāh al-Hidāya*, p. 78

38 Al-Kūfī, *Tafsīr Furāt*, p. 581

39 In order to understand the core of this tradition which is beyond the scope of this work, readers are requested to refer to pp. 11-112 of the Persian treatise *Jelweye Nūr*.

treatise on the spiritual status of Ḥaḍrat Fāṭima عليها السلام *Jelweye Nūr* says that this tradition is understandable after we believe that the reality of the entire Holy Qur᾽ān was received all at once by the heart of the Holy Prophet صلى الله عليه وآله on the night of grandeur. This is because Fāṭima عليها السلام similar to her father enjoys a receptacle that can contain the Divine message. Hence it is proper to call her *Laylat al-Qadr*.

Bearing the aforesaid in mind, the matronym *Ibnu Fāṭima* عليه السلام implies that the creation is likewise detatched from knowing the exalted status and sanctity of Imām al-Ḥusayn عليه السلام.

In a lengthy conversation, Imām ʿAlī عليه السلام says to Abū Dharr:

. . . فَإِنَّكُمْ لاَ تَبْلُغُونَ كُنْهَ مَا فِينَا وَلاَ نِهَايَتَه

> ...for surely you will not attain the zenith or of our station, nor its ultimate state...[40]

And in a brilliant tradition, Imām al-Riḍā عليه السلام, defining the station of an infallible Imām عليه السلام says:

الإِمَامُ وَاحِدُ دَهْرِهِ لاَ يُدَانِيهِ أَحَدٌ وَلاَ يُعَادِلُهُ عَالِمٌ وَلاَ يُوجَدُ مِنْهُ بَدَلٌ وَلاَ لَهُ مِثْلٌ وَلاَ نَظِيرٌ. . . فَمَنْ ذَا الَّذِي يَبْلُغُ مَعْرِفَةَ الْإِمَامِ أَوْ يُمْكِنُهُ اخْتِيَارُهُ هَيْهَاتَ هَيْهَاتَ . . .

> The Imām is unique in his time. None can come closer to him in rank, and no scholar equals him, and he has no subtitute, nor does he have an example or peer...Who then can attain the knowledge of Imām or is able to venture into knowing him? It is indeed farfetched! It is indeed

---

40 ʿAllāma Majlisī, *Biḥār al-Anwār*, v. 26, p. 1

farfetched!...[41]

يَا بْنَ فَاطِمَةَ سَيِّدَةِ نِسَآءِ الْعَالَمِينَ

O son of Faṭimah, the Mistress of the Women of the Universe

If we ponder over the appellation that follows the name Fāṭima عليها السلام we come to understand another very important implication of this verse. Ḥaḍrat Fāṭima عليها السلام is known as *Sayyidatu nisā' al-'ālamīn* (*Mistress of the women of the worlds*), which reveals her presiding status (*siyāda*) over all other women, past, present, and future. The word *sayyida* is the feminine form of the noun *sayyid*, which confers the connotation of presidence and mastership.

In order to understand the *root meaning* of mastership (*siyāda*), some authoritative scholars like Āyatullah Jawādī Amulī refer to the following tradition of Amīr al-mu'minīn عليه السلام:

بِاحْتِمَالِ الْمُؤَنِ يَجِبُ السُّؤْدُدُ

By shouldering responsibilities mastership becomes essential.

In this sense, all the fourteen infallibles are *sādāt*, for they are the fundamental beings who have shouldered the heaviest responsibility any being can ever shoulder. In the ontological and existential sense they represent the middle link between Allāh and His creation. Therefore every good is sourced through their light. Hence they have mastership over the entire caravan of the creation.

Shaykh Ṣādūq narrates in his masterpiece collection *'Ilal al-Sharāyi'* from Imām al-Ṣādiq عليه السلام:

41 Shaykh al-Kulaynī, *Al-Kāfī*, v.1, p. 201

عَنْ أَبِي عَبْدِ اللَّهِ عليه السلام قَالَ: إِنَّمَا سُمِّيَتْ فَاطِمَةُ مُحَدَّثَةً لِأَنَّ الْمَلَائِكَةَ كَانَتْ تَهْبِطُ مِنَ السَّمَاءِ فَتُنَادِيهَا كَمَا تُنَادِي مَرْيَمَ بِنْتَ عِمْرَانَ فَتَقُولُ يَا فَاطِمَةُ إِنَّ اللَّهَ اصْطَفَاكِ وَطَهَّرَكِ وَاصْطَفَاكِ عَلَى نِسَاءِ الْعَالَمِينَ يَا فَاطِمَةُ اقْنُتِي لِرَبِّكِ وَاسْجُدِي وَارْكَعِي مَعَ الرَّاكِعِينَ فَتُحَدِّثُهُمْ وَيُحَدِّثُونَهَا فَقَالَتْ لَهُمْ ذَاتَ لَيْلَةٍ أَلَيْسَتِ الْمُفَضَّلَةُ عَلَى نِسَاءِ الْعَالَمِينَ مَرْيَمَ بِنْتَ عِمْرَانَ فَقَالُوا إِنَّ مَرْيَمَ كَانَتْ سَيِّدَةَ نِسَاءِ عَالَمِهَا وَإِنَّ اللَّهَ عَزَّ وَجَلَّ جَعَلَكِ سَيِّدَةَ نِسَاءِ عَالَمِكِ وَعَالَمِهَا وَسَيِّدَةَ نِسَاءِ الْأَوَّلِينَ وَ الْآخِرِينَ

Fāṭima عليها السلام was known as *Muḥaddatha* (one spoken to by the angels) because the Angels would descend from the heaven and call her the way they would call Maryam, daughter of ʿImrān. They would say: Indeed Allāh has chosen you and purified you and chosen you over the women of the worlds. O Fatima be obedient to your Lord and prostrate and bow down with those who bow down. So she would speak to them and they would speak to her. One night she said to them: isn't the one who has more merit over all the women of the world Maryam, the daughter of ʿImrān? They said: Indeed Maryam was the Mistress of her world, and indeed Allāh, the Invincible and Magnificent made you the Mistress of the women of your and her world as well as the

> Mistress of the preceding and succeeding women.[42]

The word *al-ʿālamīn* confers the meaning that her mistressship envelops all the worlds, and she presides every woman whatsoever. This is because when the article '*al*' precedes a plural noun, it refers to *all the extensions* of the noun.

Imām al-Ḥusayn عليه السلام being *ibnu Fāṭimati Sayyidati nisā' al-ʿālamīn*, and hence a product and fruit of the mistress of the women of the world, also enjoys qualities of mastership.

Imām Zayn al-ʿĀbidīn عليه السلام reports from Imām al-Ḥusayn عليه السلام:

كَانَ رَسُولُ اللَّهِ صلى الله عليه وآله يَقُولُ فِيمَا بَشَّرَنِي بِهِ: يَا حُسَيْنُ أَنْتَ السَّيِّدُ ابْنُ السَّيِّدِ أَبُو السَّادَةِ . . .

> Among the glad tidings that the Messenger of Allāh صلى الله عليه وآله would give me, is: O Ḥusayn, you are the master (sayyid), son of the master (sayyid), father of masters (sayyids)...[43]

And in the well-known *Ziyarat al-Arbaʿīn* Imām al-Ṣādiq عليه السلام teaches us to address Imām al-Ḥusayn عليه السلام as follows:

وَجَعَلْتَهُ سَيِّداً مِنَ السَّادَةِ وَقَائِداً مِنَ الْقَادَةِ . . .

> ...and He (Allāh) made you a *sayyid* from the sayyids, and a leader from the leaders...[44]

The Path towards Mastership

When we try to to address Imām al-Ḥusayn عليه السلام with mastership, we must struggle to embark on a spiritual journey to attain a color of the

---

42 ʿAllāma Majlisī, *Biḥār al-Anwār*, v. 14, p. 206

43 Ibid., v. 36, p. 344

44 Ibid., v. 98, p. 331

same. The Ahl al-Bayt ﻊ whose light presides over the creation have also taught us the path towards *siyāda* (mastership).

One of the fundamental criteria of mastership is generosity and open-handedness (*jūd*). Consider the following narrations:

1. Imām al-Ḥusayn ﻉ is reported to have said:

مَنْ جَادَ سَادَ وَمَنْ بَخِلَ رَذِلَ

> Whosoever bestows generously reigns supreme, and one who is stingy becomes ignoble.[45]

2. The Holy Prophet ﷺ is reported to have said:

سَيِّدُ الْقَوْمِ خَادِمُهُمْ

> The sayyid of a nation is their servant.[46]

3. Imām ʿAlī ﻉ is reported to have said:

بِالْجُوْدِ تَكُوْنُ السِّيَادَةُ

> Mastership comes about through open-handedness.[47]

4. Imām ʿAlī ﻉ is reported to have said:

سَبَبُ السِّيَادَةِ اَلسَّخَاءُ

> Generosity is the cause of mastership.[48]

5. Imām ʿAlī ﻉ is reported to have said:

---

45 Shaykh Bāqir Sharīf al-Qarashī, *Ḥayāt al-Imām al-Ḥusayn* ﻉ, v.1, p. 157

46 *Man Lā Yaḥḍuruhu al-Faqīh*, v.4, p. 378

47 Al-Āmadī, *Ghurar al-Ḥikam*, p.378

48 Al-Wāsiṭī, *ʿUyūn al-Ḥikam wa al-Mawāʿiẓ*, p. 281

تَجَاوَزْ مَعَ الْقُدْرَةِ وَأَحْسِنْ مَعَ الدَّوْلَةِ تَكْمُلُ لَكَ السِّيَادَةُ

Forgive in power and do good in fortune, your mastership will turn perfect.[49]

Considering the aforesaid narrations which speak of generosity and open-handedness as the criteria of mastership, let us consider the following narration that speaks of the best kind of open-handedness:

The Holy Prophet ﷺ is reported to have said:

وَأَجْوَدَ النَّاسِ مَنْ جَادَ بِنَفْسِهِ وَمَالِهِ فِي سَبِيلِ اللَّهِ

...And the most openhanded of all people, is one who generously bestows his self and his wealth in the way of Allāh.[50]

And Imām al-Ḥusayn ؑ was that sayyid who sacrificed everything that he had for the sake of Allāh. Therefore he has *al-siyāda al-ʿuẓmā* (The greatest mastership).

Hilāl bin Nāfiʿ reports:

وروى هلال بن نافع قال: إني لواقف مع أصحاب عمر بن سعد إذ صرخ صارخ: أبشر أيها الامير فهذا شمر قد قتل الحسين، قال: فخرجت بين الصفين فوقفت عليه وإنه ليجود بنفسه فوالله ما رأيت قط قتيلا مضمخا بدمه أحسن منه ولا أنور وجها، ولقد شغلني نور وجهه وجمال

49 Al-Wāsiṭī, *ʿUyūn al-Ḥikam wa al-Mawāʿiẓ*, p. 200

50 ʿAllāma Majlisī, *Biḥār al-Anwār*, v. 73, p. 12

هيبته عن الفكرة في قتله . . .

Hilāl bin Nāfiʿ reports: I stood with the companions of ʿUmar bin Saʿd, when a caller shouted: Glad tidings to you, O Amīr, for this is Shimr, who has already killed al-Husayn ﷺ. Hilāl says: I left between the two ranks and stood besides him (al-Ḥusayn ﷺ) while surely *he was giving away his life*; I swear by Allāh I never saw a killed man smeared in his blood more beautiful and more sparkling in face than him. And indeed the light of his face and the beauty of his awe-inspiring appearance occupied me from thinking about his martyrdom...[51]

يَا ابْنَ فَاطِمَةَ سَيِّدَةِ نِسَآءِ الْعَالَمِيْنَ

O son of Faṭimah, the Leader of the Women of the Worlds

Some commentators of Ziyārat ʿĀshūrā'[52] have defined *siyāda* as *sharāfa wa ʿulluw al-martaba.* In other words, when we say Ḥaḍrat Fāṭima ﷺ is *Sayyidatu nisā' al-ʿālamīn*, we mean she is the most high-ranking of all women, past, present, and future:

Shaykh Ṣadūq in his *al-Amālī* narrates a lengthy tradition from the Holy Prophet ﷺ, who at one point says:

فَأَمَّا ابْنَتِي فَاطِمَةُ فَهِيَ سَيِّدَةُ نِسَاءِ الْعَالَمِيْنَ مِنَ الأَوَّلِيْنَ وَالآخِرِيْنَ، وَإِنَّهَا لَتَقُوْمُ فِي مِحْرَابِهَا

51 ʿAllāma Majlisī, *Biḥār al-Anwār*, v. 45, p. 57

52 Shaykh ʿAlī Ḥaydar Muʿayyad, *Aḍwā' ʿalā Ziyārat ʿĀshūrā'*, p. 131

فَيُسَلِّمُ عَلَيْهَا سَبْعُوْنَ أَلْفَ مَلَكٍ مِنَ الْمَلَائِكَةِ
الْمُقَرَّبِيْنَ، وَيُنَادُوْنَهَا بِمَا نَادَتْ بِهِ الْمَلَائِكَةُ مَرْيَمَ
فَيَقُوْلُوْنَ: يَا فَاطِمَةُ ﴿إِنَّ اللّٰهَ اصْطَفَاكِ وَطَهَّرَكِ
وَاصْطَفَاكِ عَلَى نِسَاءِ الْعَالَمِيْنَ﴾

> As for my daughter Fāṭima, *she is the Mistress of the women of the worlds from the foremost and latter ones*, and surely she stands in her place of prayer, whereupon seventy thousand angels close to Allāh, send their salutations to her, and call her with what the angels called Maryam. So they say: "O Fāṭima, indeed Allāh chose you and purified you, and chose you over the women of all the worlds."[53]

Therefore Imām al-Ḥusayn عليه السلام who is the son and edifice of *Sayyidatu nisā'i al-ʿālamīn* also is among the most elevated of people. We have already mentioned traditions that clearly distinguish Imām al-Ḥusayn عليه السلام as *sayyid*. However, because we defined the word *sayyid* here to mean *sharīf*, let us consider the following verse of the well-known salutational recital of *Ziyārat al-Jāmiʿa al-Kabīra*:

وَطَأْطَأَ كُلُّ شَرِيْفٍ لِشَرَفِكُمْ . . .

> And every *sharīf* (one who enjoys an elevated status) bows down before your elevated status (*li sharafikum*)...[54]

This clearly informs us that the Infallible Imāms of the Ahl al-Bayt عليهم السلام enjoy the highest stations, and therefore all of them are *sayyids* in relation to the people.

---

53 Shaykh Ṣadūq, *Al-Amālī*, p. 575

54 ʿAllāma Majlisī, *Biḥār al-Anwār*, v. 99, p. 132

يَابْنَ فَاطِمَةَ سَيِّدَةِ نِسَآءِ الْعَالَمِيْنَ

O son of Faṭimah, the Mistress of the Women of the Universe

Another possible meaning of *Sayyidat al-Nisā*, as understood from a tradition, is that she is *mufrūḍāt al-ṭā'a* (one who must be obeyed) with regard to all the women. That is, whatever she commands must be obeyed, and her words and deeds are are proof for them. Rather according to a tradition, she has this position with regard to all:

Imām Muḥammad al-Bāqir عليه السلام is reported to have said:

> وَلَقَدْ كَانَتْ عليها السلام مَفْرُوْضَةَ الطاعَةِ عَلَى جَمِيْعِ مِنْ خَلْقِ اللهِ مِنَ الْجِنِّ وَالإِنْسِ وَالطيْرِ وَالْوَحْشِ وَالأَنْبِيَاءِ وَالْمَلاَئِكَةِ.
>
> And indeed she عليها السلام was **one to be compulsorily obeyed by all the creation: the Jins, the human beings, the birds, the wild animals, the prophets and the angels.**[55]

And *mafrūḍat al-ṭā'a* (one who must be obeyed) in this tradition should not be merely taken as one who must be obeyed by all through their volitions. Rather it also speaks of *wilāya takwīniyya* (ontological presidence), which means that she has Divinely bestowed power and can control or lay effect on their entities of existence. This definition of mistressship is an inspiration from the following tradition:

'Allāma Majlisī narrated the following tradition in *Biḥār al-Anwār*:

55 Al-Shāhrūdī, *Mustadrak Safīnat al-Biḥār*, v.6, p. 208

وَقَالَ النَّبِيُّ ﷺ: عَلِيٌّ سَيِّدُ الْعَرَبِ فَقَالَتْ عَائِشَةُ يَا رَسُولَ اللَّهِ أَلَسْتَ سَيِّدَ الْعَرَبِ؟ قَالَ أَنَا سَيِّدُ وُلْدِ آدَمَ وَعَلِيٌّ سَيِّدُ الْعَرَبِ. فَقَالَتْ عَائِشَةُ: يَا رَسُولَ اللَّهِ وَمَا السَّيِّدُ؟ قَالَ: مَنِ افْتُرِضَتْ طَاعَتُهُ كَمَا افْتُرِضَتْ طَاعَتِي.

The Prophet ﷺ said: ʿAlī is the Sayyid of the Arabs. So ʿĀʾisha asked: O Messenger of Allāh, aren't you the Sayyid of Arabs? He ﷺ said: I am the Sayyid of the children of Adam, and ʿAlī is the Sayyid of the Arabs. So ʿĀʾisha asked: O Messenger of Allāh, and who is a sayyid? He ﷺ said: One whose obedience is made compulsory, the way my obedience is made compulsory.[56]

And the traditions of the Ahl al-Bayt عليهم السلام are clear that all the Imāms are *muftaraḍ al-ṭāʿa*. There are clear expressions about that in some interesting traditions. Observe the following traditions:

Al-ʿĀmilī in his *Wasāʾil al-Shīʿa* narrates:

قَالَ وَرُوِيَ أَنَّ الصَّادِقَ عليه السلام مَرِضَ فَأَمَرَ مَنْ عِنْدَهُ أَنْ يَسْتَأْجِرُوا لَهُ أَجِيراً يَدْعُو لَهُ عِنْدَ قَبْرِ الْحُسَيْنِ عليه السلام فَوَجَدُوا رَجُلًا فَقَالُوا لَهُ ذَلِكَ فَقَالَ أَنَا أَمْضِي وَلَكِنَّ **الْحُسَيْنَ إِمَامٌ مُفْتَرَضُ الطَّاعَةِ وَهُوَ إِمَامٌ مُفْتَرَضُ الطَّاعَةِ** فَرَجَعُوا إِلَى الصَّادِقِ عليه السلام وَأَخْبَرُوهُ فَقَالَ هُوَ كَمَا قَالَ وَلَكِنْ أَمَا عَرَفَ أَنَّ

56 ʿAllāma Majlisī, *Biḥār al-Anwār*, v.4, p.198

لِلَّه تَعَالَى بِقَاعاً يُسْتَجَابُ فِيهَا الدُّعَاءُ فَتِلْكَ الْبُقْعَةُ مِنْ تِلْكَ الْبِقَاعِ.

It is narrated that Imām al-Ṣādiq عليه السلام once got ill, and ordered someone who was near him to to tell his people to hire someone, so that he may pray for him near the grave of al-Ḥusayn عليه السلام. So they found a person, and told him to do what is required. He said: I will go, **but al-Ḥusayn عليه السلام is an Imām who must be compulsorily obeyed (muftaraḍ al-ṭā'a) and he (i.e. Imām al-Ṣādiq عليه السلام) [likewise] is an Imām who must be compulsorily obeyed.**[Aren't they equal in status?] So they went to Imām al-Ṣādiq عليه السلام and informed him what the person had said. The Imām عليه السلام said: What he said is correct. However, is he not aware that Allāh has places, wherein supplications are accepted. And that spot [i.e. near the grave of al-Ḥusayn عليه السلام] is among those places.[57]

'Allāma Majlisī narrates the following tradition in his *Biḥār al-Anwār*:

عَنْ عَبْدِ اللَّهِ بْنِ الْفَضْلِ قَالَ كُنْتُ عِنْدَ أَبِي عَبْدِ اللَّهِ عليه السلام فَدَخَلَ عَلَيْهِ رَجُلٌ مِنْ أَهْلِ طوس فَقَالَ لَهُ: يَا ابْنَ رَسُولِ اللَّهِ مَا لِمَنْ زَارَ قَبْرَ أَبِي عَبْدِ اللَّهِ الْحُسَيْنِ بْنِ عَلِيٍّ عليه السلام؟ فَقَالَ لَهُ: **يَا طوسِيُّ مَنْ زَارَ قَبْرَ أَبِي عَبْدِ اللَّهِ الْحُسَيْنِ بْنِ عَلِيٍّ عليه السلام وَهُوَ يَعْلَمُ أَنَّهُ إِمَامٌ مِنَ اللَّهِ مُفْتَرَضُ الطاعَةِ** عَلَى الْعِبَادِ غَفَرَ اللَّهُ

57 Al-'Āmilī, *Wasā'il al-Shī'a*, v.14, p. 537

لَهُ مَا تَقَدَّمَ مِنْ ذَنْبِهِ وَمَا تَأَخَّرَ وَقَبِلَ شَفَاعَتَهُ فِي سَبْعِينَ مُذْنِباً وَلَمْ يَسْأَلِ اللَّهَ جَلَّ وَعَزَّ عِنْدَ قَبْرِهِ حَاجَةً إِلاَ قَضَاهَا لَهُ.

ʿAbdullāh bin al-Fāḍl is reported to have said: I was with Abū ʿAbdillāh [al-Ṣādiq عليه السلام], and a person from the inhabitants of Ṭūs came in his presence. He said to the Imām عليه السلام: O son of the Messenger of Allāh, what reward is there for one who visits the grave of Abū ʿAbdillāh al-Ḥusayn bin ʿAlī عليه السلام? The Imām عليه السلام said to him: **O Ṭusī, whosoever visits the grave of Abū ʿAbdillāh al-Ḥusayn bin ʿAlī عليه السلام while he knows that the Imām عليه السلام is one who is compulsorily to be obeyed (*muftaraḍ al-ṭāʿa*) by the servants of Allāh**, Allāh would forgive him his past and future sins, and would accept his intercession for seventy sinners, and he would not ask any need from Allāh near the Imām's grave save that Allāh would fulfil his need.[58]

ʿAllama Majlisī narrates the following tradition in his *Biḥār al-Anwār*:

عَنْ عَبْدِ الْحَمِيدِ بْنِ نَصْرٍ قَالَ قَالَ أَبُو عَبْدِ اللَّهِ عليه السلام: يُنْكِرُونَ الإِمَامَ الْمُفْتَرَضَ الطَاعَةَ وَيَجْحَدُونَ بِهِ **وَاللَّهِ مَا فِي الأَرْضِ مَنْزِلَةٌ أَعْظَمَ عِنْدَ اللَّهِ مِنْ مُفْتَرَضِ الطاعَةِ . . .**

ʿAbd al-Ḥamiḍ bin Naṣr reports: Abū ʿAbdillāh [Imām al-Ṣādiq] عليه السلام said: They deny the Imām who

58 ʿAllāma Majlisī, *Biḥār al-Anwār*, v.4, p.198

must be compulsorily obeyed and reject him. ***I swear by Allāh there is no station in the earth greater near Allāh then one who must be compulsorily obeyed...***[59]

59 Ibid., v.25, p.141

CHAPTER 5

أَلسَّلَامُ عَلَيْكَ

يَا ثَارَ اللّٰهِ وَابْنَ ثَارِهِ

Peace be unto you, O blood of Allāh and the son of the blood of Allāh

أَلسَّلَامُ عَلَيْكَ يَا ثَارَ اللّٰهِ وَابْنَ ثَارِهِ

Peace be unto You, O Blood of Allāh and
the son of the Blood of Allāh

COMMENTARY

السَّلَامُ عَلَيْكَ يَا ثَارَ اللّٰهِ

Peace be unto You, O possessor of the blood venerated by Allāh

The word *thār* ثَار in the Arabic language has been employed for different meanings: avenging for blood, rancour, blood, the slain, etc.

Many commentators of *Ziyārat ʿĀshurāʾ* have rendered the phrase '*thār Allāh*' as 'blood of Allāh'. ʿAllāma al-Ṭabāṭabāʾī likewise is reported to have said the same thing when asked about its meaning[1].

In order for this verse to be comprehensible, a *muḍāf* (first particle of a genetive construction) is taken to be elliptical and hidden before the word *thār*. The sentence would originally read "*yā ṣāhiba thārillāh*" (O *possessor* of the blood of Allāh'. Therefore when we say "*yā thār Allāh*", we actually mean "*yā ṣāḥiba thārillāh*".

Obviously Allāh is free from any kind of anthropomorphic attribute (Qurʾān, 42:11), and thus the meaning of 'blood of Allāh' should not be taken as 'the blood that is a part of Allāh', far is He from any kind of imperfection whatsoever. The possibility that *thār Allāh* means 'the blood owned by Allāh' is although correct in the real sense, for Almighty Allāh has absolute ownership over every entity (Qurʾān, 3:189), it is not meant in the present case. This is because the appellation '*thār Allāh*' here denotes a distinct characteristic of al-Ḥusayn عليه السلام

---

1 Muḥammad Ḥusayn Rukhshād, *Dar Mahzare ʿAllameye Ṭabātabāʾī*, p. 177

whereas '*thār Allāh*' in its general sense refers to every human being. Unless, however, we would like to express the nobility (*sharāfa*) of the blood of Imām al-Ḥusayn عليه السلام, which was sacrificed in the way of Allāh. We do have similar instances in the Arabic language such as *baytullāh* (house of Allāh), *rūḥullāh* (spirit of Allāh), *nāqatallāh* (camel of Allāh: 91:13), etc. Annexing the name Allāh in such instances is in order to reveal the nobility of the first particle of the genetive construction. In short, when we say '*yā thār Allāh*' we mean 'O one whose blood is the blood that Allāh venerated and preferred over the blood of others.'[2]

أَلسَّلاَمُ عَلَيْكَ يَا ثَارَ اللَّهِ

Peace be unto you, O the spilled blood, whose avenger is Allāh

One of the most clear expositions[3] for *thār Allāh* is that it refers to that blood that has been spilled in falsehood and injustice, and is attributed to the *walī al-dam* (one who has the right to avenge for the blood). Therefore when we say *thār Allāh* we mean 'the spilled blood that belongs to Allāh', and He alone is the avenger of the same. This meaning can be understood in other salutational recitals as well. For example in one of the *ziyārāt* of Imām al-Ḥusayn عليه السلام we address him as follows:

. . . وَأَنَّكَ ثَارُ اللَّهِ فِي الأَرْضِ وَالدَّمُ الَّذِيْ لاَ يُدْرِكُ ثَارَهُ أَحَدٌ مِنْ أَهْلِ الأَرْضِ وَلاَ يُدْرِكُهُ إِلاَّ اللَّهُ وَحْدَهُ

...and that you are the blood of Allāh (*thār Allāh*) in the earth and **the blood** that none of the inhabitants of the earth can avenge, and none save Allāh alone

2 Habībullāh Kāshānī, *Sharḥu Ziyārat 'Āshūrā'*, p. 45

3 Sayyid Mahdī Mīr Bāqirī, *Ṣabr-e-Jamīl Sayr o Sulūk bā 'Āshūrā'*, pp. 75-76

can avenge it.[4]

This, however, does not contradict those salutational recitals and supplications that encourage us to ask Almighty Allāh to enable us avenge the blood of Imām al-Ḥusayn عليه السلام with our present Imām عليه السلام, for he is a vicegerent of Allāh on earth and His medium, and can thus serve as Allāh's representative in avenging the blood of Imām al-Ḥusayn عليه السلام.

The Holy Qur'ān says:

وَلا تَقْتُلُوا النَّفْسَ الَّتِي حَرَّمَ اللَّهُ إِلاَّ بِالْحَقِّ **﴿وَمَنْ**
قُتِلَ مَظْلُوماً فَقَدْ جَعَلْنَا لِوَلِيِّهِ سُلْطَاناً﴾ فَلا يُسْرِفْ
فِي الْقَتْلِ إِنَّهُ كَانَ مَنْصُوراً

> Do not kill a soul [whose life] Allāh has made inviolable, except with due cause, and whoever is killed wrongfully, We have certainly given his heir an authority. But let him not commit any excess in killing, for he enjoys the support [of law.] (17:33)

Al-Baḥrānī in his *Tafsīr al-Burhān*, while commenting on the above verse narrates the following tradition:

عَنْ مُحَمَّد بن سِنَان، عَنْ رَجُلٍ، قَالَ: سَأَلْتُ أَبَا
عَبْدِ اللهِ عليه السلام عَنْ قَوْلِهِ تَعَالَى: وَمَنْ قُتِلَ مَظْلُوماً
فَقَدْ جَعَلْنَا لِوَلِيِّهِ سُلْطَاناً فَلا يُسْرِفْ فِي الْقَتْلِ إِنَّهُ
كَانَ مَنْصُوراً.قَالَ: **ذَلِكَ قَائِمُ آلِ مُحَمَّدٍ عليه السلام،**
يَخْرُجُ فَيَقْتُلُ بِدَمِ الْحُسَيْنِ عليه السلام . . .

---

4 Ibn Qūlawayh, *Kāmil al-Ziyārāt*, v.1, p. 216

> Muḥammad bin Sinān narrates from a person who said: I asked Abā ʿAbdillāh [al-Ṣādiq ﷺ] about the verse "and whoever is killed wrongfully, We have certainly given his heir an authority", and he said: **That is the Qā'im of the progeny of Muḥammad ﷺ. He will come out and rise to avenge the blood of al-Ḥusayn ﷺ...**[5]

We also read in the supplication of *al-Nudba*:

اَيْنَ الطالِبُ بِدَمِ الْمَقْتُوْلِ بِكَرْبَلاَءِ

> Where is the one who would avenge the blood of the one who was killed in Karbalā'...[6]

Therefore whether we say that Allāh Himself will avenge the blood of Imām al-Ḥusayn ﷺ or the present Imām ﷺ will do the same, there is no difference. This is because the Imām ﷺ is an entirely submissive servant of Almighty Allāh and whatever he does is whatever Allāh wants.

أَلسَّلَامُ عَلَيْكَ يَا ثَارَ اللهِ

Peace be unto you, O one whose blood is the blood of Allāh

One of the possible meanings of the phrase *yā thār Allāh* is '*yā man thāruhu thār Allāh'* (O one whose blood is the blood of Allāh)[7]. Here the *zā'ir* declares that Imām al-Ḥusayn ﷺ enjoys the lofty spiritual state of *al-baqāʿ bi Allāh baʿd al-fanāʿ* (survival in Allāh after

5 Al-Baḥrānī, *Al-Burhān fī Tafsīr al-Qur'ān*, v.3, p. 528

6 Al-Mashhadī, *al-Mazār*, p. 579

7 Habībullāh Kāshānī, *Sharḥu Ziyārat 'Āshūrā'*, p. 45

dissolution in Him) which the mystic-scholars expound in their works. Due to the comprehensive and profound meaning it entails, we would not like to go into the details of this reality here.

Those who have attained heights of human perfection through supererogatory worship and obedience (*nawāfil*) come to a station where they vision and comprehend that every act of theirs is done through Almighty Allāh. In other words, Almighty Allāh becomes their means of action. In a sacred tradition [*hadīth al-qudsī*], Almighty Allāh is reported to have said:

مَا يَتَقَرَّبُ إِلَيَّ عَبْدٌ مِنْ عِبَادِي بِشَيْءٍ اَحَبُّ إِلَيَّ مِمَّا افْتَرَضْتُ عَلَيْهِ. وَإِنَّهُ لَيَتَقَرَّبُ إِلَيَّ بِالنَّافِلَةِ حَتَّي أُحِبَّهُ، فَاذَا اَحْبَبْتُهُ، كُنْتُ اذاً سَمْعَهُ الَّذِي يَسْمَعُ بِهِ وَبَصَرَهُ الَّتِي يَبْصُرُ بِهَا وَلِسَانَهُ الَّذِي يَنْطِقُ بِهِ وَيَدَهُ الَّتِي يَبْطِشُ بِهَا، إِنْ دَعَانِي اَجَبْتُهُ.

> My servant does not draw near to me with anything more lovable to Me than what I have made obligatory on him. And surely he never ceases to draw near to Me through supererogatory acts until I love him. And when I love him, I am his hearing through which he hears, his sight through which he sees, his tongue through which he speaks, his hand through which he grasps. When he calls on Me I respond to him.

This tradition speaks of two fundamental kinds of proximity: (a) proximity attained through obligatory deeds (*qurb al-farā'iḍ*), and (b) proximity attained through supererogatory deeds (*qurb al-nawāfil*). *Thār Allāh* refers to the first level. In this level it is the servant who becomes the instrument of Allāh. Almighty Allāh Sees, Hears, and

Speaks through His servant. This should not lead one to conjecture that Allāh is in need of His servant, for the latter's very existence as well as subsistence entirely depend on Allāh's volition. Being an instrument of Allāh rather shows the utter obedience of the servant and his unity with Divine volition. Perhaps Imām al-Ḥusayn عليه السلام's well-known dictum '*Riḍa Allāh Riḍānā Ahl al-Bayt'* (The pleasure of Allāh is our pleasure, the Ahl al-Bayt عليهم السلام[8] refers to this very state. The servant in this state becomes عَيْنُ الله *'aynullāh* (the eyes of Allāh), يَدُالله *yadullāh* (the hand of Allāh) or ثَارَالله "*thārullāh*" (blood of Allāh), which means that He employs these intermediaries of the elevated human being to do what He decides. Hāshim bin ʿUmāra narrates: I heard Amīr al-mu'minīn ʿAlī عليه السلام say:

أَنَا عَيْنُ اللّٰهِ وَأَنَا يَدُ اللّٰهِ وَأَنَا جَنْبُ اللّٰهِ وَأَنَا بَابُ اللّٰهِ

> I am the eye of Allāh, and I am the hand of Allāh; and I am the side of Allāh and I am the door of Allāh.[9]

And Aswad bin Saʿīd reports: I was with Abū Jaʿfar عليه السلام, and he said:

نَحْنُ حُجَّةُ اللّٰهِ وَنَحْنُ بَابُ اللّٰهِ وَنَحْنُ لِسَانُ اللّٰهِ
وَنَحْنُ وَجْهُ اللّٰهِ وَنَحْنُ عَيْنُ اللّٰهِ فِي خَلْقِهِ . . .

> We (the Ahl al-Bayt) are the proof of Allāh, we are the door of Allāh, and we are the tongue of Allāh, and we are the face of Allāh, and we are the eye of Allāh in His creation...[10]

Scholars of insight when expounding this exalted state also refer to the following verse of the Holy Qur'ān:

---

8 Imām Khumaynī, *Glosses on the Commentary of Fuṣūṣ al-Ḥikam*, pp. 281-282

9 Shaykh al-Kulaynī, *Al-Kāfī*, v.1, p. 145

10 'Allama Majlisī, *Biḥār al-Anwār*, v.25, p. 384

﴿فَلَمْ تَقْتُلُوهُمْ وَلَكِنَّ اللَّهَ قَتَلَهُمْ وَمَا رَمَيْتَ إِذْ
رَمَيْتَ وَلَكِنَّ اللَّهَ رَمَى وَلِيُبْلِيَ الْمُؤْمِنِينَ مِنْهُ بَلَاءً
حَسَنًا إِنَّ اللَّهَ سَمِيعٌ عَلِيمٌ﴾

You did not kill them; rather it was Allāh who killed them; and you did not throw when you threw, rather it was Allāh who threw, that He might test the faithful with a good test from Himself. Indeed Allāh is All-Hearing, All-Knowing.(8:17)

This verse speaks of the Battle of Badr. The Holy Prophet ﷺ asks Imām ʿAlī عليه السلام to give him a handful of pebbles, whereafter he ﷺ throws them at the faces of the polytheists of Quraysh.[11] Almighty Allāh describes this as His own action. In other words, the Holy Prophet ﷺ was Allāh's agent and medium. He is told: *You did not throw when you threw, but Allāh threw.* In reality no kind of selfhood remained in the Prophet ﷺ. His entire being manifested the Divine.

Thār Allāh, according to some Divine scholars, refers to this very kind of perfection. Imām al-Ḥusayn عليه السلام's entire movement and sacrifice manifested the attributes of Allāh.

Scholars of insight, considering the reality that Imām al-Ḥusayn عليه السلام is *thār Allāh* say that the compensatory price of the blood of al-Ḥusayn عليه السلام therefore is Allāh Himself. The late scholar Āyatullāh Mūḥammad Riḍā Rabbānī in his *Jalawāt-e-Rabbānī* says:

آن حضرت مقام ثاراللهی را واجد است و بهمین جهت
است که خونبهای او خود خداست

That Ḥaḍrat occupies the station of *thār Allāh* and for this very reason his compensatory price is God

11 Shaykh al-Baḥrānī, *Al-Burhān fī Tafsīr al-Qurʾān*, v.2, p. 662

> Himself.[12]

And in his comments over ʿAllāma al-Ṭabāṭabāʾi's translation of *thār Allāh* as '*blood of Allāh*' Shaykh Rukhshād, a former student of ʿAllāma says:

> منظور این است که خداوند متعال خـود خونبهـای امـام حسین – علیه السلام – می باشد؛ زیرا در برابر شـهادت و فداکاری آن حضرت هیچ نعمتی از نعمتهـای آخرتـی جز دیدار پروردگار قرار نمی گرفت.
>
> This implies that Almighty God Himself is the compensatory price of the blood of Imām al-Ḥusayn عليه السلام. This is because in exchange for the Imām's martyrdom and sacrifice, there was no blessing of the Hereafter other than the vision of God.[13]

Perhaps the reason why the compensatory price of al-Ḥusayn عليه السلام is Allāh Himself is the Imām's state of utter dissolution in the Beloved and survival by Him (*al-fanāʾ fī Allāh wa al-baqāʾ bihi*)[14]. As we said earlier, Imām al-Ḥusayn عليه السلام, due to his very exalted station, was a medium of Allāh's works. Therefore, like the Prophet ﷺ who is told '*you did not throw when you threw, rather it was Allāh who threw*'(8:17), Imām al-Ḥusayn did not fight gallantly when he fought gallantly in the plains of Karbalāʾ but Allāh fought gallantly in the plains of Karbalāʾ. This is because every element of Imām al-Ḥusayn

---

12 Āyatullāh Muḥammad Riḍā Rabbānī, *Jalawāt-e-Rabbānī*, v.1, p.305

13 Muḥammad Ḥusayn Rukhshād, *Dar Mahzare ʿAllāmeye Ṭabātabāʾī*, p. 177

14 One should not misconceive such kind of unity being a kind of compositional unity (*ittiḥād*) or incarnation (*ḥulūl*); far is Allāh from every kind of deficiency whatsoever. Those endowed with a sharp vision say that such a state is nothing but 'the unveiling of the reality.' The utterly submissive human being understands that he is nothing but an action of Allāh.

عليه السلام was for Allāh. Hence he can rightly be known as *'aynullāh* (eye of Allāh), *yadullāh* (hand of Allāh), *lisānullāh* (tongue of Allāh), *thārullāh* (blood of Allāh), etc.

Mentioning the lofty station of Imām al-Ḥusayn عليه السلام and his companions, al-Naräqī in his *Mathnawī-e-Ṭāqdīs* says:

این فنای بنده در مولا بُوَد

این فنا از صد بقا اولی بُوَد

این عدم باشد رهِ کویِ بقا

فهم آن خواهی برو تا کربلا

This is the dissolution of the servant in his Master

This dissolution is better than a hundred lives

This dissolution is a path towards the alley of survival

If you would like to know its reality go upto Karbala.[15]

Although the compensatory price for the horrendous massacre cannot be paid, the meaning of 'avenging the blood of Imām al-Ḥusayn عليه السلام', as we shall come to understand later in this *Ziyārat*, would in reality be a struggle to eradicate all those enemies who are openly against a Divine government being established, where the laws of Allāh are executed and the religion is practised in the best possible manner, so that an environment for human perfection is facilitated for every human being.

15 Mawlā al-Narāqī, *Mathnawī-e-Ṭāqdīs*, p. 273

يَا ثَارَ اللهِ

O one who has been killed for the sake of Allāh

Thār has also been translated as *qatīl* (the one who is killed). And when Allāh is annexed to the word *thār*, it confers the meaning *qatīlullāh* (the one killed for Allāh or in His way). The expression *qatīlu Allāh* has come in different *ziyārāt* related to Imām al-Ḥusayn ﷷ. For example in a *Ziyārat* taught by Imām al-Ṣādiq ﷷ we address the Imām ﷷ saying:

أَلسَّلاَمُ عَلَيْكَ يَا قَتِيلَ اللّٰهِ وَابْنَ قَتِيلِهِ أَلسَّلاَمُ عَلَيْكَ يَا ثَارَ اللّٰهِ وَابْنَ ثَارِهِ

> Peace be unto you O martyr, the son of a martyr, peace be unto you, O blood of Allāh, the son of the blood of Allāh...[16]

Observe that the phrase '*thār Allāh wabna thārih*' has also come in this *Ziyārat*. Does it mean therefore that *thār Allāh* has a different meaning from *qatīl Allāh*? Obviously in this place it is possible. However we can also take *thār Allāh* as an emphasis of *qaṭīl Allāh*. In our case, i.e. in Ziyārat 'Āshurā', however, it is possible that this phrase would like to confer the meaning of both the phrases depicted in the above quotation. And Allāh is All-Knowing.

16 'Allama Majlisī, *Biḥār al-Anwār*, v.98, p. 151

وَابْنَ ثَارِهِ

And the offspring of the blood of Allāh

This phrase talks about Imām ʿAlī عليه السلام also occupying the exalted station of *thār Allāh.* Perhaps it would like us to know that Imām al-Ḥusayn عليه السلام being the product (*ibn*) of a *thār Allāh* inherited the same appellation from his father.

CHAPTER 6

الْوِتْرَ الْمَوْتُورَ

The exceptionally unique

الْوِتْرَ الْمَوْتُورَ

The Exceptionally Unique

COMMENTARY

الْوِتْرَ الْمَوْتُورَ

The Exceptionally Unique

The original meaning of *al-witr* in the Arabic language is *al-fard* (single) and *man lā thāniya lah* (one who does not have a second)"[1]. And *al-mawtūr* which is an adjective of *al-witr* also means the same, but is brought as an emphasis[2] in this case. A similar example[3] has come in the Qur'ān with regard to *ḥijr* (forbidden) and *maḥjūr* (prohibited), the latter being an emphasis of the former:

﴿يَوْمَ يَرَوْنَ الْمَلَائِكَةَ لَا بُشْرَى يَوْمَئِذٍ لِّلْمُجْرِمِينَ وَيَقُولُونَ حِجْرًا مَّحْجُورًا﴾

On the day when they shall see the angels, there shall be no joy on that day for the guilty, and they shall say: **It is a forbidden thing totally prohibited.** (25:22)

---

1 Sayyid Ḥusayn al-Hamadānī, *Sharḥ al-Asmā' al-Ḥusnā*, p.143

2 This variable has been discussed by great scholars like al-Narāqī in his *Mushkilāt al-Akhbār* (p. 301) and al-Shubbar in his *Maṣābīḥ al-Anwār* (p. 341). 'Allāma al-Ṭabāṭabā'i also translated *al-witr al-mawtūr* as 'the unique one' (Rukhshād, *Dar Maḥzar-e-'Allāmeye Ṭabāṭabā'ī*, p. 184)

3 Other examples that have come in Arabic literature are: *bardun bārid, shi'run shā'ir*, etc.

And in the well-known supplication of *al-Ṣabāḥ*, Amīr al-mu'minīn 'Alī ﷺ tries to emphasize *al-layl* (the night) with the adjective *al-alyal* (nightly):

صَلِّ اللَّهُمَّ عَلَى الدَّلِيلِ إِلَيْكَ فِي اللَّيْلِ الأَلْيَلِ
وَالْمَاسِكِ مِنْ أَسْبَابِكَ بِحَبْلِ الشَّرَفِ الأَطْوَلِ

> Bless, oh Allāh, the guide to You in the darkest night, him who, of Thy ropes, clings to the cord of the longest nobility...[4]

Some scholars opine[5] that *al-witr* refers to Imām al-Ḥusayn ﷺ's unique spiritual status which the Holy Prophet ﷺ and the Infallible Imāms of the Ahl al-Bayt ﷺ also possess. Hence, in relation to the rest of the creation an infallible leader (*al-imām al-ma'ṣum*) the like of Imām al-Ḥusayn ﷺ occupies a unique station, and hence is *al-witr al-mawtūr.* Amīr al-mu'minīn 'Alī ﷺ describing an Infallible Imām as:

لاَ يُوجَدُ لَهُ مَثِيلٌ وَلاَ يَقُومُ لَهُ بَدِيل

> **He is peerless**, no substitute can represent him.[6]

And in another tradition, Imām al-Riḍā ﷺ describing the qualities of an infallible Imām, says:

الإِمَامُ وَاحِدُ دَهْرِهِ لاَ يُدَانِيهِ أَحَدٌ

> The Imām is unique in his time. **None can come closer to him in rank...**[7]

---

4 'Allāma al-Majlisī, *Biḥār al-Anwār*, v. 84, p. 339

5 I heard this opinion from Āyatullāh Anṣārī Shīrāzī, from whom I would study the 9th volume of the magnum opus *al-Asfār* of Mullā Ṣadrā.

6 'Allāma al-Majlisī, *Biḥār al-Anwār*, v. 25, pp. 169-170

7 Shaykh al-Kulaynī, *Al-Kāfī*, v.1, p. 201

We may also say that Imām al-Ḥusayn عليه السلام is a manifestation of the Divine Name *al-Witru*. The Holy Prophet ﷺ, after speaking about the Divine Names, is reported to have said:

إِنَّهُ وِتْرٌ، يُحِبُّ الوِتْرَ

> Surely He [Allāh] is Unique, and He Loves the unique[8]

Expounding the meaning of *Yā Witru* in his commentary on the supplication of *al-Jawshan al-Kabīr*, Mullā Hādī Sabzawārī says:

(يَا وِتْرُ) ايْ انه الوجود الصرف البسيط الذى لا يخالطه سنخ اخر من ماهية أو مادة أو قوة أو استعداد . . .

> *Yā Witru* means that He is Sheer Existence, which is Simple [Non-composite], and nothing accompanies it like quiddity (*māhiyya*), matter (*mādda*), potentiality (*quwwa*) or potential (*isti'dād*)...[9]

The corollary of being 'sheer existence' (*al-wujūd al-ṣirf*) and 'non-compositeness' (*al-basāṭa*) is uniqueness. This is because it is impossible for a non-composite entity to have a second. Hence, no entity can be likened to His Sacred Essence, nor can any entity be compared to Him.

Imām 'Alī عليه السلام explaining the meaning of the phrase *Allāhu Akbar* says:

يَعْنِي اَلْوَاحِدُ الاَحَدُ الَّذِيْ لَيْسَ كَمِثْلِهِ شَيْءٌ لاَ يُقَاسُ بِشَيْءٍ . . .

> It means that He is One, Non-composite, the like of

8 'Allāma al-Ṭabāṭabā'ī, *al-Mīzān*, v.8, p. 359

9 Mullā Hādī Sabzawārī, *Sharḥ al-Asmā' al-Ḥusnā*, p. 722

> which there is nothing, and nothing can be compared to Him...[10]

The Ahl al-Bayt عليهم السلام, being the most perfect manifestations of the Divine Names, enjoy such an exalted station near Allāh, that non can be compared to them. They undoubtedly are manifestations of the Divine Name *al-Witr*, which means مَنْ لاَ ثَانِيَ لَهُ (One who does not have a second). In a tradition narrated from Zurāra, Imām al-Bāqir عليه السلام says:

> وَإِنَّا لاَ نُوصَفُ وَكَيْفَ يُوصَفُ قَوْمٌ رَفَعَ اللَّهُ عَنْهُمُ
> الرِّجْسَ وَهُوَ الشَّكُ

> And surely we cannot be described, and how can a people be described from whom Allāh has removed impurity, which is doubt...[11]

Apparently the doubt that is spoken about in this tradition is related to the realities of the Creator and His creation. The Ahl al-Bayt عليهم السلام, due to their lofty spiritual status, transcend the lower levels of conviction and enjoy the level of *ḥaqq al-yaqīn* or even higher. Therefore the absence of doubt should not be conjectured to be merely in the conceptual level.

الْوِتْرَ الْمَوْتُورَ
The Exceptionally Unique

Some commentators give the possibility that this verse refers to Imām al-Ḥusayn عليه السلام's uniqueness with regard to everyone, including Prophet Muḥammad ﷺ and the other members of his infallible progengy عليهم السلام.

---

10 Shaykh al-Ṣadūq, *'Ilal al-Sharā'i'*, v.2, p. 320

11 Shaykh al-Kulaynī, *al-Kāfī*, v.2, p. 182

This however is not because his spiritual station is higher than theirs, for all of them unite in the Muḥammadan Light (al-Nūr al-Muḥammadī). In a conversation with Salmān and Jundub, Imām ʿAlī عليه السلام says:

اَنَـا اُحْيِـي وَاُمِيـتُ بِـاذْنِ رَبِّـي، اَنَـا اُنَبِّـئُكُمْ بِمَـا تَـأكُلُوْنَ وَمَـا تَدَّخِرُوْنَ فِـيْ بُيُوْتِكُمْ بِـاذْنِ رَبِّـي، وَاَنَـا عَـالِمٌ بِضَـمَائِرِ قُلُـوْبِكُمْ وَالْأئِمَّـةِ مِـنْ اَوْلَادِيْ عليهم السلام يَعْلَمُـوْنَ وَيَفْعَلُـوْنَ هَـذَا إذَا اَحَبُّـوْا وَاَرَادُوْا لِأَنَّـا كُلَّنَا وَاحِدٌ، اَوَّلُنَا مُحَمَّدٌ وَآخِرُنَا مُحَمَّدٌ وَاَوْسَطُنَا مُحَمَّدٌ وَكُلَّنَا مُحَمَّدٌ فَلَاتُفَرِّقُوْا بَيْنَنَا . . .

I revive the dead, and make the living ones die by my Lord's permission; I can inform you about what you eat and what you store in your homes by my Lord's permission; and I know what is hidden in your hearts; and the Imāms from my progeny عليه السلام can [also] know this and do the aforesaid if they desired and wanted, because all of us are one: **the first among us is Muḥammad, the middle one among us is Muḥammad, the last among us is Muḥammad, and all of us are Muḥammad; therefore do not differentiate between us.**[12]

The reason, as some great scholars like the late ʿAllāma al-Ṭabāṭabāʾī[13] and Āyatullāh Saʿādat Parwar (may Allāh elevate their noble spirits) expound[14], why Imām al-Ḥusayn عليه السلام occupies a unique station, is his

---

12 ʿAllāma al-Majlisī, *Biḥār al-Anwār*, v.26, p.6

13 Muḥammad Ḥusayn Rukhshād, *Dar Maḥzare ʿAllameye Ṭabāṭabāʾī*, p. 184

14 Āyatullāh Saʿādat Parwar, *Furūgh-e-Shahādat*, p.40

utilization of the greater opportunity to manifest his perfect qualities by carrying out his great movement and sacrificing everything he had for the sake of the Only Beloved. The Holy Qur'ān says that for everyone are stations according to what they did:

﴿وَلِكُلٍّ دَرَجَاتٌ مِّمَّا عَمِلُوا وَلِيُوَفِّيَهُمْ أَعْمَالَهُمْ وَهُمْ لاَ يُظْلَمُونَ﴾

> And for all are degrees according to what they did, and that He may pay them back fully their deeds and they shall not be wronged. (46:19)

If the other Imāms عليهم السلام faced the same conditions that Imām al-Ḥusayn عليه السلام had encountered, they too would have done what he did. The opportunity however was gifted to Imām al-Ḥusayn عليه السلام and accordingly he acquired a station that is unparalleled. The following tradition refers to a unique station for Imām al-Ḥusayn عليه السلام:

رُوِيَ عَنِ الرَّسُوْلِ الأَعْظَمِ ﷺ قَالَ لِزَوْجَتِهِ أُمِّ سَلَمَةَ: اَوْحي اللّٰهُ عَزَّ وَجَلَّ إِلَيَّ اَنَّ لَهُ (اَيْ لِلْحُسَيْنِ) دَرَجَةٌ لاَ يَنَالُهَا اَحَدٌ مِنَ الْمَخْلُوْقِيْنَ.

> The Most Noble Messenger ﷺ said to his wife Umm Salama: Allāh Revealed unto me that verily he (al-Ḥusayn) has a station which none of the creation would attain.[15]

And Imām al-Ḥusayn عليه السلام just before his departure from Madīna sees the Prophet ﷺ in his dream saying to him:

وَ إِنَّ لَكَ فِي الْجَنَّةِ دَرَجَاتٍ لاَ تَنَالُهَا إِلاَّ بِالشَّهَادَةِ

15 ʿAllāma al-Majlisī, *Biḥār al-Anwār*, v. 44, p.225

And indeed you have stations in the Paradise that you shall not attain save with martyrdom.[16]

A Peerless Contingent Being

In his masterpiece *Jalawāt-e-Rabbānī* Āyatullāh Muḥammad Riḍā Rabbāni (may Allāh elevate his spirit) believes and tries to establish that Imām al-Ḥusayn عليه السلام is a peerless contingent being (*mumkin al-wujūd bilā sharīk*). At one place he says: In our book *Tawḥīd-e-Rabbānī we* have comprehensively explained the meaning of the magnificent name Allāh. One of its meanings is, "*aliha al-khalq 'an darki mā'iyyatih wal iḥāṭa bikayfiyyatih*" (The creation is baffled in comprehending His whatness and apprehending His howness)[17], which the cleaver of the knowledge of the disciplines of the foremost and latter ones and the fifth brilliant star of Divine Leadership and Guardianship, Ḥaḍrat Imām al-Bāqir عليه السلام has mentioned. Imām al-Bāqir عليه السلام has said that Allāh is that God before Whose Essence and Attributes the intellects of the entire creation are bewildered, confounded and mystified.

Sa'dī, the Persian poet says:

جهان متفق بر الهيتش

فرو مانده در كنه ماهيتش.

The entire creation is unanimous in his Godhood

Unable to apprehend the Essence of His Being

Thereafter Rabbanī says that Imām al-Ḥusayn عليه السلام, who is a manifestation of the Name Allāh, likewise, confounds the intellects and overcomes the human beings with perplexity and amazement.

فيك يا أعجوبة الكون غدا الفكر كليلاً. أنت

16 'Allāma al-Majlisī, *Biḥār al-Anwār*, v. 58, p.182

17 'Allāma al-Majlisī, *Biḥār al-Anwār*, v.3, p. 222

حيّرت ذوي اللب وبلبلت العقولا.

O the marvel of existence, the intellect is exhausted in You; You confounded people of insight and confused the intellects

این حسین کیست که عالم همه دیوانه اوست

این چه شمعی است که جانها همه پروانه اوست

Who is this Husayn, that the entire world is mad after him; What candle is this, that all the souls are its moth(s)?

Imām Husayn ﷤ not only puzzled and astounded the human world and realm of humanity, but also made the most exalted angels and the residents of the Divine throne as well as the entire chain of the sacred intellects, astonished at his display of intense love and self-sacrifice in the path of the Eternal and Infinite Beloved.[18]

الْوِتْرَ الْمَوْتُورَ

The martyr, whose near ones have been killed, but their blood have not been avenged for

Lexicologists like al-Ṭurayḥī in his *Majma' al-Baḥrayn*, have defined the word *mawtūr* as one whose near one has been unjustly killed but his blood has not been avenged for as yet[19]. And since he is *mawtūr*, he necessarily is the *thā'ir* (avenger of the blood) as well. Muḥammad bin Muslima in the battle of Khaybar employs a similar expression when he

18 Āyatullah Muḥammad Riḍā Rabbānī, *Jalawāt-e-Rabbānī*, v.1, pp. 278-279.

19 Shaykh al-Ṭurayḥī, *Majma' al-Baḥrayn*, v.4, p. 463

tells the Holy Prophet ﷺ:

أَنَا الْمَوْتُورُ الثَّائِرُ

> I am one whose kin has been unjustly killed but his blood not yet avenged, and I am the avenger.[20]

The word *witr* also signifies 'the blood that has been spilled unjustly'[21]. Therefore when we address Imām al-Ḥusayn عليه السلام as *al-witr al-mawtūr* we mean he is the martyr whose near ones and companions were unjustly killed, but their blood has not been avenged for. Hence he is the avenger of their blood. Some commentators opine that if we consider the Imām عليه السلام to be the one who would avenge the blood of his near ones, then that would transpire during his return to this world (*raj'a*). With regard to *raj'a*, Ḥamrān narrates from Imām Muḥammad al-Bāqir عليه السلام:

إِنَّ أَوَّلَ مَنْ يَرْجِعُ لَجَارُكُمُ الْحُسَيْنُ عليه السلام فَيَمْلِكُ حَتَّى تَقَعَ حَاجِبَاهُ عَلَى عَيْنَيْهِ مِنَ الْكِبَرِ

> Indeed the first one to return is your refuge al-Ḥusayn عليه السلام, who will rule [for so many years] until his eyebrows would hang over his eyes, out of old age.[22]

الْوِتْرَ الْمَوْتُورَ

The Alone who was Rendered Solitary

---

20 Al-Zubaydī, *Tāj al-'Arūs*, v.7, p. 582

21 Mīrza Tehrānī, *Shifā'al-Ṣudūr*, p. 165

22 'Allāma al-Majlisī, *Biḥār al-Anwār*, v.53, p.43

Sometimes the word *witr* is translated as 'alone', whereas the word *mawtūr* as 'one whose relation is slain, and so is separated from him and rendered solitary'.[23] Imām al-Ḥusayn عليه السلام was rendered solitary after he lost his near ones and noble companions and stood alone to fight against the forces of evil.

Some analysts of this radiant *Ziyārat* believe that the enemies of Islam right from the time of the Holy Prophet ﷺ planned how to isolate and make people be indifferent of the household of the Holy Prophet ﷺ. The word *al-witr* can also allude to this situation that the Imām عليه السلام experienced. Therefore he was the lonely one, whose relation was slain and who was rendered solitary.

We must understand that the Imām عليه السلام, due to his sublime rank was even lonlier than his companions and family members in the plains of Karbalā. The station of Imāmate is unique and has no parallel. In this sense he was not only from the strangers (*ghurabā'*) like his companions, but also *gharīb al-ghurabā'* (the stranger of the strangers). In a *Ziyārat* narrated from Imām al-Ṣādiq عليه السلام we address Imām al-Ḥusayn عليه السلام as follows:

السَّلاَمُ عَلَيْكَ يَا غَرِيبَ الْغُرَبَاء

Peace be unto you, o stranger of the strangers.[24]

In this state of intense *ghurba*, the enemies did not spare the lives of his noble family members and companions, and rendered him solitary and alone. It is in these moments that he cried from the depths of his heart:

هَلْ مِنْ نَاصِرٍ يَنْصُرُ الذُّرِّيَّةَ الأَطهَار ، هَلْ مِنْ مُجِيْرٍ
لأَبْنَاءِ الْبَتُولِ، هَلْ مِنْ ذَابٍّ يَذُبُّ عَنْ حَرَمِ

23 Al-Zubaydī, *Tāj al-'Arūs*, v. 7, p.583

24 'Allāma al-Majlisī, *Biḥār al-Anwār*, v.98, p.230

الرَّسُوْلِ ؟

Is there any helper to help the immaculate progeny?
Is there any protector for the children of al-Batūl
ﻉﻠﻴها؟ Is there any defender to guard the sanctuary of
the Messenger of Allāh?

Perhaps Imām al-Ḥusayn ﻉﻠﻴه summed up his message to his lovers in
these short, but very meaningful expressions. The call was made to 'the
future' and every receptive heart can hear it every moment. Imām al-
Ḥusayn ﻉﻠﻴه was the epitome of Islam, and his call was the call for the
emancipation of Islam. If we are receptive enough to hear his call, then
every step of ours must be geared towards assiting Islam. If we struggle
to eradicate sin and try to perfect ourselves as well as others and revive
Islam, then we do respond to his call. Otherwise we should not be
surprised if we also rank among those who left him alone. May Allāh
protect us from being among those who leave him alone.

الْوِتْرَ الْمَوْتُورَ

The Alone and Deprived

Sometimes the word *al-mawtūr* is employed to mean 'one who is
deprived' (*al-manqūṣ*). The following tradition of the Holy Prophet ﷺ
is translated taking this meaning into consideration:

الْمَوْتُورُ أَهْلُهُ وَمَالُهُ مَنْ ضَيَّعَ صَلاَةَ الْعَصْرِ

One who is deprived of his family and wealth is one
who wastes the prayer of 'Aṣr[25]

---

25 'Allāma al-Majlisī, *Biḥār al-Anwār*, v.80, p.28

Therefore if we take the word *witr* to mean 'alone', the phrase would mean 'the alone who was deprived of his hometown, family and wealth'.

CHAPTER 7

أَلسَّلامُ عَلَيْكَ وَعَلَى الأَرْوَاحِ
الَّتِي حَلَّتْ بِفِنَائِكَ

Peace be unto you and unto the spirits who descended in your courtyard

أَلسَّلاَمُ عَلَيْكَ وَعَلَى الأَرْوَاحِ الَّتِي حَلَّتْ بِفِنَائِكَ

Peace be unto you and unto the spirits who descended in your courtyard

---

COMMENTARY

أَلسَّلاَمُ عَلَيْكَ وَعَلَى الأَرْوَاحِ

Peace be unto you and unto the spirits...

In this verse not only do we declare that Imām al-Ḥusayn عليه السلام is in the state of *salām*, but also bear witness that his noble companions who sacrificed their lives for Allāh and attained the great station of martyrdom, also enjoy the state of peace and protection from calamities. And if we take the verse to be invocative, then we also pray for higher states of *salām* for them.

وَعَلَى الأَرْوَاحِ

And unto the spirits (*arwāḥ*)

The word a*rwāḥ* in the above phrase is the plural of *rūḥ*. And the word *rūḥ* (spirit) comes from the word *rīḥ* (wind)[1]. *Rūḥ* has the quality of *rīḥ*, which moves (*mutaḥarrik*) and makes things move (*muḥarrik*). The *ruḥ* likewise moves and makes the body move. In a tradition narrated in *al-Kāfī*, Imām al-Ṣādiq عليه السلام tells Muḥammad bin Muslim:

---

1 Al-Muṣṭafawī, *Al-Taḥqīq fī Kalimāt al-Qur'ān al-Karīm,* v.4, p. 254

إِنَّ الرُّوْحَ مُتَحَرِّكٌ كَالرِّيْحِ وَإِنَّمَا سُمِّيَ رُوْحًا لأَنَّهُ اشْتُقَّ اِسْمُهُ مِنَ الرِّيْحِ . . .

Indeed *rūḥ* (spirit) is in motion like *rīḥ* (lit. wind), and ***it was named rūḥ because its name was gotten from al-rīḥ...***[2]

In fact the entire universe, constantly moves and travels towards Allāh, for the Holy Qur'ān explicitly tells us that every entity does *tasbīh*, which, according to authoritative lexicographers like Rāghib al-Iṣfahānī, fundamentally means:

اَلْمَرُّ السَّرِيْعُ فِيْ عِبَادَةِ اللّٰهِ

"...to travel swiftly in the path of Divine worship."[3]

Almighty Allāh says

﴿تُسَبِّحُ لَهُ السَّماواتُ السَّبْعُ وَالأَرْضُ وَمَنْ فِيهِنَّ وَإِنْ مِنْ شَيْءٍ إِلاَّ يُسَبِّحُ بِحَمْدِهِ وَلكِنْ لا تَفْقَهُونَ تَسْبِيحَهُمْ إِنَّهُ كانَ حَلِيماً غَفُوراً﴾

The seven heavens glorify Him, and the earth [too], and whoever is in them. There is not a thing but that it glorifies Him with praise, but you do not understand their glorification. Indeed He is all-forbearing, all-forgiving. (17:44)

Spirit- A Higher Level of the Body

Some of us conjecture that the human being is "composed"- in the physical sense- of a body and a spirit, and that the spirit comes down to,

2 Thiqat al-Islām al-Kulaynī, *Al-Kāfī*, v. 1, p. 133

3 Al-Iṣfahānī, Al-*Mufradāt fī Gharīb al-Qur'ān*, p. 392

and settles in the body as a separate thing. This stereotype is incorrect, for the human being is a unit of different levels of reality, the spirit being one of them. The spirit is a higher reality of the very body, and the body serves as a lower manifestation of the spirit. Observe the following verse of the Qur᾽ān which talks about how the human spirit is blown:

﴿وَلَقَدْ خَلَقْنَا الإِنْسَانَ مِنْ سُلاَلَةٍ مِنْ طِينٍ. ثُمَّ جَعَلْنَاهُ نُطْفَةً فِي قَرَارٍ مَكِينٍ. ثُمَّ خَلَقْنَا النُّطْفَةَ عَلَقَةً فَخَلَقْنَا الْعَلَقَةَ مُضْغَةً فَخَلَقْنَا الْمُضْغَةَ عِظَامًا فَكَسَوْنَا الْعِظَامَ لَحْمًا ثُمَّ أَنْشَأْنَاهُ خَلْقًا آخَرَ فَتَبَارَكَ اللّٰهُ أَحْسَنُ الْخَالِقِينَ﴾

> And certainly We created man of an extract of clay, Then We made him a small seed in a firm resting-place, Then We made the seed a clot, then We made the clot a lump of flesh, then We made (in) the lump of flesh bones, then We clothed the bones with flesh, then **We made it another creation**, so blessed be Allāh, the best of the creators. (23:12-14)

Here Almighty Allāh explicitly tells us that it is the very body that He creates in another form: *thumma ansha᾽nāhu khalqan ākhara* (then we made ***it*** another creation). In this verse the third person pronoun "*hu*" refers to the material body. In other words, Allāh perfects the very body and brings it to a higher state.

The great philosopher and mystic, Mullā Hādī Sabzawārī, in his poetical masterpiece *al-Manẓūmah* says:

اَلنَّفْسُ فِي الْحُدُوثِ جِسْمَانِيَّةٌ

وَفِي الْبَقَا تَكُوْنُ رُوْحَانِيَّــــة

The soul in its origination is material,

but in its survival is spiritual.[4]

Perhaps the first person to expound this body-spirit relation in a logical manner was Ṣadr al-Muta'allihīn. Al-Kharrazī[5] writes:

> Mullā Ṣadrā believes that soul is created corporeally. That is, there exists at first corporeal soulless matter. Then, under certain conditions, soul comes into being gradually through matter and its substantial motion. When the fetus settles in its place it starts its evolution on the strength of trans–substantial motion. The fetus first takes a natural mineral shape. Then, because of further evolution, it takes a vegetative form. At this stage, the corporeal matter is mature enough to take on perception; but as long as it is devoid of sense under the influence of environment, there exists no room for soul therein. After having found vegetative form within the womb, and been influenced both by external factors, and their stimulants, the corporeal matter passively takes on sense, and then the earliest form of perception takes place. Thus, the first manifestation of soul occurs. Here it could be said that soul is created out of corporeal matter... (Mullā Ṣadrā, *Asfār*, vol.9, p. 112)

---

4 Mullā Hādī Sabzawārī, *Sharḥ al-Manṣuma*, v.5, p. 113

5 Kamāl Kharrāzī, *Mulla Sadra's Idea of Soul-Body Relation and its Consquences in Psychology*, http://www.mullasadra.org/New_Site/English/Paper%20Bank/Anthropology/kamal%20Kharazi.htm

There is a tradition from Imām ʿAlī ؑ worthy of contemplation:

مَا أَضْمَرَ أَحَدٌ شَيْئًا الاَّ ظَهَرَ فِي فَلَتَاتِ لِسَانِهِ وَصَفَحَاتِ وَجْهِهِ

No one hides anything save that it appears in the lapses of his tongue and the cheeks of his face.[6]

This shows a unity between the outer side of the human being which is his physical structure and his inner side which is the spirit. The physical can only reveal what is hidden of the spiritual if it is united with the latter.

وَعَلَى الاَرْوَاحِ

And unto the spirits (*al-arwāḥ*)

Some commentators of this sacred *Ziyārat* have given the possibility that the *arwāḥ* mentioned in this verse refers to the angels who live around the radiant *rawḍa* of Imām al-Ḥusayn ؑ. Explaining the reality of angels, Shaykh al-Ṭabrasī in his *Tafsīr Majma' al-Bayān* says:

وَالْمَلاَئِكَةُ رُوْحَانِيُّوْنَ خُلِقُوْا مِنَ الرِّيْحِ فِي قَوْلِ بَعْضِهِمْ، وَمِنَ النُّوْرِ فِيْ قَوْلِ الْحَسَنِ، لاَ يَتَنَاسَلُوْنَ وَلاَ يَطْعَمُوْنَ وَلاَ يَشْرَبُوْنَ.

And angels are spiritual entities (*rūḥāniyyūn*). They were created from *al-rīḥ (the wind)* according to some, and from light (*al-nūr*) according to al-Ḥasan,

6 Imām ʿAlī ؑ, *Nahj al-Balāghah*, v.4, p. 7

> they neither mate, not eat, nor drink.[7]

We should note however that words like *al-rīḥ* and *al-nūr* must not quickly transport us to their material extensions. Words, as has been established in its own place, have been coined for the spirits of their meanings. Therefore these terms have a subtler meaning, the discussion of which is beyond the scope of this work. One should however at least understand that they do not necessarily refer to the wind that we can feel, or the physical light that we can vision.

According to authoritative scholars like Mīr Dāmād and Mullā Hādī Sabzawārī, *al-rūhāniyyūn* (the spiritual entities) are the highest of the classes of the angels. In his *Sharḥ al-Asmā'* Sabzawārī says:

> ... فَالأَعْلَى طَبَقَةً اَلَّذِيْنَ طَعَامُهُمْ التَّسْبِيْحُ وَشَرَابُهُمُ التَّقْدِيسُ اَلرُّوْحَانِيُّوْنَ....
>
> ...The angels of the highest level, whose food is glorification (*al-tasbīḥ*) and whose drink is sanctification (*al-taqdīs*), are the *rūḥāniyyūn*...[8]

There are ample traditions that explicitly mention the existence of so many angels in the proximity and neighborhood of the grave of Imām al-Ḥusayn ﵇. The following is an example:

> عَنْ مُحَمَّد بْن مَرْوَان، عَنْ أَبِيْ عَبْدِ اللّٰه﵇، قَالَ: سَمِعْتُهُ يَقُوْلُ: زُوْرُوْا الْحُسَيْنَ﵇ وَلَوْ كُلَّ سَنَة، فَإنَّ كُلَّ مَنْ أَتَاهُ عَارِفًا بِحَقِّهِ غَيْرَ جَاحِدٍ لَمْ يَكُنْ لَهُ عِوَضٌ غَيْرُ الْجَنَّةِ، وَرُزِقَ رِزْقًا وَاسِعًا، وَأَتَاهُ اللّٰهُ

---

7 Shaykh al-al-Ṭabrasī, *Majma' al-Bayān fī Tafsīr al-Qur'ān*, v.1, p. 190

8 Mullā Hādī Sabzawārī, *Sharḥ al-Asmā' al-Ḥusnā*, v.2, p. 51

بِفَرَجٍ عَاجِلٍ، إِنَّ اللّٰهَ وَكَّلَ بِقَبْرِ الْحُسَيْنِ بْنِ عَلِيٍّ عليه السلام **أَرْبَعَةَ آلاَفِ مَلَكٍ** كُلُّهُمْ يَبْكُوْنَهُ وَيُشَيِّعُوْنَ مَنْ زَارَهُ إِلى أَهْلِهِ، فَإِنْ مَرِضَ عَادُوْهُ، وَإِنْ مَاتَ شَهِدُوا جَنَازَتَهُ بِالاِسْتِغْفَارِ لَهُ وَالتَّرَحُّمِ عَلَيْهِ

Muhammad bin Marwān is reported to have said: I heard him [Imām al-Ṣādiq عليه السلام] say: Visit al-Ḥusayn عليه السلام, even if it is once a year, for whosoever comes to him, with knowledge of his station, and not a non-believer, would not be given other than Paradise, and he would be bestowed with extensive sustenance, and Allāh would quickly relieve him (from his problems). **Indeed Allāh entrusted four thousand *angels on the grave of al-Ḥusayn***, all of who weep for him. They accompany the visitor until he returns to his family, and if the visitor gets sick they visit him, and if he dies, they witness his bier and seek for his forgiveness and mercy.[9]

Therefore *salām* can also be expressed for these spirits who accompany the grave of al-Ḥusayn عليه السلام. In another *ziyara* of bidding farewell to Imām al-Ḥusayn عليه السلام we explicitly send our salāms to the angels. Al-Mashhadī in his *al-Mazār* narrates the following *Ziyārat*:

اَلسَّلاَمُ عَلَيْكُمْ يَا مَلاَئِكَةَ رَبِّي **الْمُقِيْمِيْنَ فِيْ هَذَا الْحَرَمِ**

Peace be on you o angels of my Lord, **who inhabit**

9 Ibn Qūlawayh, *Kāmil al-Ziyārāt*, pp. 175-176

this sanctuary.[10]

According to this nondescript, the most probable meaning of *al-arwāh* refers to the companions, but there is no harm if we intend the angels too.

...الَّتِي حَلَّتْ بِفِنَائِكَ

...who descended in your courtyard

The past tense verb حَلَّتْ '*ḥallat*' means نَزَلَتْ '*nazalat*' (they came down, or descended). And the word *finā'* in the phrase "*bi finā'ik*" means 'open space in front or at either side of the house' or 'the courtyard'. The above phrase indicates that the spirits of the companions of al-Ḥusayn عليه السلام enjoy his company and neighborhood after their martyrdom. The implication that the word '*ḥallat*' gives, as some commentators have stated, is that the station of the companions is lower than that of the Imām عليه السلام, a reality which by now is quite clear to the readers, for the Imām عليه السلام is in an apex which none can comprehend and fathom.

Outstanding Qualities of the Companions of Imām al-Ḥusayn عليه السلام

It would not be without benefit to mention some of the outstanding qualities of the companions of Imām al-Ḥusayn عليه السلام, for that would make us understand better their sanctity and elevated spirits:

1. The Best Companions (*Khayru Aṣḥāb*)

The Holy Qur'ān says:

﴿لاَ يَسْتَوِي أَصْحَابُ النَّارِ وَأَصْحَابُ الْجَنَّةِ أَصْحَابُ الْجَنَّةِ هُمُ الْفَائِزُونَ﴾

---

10 Al-Mashhadī, *Al-Mazār*, p. 426

> The companions of Hell Fire and the companions of the Paradise are not alike; the companions of the Paradise are the achievers. (59:20)

Imām al-Ḥusayn عليه السلام is reported to have said about his noble companions:

> إِنِّيْ لاَ أَعْلَمُ أَصْحَاباً أَوْفَى، وَلاَ خَيْراً مِنْ أَصْحَابِيْ
>
> 'Surely I do not know companions more faithful and better than my companions'.[11]

In one of the radiant *ziyārāt*, we address the companions of Imām al-Ḥusayn عليه السلام as follows:

> السَّلاَمُ عَلَيْكُمْ يَا خَيْرَ أَنْصَارٍ . . .
>
> Peace be unto you O best helpers.

It is important for us to know the literal meaning of *aṣḥāb*, so that we can understand the traditions narrated about the *aṣḥāb* of lofty personalities like Imām al-Ḥusayn عليه السلام. There has been a tendency among many people to conjecture that *aṣhāb* merely refers to those who physically accompany someone. For example, those who physically accompanied the Holy Prophet ﷺ are known as *aṣhābu Rasūlillāh* ﷺ. Although such usage of the word is common, it is not always meant. Before we establish our contention, let us consider the meaning of *aṣhāb*: Rāghib al-Iṣfahānī in his lexicon of Qur'ān under the discussion of the root word صحب *"ṣ ḥ b"* says:

> الصاحب الملازم إنسانا كان أو حيوانا أو مكانا
>
> أو زمانا ولا فرق بين أن تكون مصاحبته بالبدن

11 Shaykh al-Mufīd, *Kitāb al-Irshād*, p. 43

وهو الاصل والاكثر أو بالعناية والهمة وعلى هذا قال:

لَئِنْ غِبْتِ عَنْ عَيْنِيْ   لَمَا غِبْتِ عَنْ قَلْبِيْ

Al-ṣāḥib [pl. *aṣḥāb*] is one who accompanies whether a human being, an animal, a place or an age. And it makes no difference whether his company is with his body, which is primarily and mostly the case, or through concern and ambition. And based on this it is said:

If you hide from my eyes

You cannot hide from my heart.[12]

In verse 59:20 quoted in the beginning, we observed that the noun *aṣḥāb* is annexed to Paradise and Hell Fire. The literal import of the verse, which also is an established reality, reveals that despite their physical existence in this corporeal world, the *aṣḥāb*, depending on their state, either spiritually accompany Paradise or Hell Fire. Therefore the criteria of sharing the company of someone or something is not always physical and material.

A well-known tradition narrated by some Muslims to establish the purity of all those who physically accompanied the Holy Prophet ﷺ is as follows:

اَصْحَابِيْ كَالنّجُوْمِ بِأَيّهِمْ اِقْتَدَيْتُمْ اِهْتَدَيْتُمْ

My companions are like stars, whosoever among them were you to follow, you will be guided.[13]

---

12 Al-Rāghib al-Iṣfahānī, *Mufradātu Alfāẓ al-Qur'ān*, p. 475

13 Al-Tha'labī, *Tafsīr al-Tha'labī*, v.3, p. 334

The Holy Qur'ān, traditions of the Holy Prophet ﷺ, the intellect as well as history falsifies this tradition if we were to interpret the word *aṣḥāb* to merely mean 'whosoever met the Holy Prophet ﷺ or physically accompanied him'. For the sake of brevity, we would not like to explain this matter here. Interested readers may refer to a host of scholarly books written on this subject, especially sparkling works like the outstanding masterpiece *ʿAbaqāt al-Anwār* of the esteemed Indian scholar Sayyid Mīr Ḥāmid al-Ḥusaynī al-Hindī.

Weren't the enemies who fought against Imām Amīr al-Mu'minīn ʿAlī عليه السلام in the battle of Jamal and Ṣiffīn not among those who physically accompanied the Holy Prophet ﷺ? And what about the battle of Ṣiffīn? Can Muʿāwiya, who did meet and share the company of the Holy Prophet ﷺ but fought against the Divinely appointed leader of the time, be considered as a *najm* (a star) through which one can achieve guidance? It is absurd to attribute something like this to the Holy Prophet ﷺ or misinterpret what he ﷺ said.

There is another tradition narrated by Shīʿī sources however, that is somewhat similar to the abovementioned traditon, but sound and more meaningful: Imām al-Bāqir عليه السلام narrates from the Holy Prophet ﷺ:

مَا وَجَدْتُمْ فِيْ كِتَابِ اللّهِ عَزّ وَجَلّ فَالْعَمَلُ بِهِ لاَزِمٌ
لاَ عُذْرَ لَكُمْ فِيْ تَرْكِهِ، وَمَا لَمْ يَكُنْ فِيْ كِتَابِ
اللّهِ وَكَانَتْ فِيْهِ سُنّةٌ مِنِّي لاَ عُذْرَ لَكُمْ فِيْ تَرْكِ
سُنّتِيْ، وَمَا لَمْ يَكُنْ فِيْهِ سُنّةٌ مِنّيْ فَمَا قَالَ
اَصْحَابِيْ فَخُذُوْهُ، فَإِنّمَا مَثَلُ اَصْحَابِيْ فِيْكُمْ
كَمَثَلِ النّجُوْمِ، بِاَيّهَا اُخِذَ اهْتُدِيَ فَبِاَيّ اَقَاوِيْلِ
اَصْحَابِيْ اَخَذْتُمْ اِهْتَدَيْتُمْ، وَاخْتِلاَفُ اَصْحَابِيْ
لَكُمْ رَحْمَةٌ، قِيْلَ: يَا رَسُوْلَ اللّهِ مَنْ اَصْحَابُكَ؟

قَالَ: اَهْلُ بَيْتِي

It is essential to act according to what you find in the Book of Allāh; and you have no excuse to abandon it. Likewise you have no excuse to abandon whatever is not in the Book but there is a tradition about it from me. And when there is no tradition about something from me, then take whatever my *aṣhāb* say. For surely the example of my *aṣḥāb* among you is like the example of stars (*kamathal al-nujūm*), from whosoever among them advice is taken, guidance is achieved; therefore whichever statements of my *aṣhāb* you take, you would get guided; and frequenting my *aṣhāb* is a mercy for you. The Holy Prophet ﷺ was asked: **'O Apostle of Allāh, who are your *aṣḥāb*? He ﷺ said: 'My progeny'.**[14]

Here the meaning of *aṣḥāb* is used very aptly because the essence of the human being is in his spirit and not his body. The Ahl al-Bayt عليهم السلام being in the heights of perfection and united in the Muḥammadan Spirit, truly accompany the Holy Prophet ﷺ even if the confines of time and place were to separate them. Hence they really are stars perpetually radiating light.

The aforesaid discussion was to illustrate the meaning of *aṣḥāb* when Imām al-Ḥusayn عليه السلام said:

إِنِّي لاَ اَعْلَمُ اَصْحَاباً اَوْفَى وَلاَ خَيْراً مِنْ اَصْحَابِي

'Surely I do not know companions more faithful and better than my companions'[15]

---

14 Shaykh al-Ṣadūq, *Ma'ānī al-Akhbār*, p. 156

15 Shaykh al-Mufīd, *Kitāb al-Irshād*, p. 43

Here the Imām عليه السلام is not merely referring to their physical presence, but also alludes to their spiritual sanctity. In fact their apparent presence in the ranks of Imām al-Ḥusayn عليه السلام in the plains of Karbalā and their physical company depicted nothing but their spiritual company as well. This is because it required exalted spirits to remain steadfast in the ranks of the Imām عليه السلام despite the knowledge about their ephemeral end.

2. The Most Loyal Companions (*al-awfā*)

As earlier mentioned, the Imām clearly said:

> إِنِّي لاَ أَعْلَمُ أَصْحَاباً أَوْفَى وَلاَ خَيْراً مِنْ أَصْحَابِي
>
> 'Surely I do not know ***companions more loyal*** and better than my companions'[16]

Here the word *awfā* is employed thus showing that they were the most loyal of all companions. Whenever loyalty is talked about, there is always a pledge behind it. Perhaps the best expression of their state is conferred by the following verse of the Qur'ān:

> ﴿مِنَ الْمُؤْمِنِينَ رِجَالٌ صَدَقُوا مَا عَاهَدُوا اللَّهَ عَلَيْهِ فَمِنْهُمْ مَنْ قَضَى نَحْبَهُ وَمِنْهُمْ مَنْ يَنْتَظِرُ وَمَا بَدَّلُوا تَبْدِيلاً﴾
>
> Among the faithful are **men who fulfill what they have pledged to Allāh**. Of them are some who have fulfilled their pledge, and of them are some who still wait, and they have not changed in the least. (33:23)

One of the places where the loyalty of the companions of Imām al-Ḥusayn عليه السلام was radiantly manifested was on the night of 'Āshūrā'

---

16 Ibid.

when Imām al-Ḥusayn عليه السلام said to them that the enemies were after him and that they were free to leave. All of the loyal companions in unison expressed their loyalty and said that they would never leave the Imām عليه السلام and were ready to be martyred with him.

3. Intense Lovers of Allāh (*'Ushhāq*)

The Holy Qur'ān says:

﴿. . . وَالَّذِينَ آمَنُواْ أَشَدُّ حُبًّا لِّلَّهِ. . . ﴾

> ...and those who believe are more intense in their love for Allāh... (2:165)

It is narrated from Imām al-Bāqir عليه السلام:

> خَرَجَ عَلِيٌّ عليه السلام يَسِيرُ بِالنَّاسِ حَتَّى إِذَا كَانَ بِكَرْبَلاَءَ عَلَى مِيلَيْنِ أَوْ مِيلٍ تَقَدَّمَ بَيْنَ أَيْدِيهِمْ حَتَّى طَافَ بِمَكَانٍ يُقَالُ لَهَا الْمِقْذَفَانِ فَقَالَ قُتِلَ فِيهَا مِائَتَا نَبِيٍّ وَمِائَتَا سِبْطٍ كُلُّهُمْ شُهَدَاءُ وَمَنَاخُ رِكَابٍ وَمَصَارِعُ عُشَّاقٍ شُهَدَاءَ لاَ يَسْبِقُهُمْ مَنْ كَانَ قَبْلَهُمْ وَلاَ يَلْحَقُهُمْ مَنْ بَعْدَهُمْ

> [Imām] 'Alī عليه السلام went out with some people until he reached a place one or two miles near Karbalā', whereupon he went forward and circumambulated around a place known as *al-miqdhafān*, and said: 'This is the place where two hundred Prophets and their grandsons were killed, all of who were martyrs; and it is the halting place of horsemen and the battle ground of intense lovers (*'ushshāq*) and martyrs, whom neither those who came before them or will

come after them can prevail [in status].[17]

The word عُشّاق *'ushshāq* that is employed in the above tradition is worthy of consideration. It is the plural of the word *'āshiq* (passionate lover), which is known to be derived from عَشَقَة *'ashaqa* a plant that coils around a tree from its roots to its branches, and thus envelops it the way passionate love embraces one's entire heart[18]. Ibn 'Arabī translates *'ishq* as follows:

ثم العشق وهو التفافه بالقلب مأخوذ من العشقة اللبلابة المشوكة التي تلتف على شجرة العنبة وأمثالها فهو يلتف بقلب المحب حتى يعميه عن النظر إلى غير محبوبه

Then comes *'ishq* which is when love coils the heart; it is gotten from *al-'ashaqa*, which is the thorned convolvulus (or bindweed), that, twisting in a spiral, wraps around the grapevine and other similar plants. In this way, blinding love (*'ishq*) wraps around the heart of the lover, blinding him so that he can see no one other than his beloved.[19]

In the well-known *Ziyārat al-Shuhadā'* we address the companions of Imām al-Ḥusayn عليه السلام as follows:

اَلسَّلاَمُ عَلَيْكُمْ يَآ أَوْلِيَآءَ اللّٰهِ وَأَحِبَّآءَهُ

Peace be unto you, O friends and **beloveds of Allāh**[20]

---

17 'Allāma al-Majlisī, *Biḥār al-Anwār*, v.41, p. 295

18 Sayyid al-Jazā'irī, *al-Anwār al-Nu'māniyya*, v.3, p. 166

19 Ibn 'Arabī, *al-Futūḥāt al-Makkiyya*, v.4, p. 259

20 Al-Mashhadī, *al-Mazār*, p. 464

This verse has so much to reveal. The word *aḥibā'* is the plural of the word *ḥabīb*, which is commonly translated to mean *maḥbūb* (beloved). However, its linguistic form *fa'īl* (فعيل) can confer both the meanings of an active participle (فاعل) and a passive participle (مفعول), which means we can employ the word *ḥabīb* either to means 'the lover'[21] or 'the beloved' or both. If we only take the common meaning, however, and translate the word *ḥabīb* as *maḥbūb*, the result is the same. This is because whosoever is the beloved of Allāh, is necessarily His lover. The Holy Qur'ān says:

﴿يَا أَيُّهَا الَّذِينَ آمَنُواْ مَن يَرْتَدَّ مِنكُمْ عَن دِينِهِ فَسَوْفَ يَأْتِي اللّهُ بِقَوْمٍ يُحِبُّهُمْ وَيُحِبُّونَهُ أَذِلَّةٍ عَلَى الْمُؤْمِنِينَ أَعِزَّةٍ عَلَى الْكَافِرِينَ يُجَاهِدُونَ فِي سَبِيلِ اللّهِ وَلاَ يَخَافُونَ لَوْمَةَ لآئِمٍ ذَلِكَ فَضْلُ اللّهِ يُؤْتِيهِ مَن يَشَاءُ وَاللّهُ وَاسِعٌ عَلِيمٌ﴾

O you who believe! whoever from among you turns back from his religion, then Allāh will bring a people, ***He shall love them and they shall love Him,*** lowly before the believers, mighty against the unbelievers, they shall strive hard in Allāh's way and shall not fear the censure of any censurer; this is Allāh's grace, He gives it to whom He pleases, and Allāh is Ample-giving, Knowing. [5: 54]

Furthermore the linguistic pattern *fa'īl* (فعيل) is both a hyperbolic form *(ṣīgha mubāligha)*, which gives the connotation of abundance and, an assimilate epithet[22] (*ṣīfa mushbiha*), which confers the sense of

21 Al-Zubaydī, *Tāj al-'Arūs*, v.1, p. 393

22 Pierre Cachia (University of Edinburgh), "*THE MONITOR, A Dictionary of Arabic Grammatical Terms*", p. 107, published in 1973 by Longman Group Ltd.

continuity. Therefore, the companions of the Imām عليه السلام were abundantly and perpetually in love of Allāh.

If we try to study the origin of the word *ḥabīb*, we may be able to unravel other noteworthy secrets. Expounding on the etymology of the word *'ḥubb'* Sayyid al-Jazā'irī in his ethical masterpiece *al-Anwār al-Nu'māniyya* says:

> سمّي الحب حبا لوصوله إلى حَبّة القلب التي هي منبع الحياة، وإذا اتصل بها سرى مع الحياة في جميع اجزاء البدن واثبت في كل جزء صورة المحبوب
>
> The infinitive noun '*ḥubb*' (lit. love) was called *ḥubb* because it reaches the *ḥabbat al-qalb* (the seed of the heart), which is the source of life. And when it reaches the seed of the heart it penetrates with life to all the parts of the body and leaves the picture of the beloved in every part.[23]

And the only Master who plants, splits, and makes germinate the seed of love is the *Fāliq al-ḥabbi wa al-nawā* (*the Splitter of the grain and the pit- 6:95*), and it is He alone who rears this love and leads it to its perfection, for it is He alone who is *Rabb al-falaq* (the Lord of splitting- *113:1*).

Another interesting expression we employ when we address the companions is the following:

> اَلسَّلاَمُ عَلَيْكُمْ يَا أَصْفِيَاءَ اللّٰهِ وَأَوِدَّاءَهُ
>
> Peace be unto you, O chosen ones of Allāh and His

23 Al-Jazā'irī, *Al-Anwār al-Nu'māniyya*, v.3, p. 161

lovers[24]

The word *awiddā'* is the plural of وَدِيْد *wadīd*[25] in the linguistic pattern of *fa'īl* (فعيل) which, as discussed above, gives the connotations of permanence and abundance. In addition, it also confers the meaning of both the active participle (*fā'il*) and the passive participle (*maf'ūl*), which means that there is constant mutual love between the lovers and the Beloved. Also, the origin of the word *wadīd* and other words of the same family, is *watad* (nail), which confers the meaning of stable and constant love.

Hā'irī in his *Muqtaniyāt al-Durar* says:

وأصل الودّ من الوتد وهو أثبت من المحبّة

> ...and the origin of *al-wudd* is *al-watad* (nail) and it is more firm than *al-maḥabba* (germinal love)...[26]

And in his *Tafsīr Ruḥ al-Bayān* Ḥaqqī says:

الود أثبت فى أرض القلب من المحبة لاشتقاقه من الوتد

> *Al-wudd* is more firm in the earth of the heart than *al-maḥabba*, because it is derived from *al-watad* (nail)...[27]

Having known that the companions of Imām al-Ḥusayn عليه السلام were among the intense lovers of Allāh, let us briefly look at the origin of their intense love. What actually makes one a lover for another?

Every sound conscience will agree that knowledge for perfection would

24 Al-Shahīd al-Awwal, *al-Mazār*, p. 129

25 Al-Zubaydī, *Tāj al-'Arūs*, v.5, p. 306

26 Hā'irī, *Muqtaniyāt al-Durar wa Multaqaṭāt al-Thamar*, v.12, p. 115

27 Ḥaqqī, *Tafsīr Rūḥ al-Bayān*, v.10, p. 393

reap love and attachment for the same. So long as one is ignorant of another, one cannot develop love for him. It is after acquiring knowledge about the perfect qualities of a certain person that one develops love and attachment for the beloved. Furthermore, love requires the lover to be naturally inclined to the qualities of the beloved, otherwise the knowledge of the attributes of the beloved would not reap love. If a person, for example, has no inclination towards physical beauty, despite his knowledge of the physically beautiful, he would not develop love for the physically beautiful. It is when the heart naturally loves and appreciates beauty that when the beautiful is beheld, the spark of love is ignited and a raging fire follows.

The noble companions of Imām al-Ḥusayn عليه السلام, having retained their innate nature, were natural lovers of Absolute Perfection (*al-kamāl al-muṭlaq*) and also enjoyed the *ma'rifa of Almighty Allāh,* and that is what made them crave to meet their Only Beloved.

Knowledge of Allāh is sometimes classified into two:

- Conceptual & Acquired Knowledge (*al-ʿilm al-ḥuṣūlī*)
- Presential & Divinely Endowed Knowledge (*al-ʿilm al-ḥuḍūrī*)

Conceptual knowledge is very limited and a kind of narration of what is behind the curtain. Presential knowledge, on the contrary, is to lift the curtain from the face of the Beloved[28]. In clearer terms, it is to beautify oneself with the attributes of the Beloved. Between the conceptual appreciation of the Beloved and lifting the veil of the Beloved there is utter remoteness. It is the presential knowledge of Allāh that makes one perpetually an amorous lover. Such a lover manifests the love of the Only Beloved in every move he makes. Expressions like the following reveal how intense was the love that glowed in the hearts of the Imām عليه السلام's companions:

28 In more accurate terms, the Beloved has no veil. We are full of veils. We must therefore struggle to eradicate the veils from our side so that we can vision the face of the Only Beloved.

وَقَامَ إِلَيْهِ رَجُلٌ يُقَالُ لَهُ زُهَيْر بن اَلْقَيْنِ اَلْبَجلي، فَقَالَ: يَا بْنَ رَسُولِ اللّه، وَدَدْتُ أَنِّي قُتِلْتُ ثُمَّ نُشِرْتُ، ثُمَّ قُتِلْتُ ثُمَّ نُشِرْتُ، ثُمَّ قُتِلْتُ ثُمَّ نُشِرْتُ فِيكَ وَفِي الَّذِيْنَ مَعَكَ مائَةَ قَتْلَة

A man called Zuhayr bin al-Qayn al-Bajlī came to the Imām ﷺ and said: 'O son of the Apostle of Allāh, I wish I would be martyred and then resurrected and again be killed and resurrected, and again be killed and resurrected in your way and in the way of those who are with you, a hundred times.[29]

All this fervor shows nothing but passionate love for Almighty Allāh, for sacrificing oneself for al-Ḥusayn ﷺ who is a manifestation of Allāh's Attributes is nothing but to sacrifice oneself for Allāh, the Only Beloved.

The following verse of the Holy Qur'ān also depicts the reality of which we have so far spoken:

﴿قُلْ إِن كُنتُمْ تُحِبُّونَ اللّهَ فَاتَّبِعُونِي يُحْبِبْكُمُ اللّهُ وَيَغْفِرْ لَكُمْ ذُنُوبَكُمْ وَاللّهُ غَفُورٌ رَّحِيمٌ﴾

Say: If you love Allāh, **then follow me, Allāh will love you** and forgive you your faults, and Allāh is Forgiving, Merciful. (3:31)

We should remember that it is only after embellishing ourselves with the Attributes of Allāh, that our actions would be according to what Allāh and His messenger wants.

---

29 'Allāma al-Majlisī, *Biḥār al-Anwār*, v.44, p. 316

4. Sharp Inner Vision (*Kushifa lahum al-Ghiṭā'*)

The Holy Qur'ān says:

﴿لَقَدْ كُنتَ فِي غَفْلَةٍ مِّنْ هَذَا فَكَشَفْنَا عَنكَ غِطَاءَكَ فَبَصَرُكَ الْيَوْمَ حَدِيدٌ﴾

> Certainly you were heedless of it, but now We have removed from you your veil, so your sight today is sharp. (50:22)

Ibn 'Amāra reports from his father who reports:

قُلْتُ لَهُ اَخْبِرْنِي عَنْ اَصْحَابِ الْحُسَيْنِ وَإِقْدَامِهِمْ عَلَى الْمَوْتِ فَقَالَ: **إِنَّهُمْ كُشِفَ لَهُمُ الْغِطَاءِ** حَتَّى رَاَوْا مَنَازِلَهُمْ مِنَ الْجَنَّةِ. . .

> I asked Imām al-Ṣādiq ﷷ: Tell me about the companions of al-Ḥusayn ﷷ and how they would advance to their death, and he said: '**Indeed the curtain was unveiled for them**, until they saw their dwellings in Paradise...[30]

In one of the *ziyārāt*, we address the companions of Imām al-Ḥusayn ﷷ in the following manner:

. . . أَشْهَدُ لَقَدْ كَشَفَ اللهُ لَكُمُ الْغِطَاءَ. . .

> ...I bear witness that most surely Allāh unveiled for you the curtain...[31]

Sharp inner vision is attainable by every human being who purifies his

30 'Allāma al-Majlisī, *Biḥār al-Anwār*, v.44, p.297

31 'Allāma al-Majlisī, *Biḥār al-Anwār*, v. 45, p.70

spirit. The reason why many of us do not enjoy this kind of vision, is the murkiness of our hearts. Following is a tradition narrated from the Holy Prophet ﷺ worthy of reflection:

لَوْلاَ تَكْثِيْرٌ فِيْ كَلاَمِكُمْ وَتَمْرِيْجٌ فِيْ قُلُوْبِكُمْ لَرَأَيْتُمْ مَا أَرَى وَلَسَمِعْتُمْ مَا أَسْمَعُ

> Was it not for your loquaciousness and confusion in your hearts, you would have surely seen what I see, and you would have surely heard what I hear.[32]

In fact the faithful human being is required to behold the kernel of the universe. Almighty Allāh says:

﴿أَوَلَمْ يَنْظُرُوا فِي مَلَكُوتِ السَّمَاوَاتِ وَالأَرْضِ وَمَا خَلَقَ اللَّهُ مِنْ شَيْءٍ وَأَنْ عَسَى أَنْ يَكُونَ قَدِ اقْتَرَبَ أَجَلُهُمْ فَبِأَيِّ حَدِيثٍ بَعْدَهُ يُؤْمِنُونَ﴾

> ***Have they not contemplated the dominions of the heavens and the earth***, and whatever things Allāh has created, and that maybe their time has already drawn near? So what discourse will they believe after this?! (7:185)

5. Immersed in God (*Rabbāniyyūn*)

The Holy Qur'ān says:

﴿وَلَكِن كُونُوا رَبَّانِيِّينَ﴾

> But be godly people...(3:79)

And in one of the salutational recitals we address the companions of

---

32 'Allāma al-Ṭabāṭabā'ī, *Tafsīr al-Mīzān*, v.5, p. 270

Imām al-Ḥusayn عليه السلام in the following way:

اَلسّلاَمُ عَلَيْكُمْ ايّهَا الرّبانيّون

Peace be unto you, ***O Rabbāniyyūn***...[33]

This verse talks about the great spiritual status of the noble companions of Imām al-Ḥusayn عليه السلام. *Rabbāniyyūn* is the plural of *Rabbānī*, which according to some lexicographers like al-Ṭurayhī denotes 'one who is perfect in both knowledge and action'[34] Others translate '*Rabbānī*' more accurately and say:

الربّاني هو المنسوب الى الرّب وزيادة الالف والنون فيه تدل علي المبالغة في النسبة فتكون المعنى: من كان شديد الاختصاص بالرب وكثير الاشتغال بعبوديته وعبادته، ويجوز ايضا ان يكون منسوبا الى الرّب بمعناه المصدرى فيدل علي المبالغة في تربية الناس وتدبيرهم...

Rabbānī رَبَّانِي is one who is attributed to الربَ 'the Lord' and the additional '*alif*' and '*nūn*' in the word is to denote intensification in attribution, and hence the meaning of the word would be: One who is intensely attributed to the Lord and absorbed in His submission and worship; and the word can also be related to الربّ the Lord in its infinitive (*maṣdar*) sense, so that it would mean intensity in training the

33 Shaykh al-Kulaynī, *Al-Kāfī*, v.4, p. 574

34 Al-Ṭurayḥī, *Tafsīr Gharīb al-Qur'ān*, p. 100

people and controlling their affairs...[35]

And both the meanings can be true together.

6. Spiritual Sovereignty

The Holy Qur᾽ān says:

﴿قُلْنَا يَا نَارُ كُونِي بَرْدًا وَسَلَامًا عَلَى إِبْرَاهِيمَ﴾

We said: O fire! be a comfort and peace to Ibrahim! (21:59)

Jābir narrates from Imām al-Bāqir عليه السلام:

قَالَ الْحُسَيْنُ بْن عَلِيّ عليهما السلام لأَصْحَابِهِ قَبْلَ أَنْ يُقْتَلَ: إِنَّ رَسُوْلَ اللّٰه صلى الله عليه وآله قَالَ: يَا بُنَيَّ إِنَّكَ سَتُسَاقُ إِلَى الْعِرَاقِ، وَهِيَ أَرْضٌ قَدْ الْتَقَى بِهَا النَّبِيُّوْنَ، وَأَوْصِيَاءُ النَّبِيِّيْنَ، وَهِيَ أَرْضٌ تُدْعى "عَمُوْرَا" وَإِنَّكَ تُسْتَشْهَدُ بِهَا وَيُسْتَشْهَدُ مَعَكَ جَمَاعَةٌ مِنْ أَصْحَابِكَ لاَ يَجِدُوْنَ أَلَمَ مَسِّ الْحَدِيْدِ، وَتَلاَ: ﴿قُلْنَا يَا نَارُ كُوْنِي بَرْدًا وَسَلاَمًا عَلَى إِبْرَاهِيْم﴾ تَكُوْنُ الْحَرْبُ عَلَيْكَ وَعَلَيْهِمْ بَرْدًا وَ سَلاَمًا

Before his martyrdom, Imām al-Ḥusayn bin ʿAlī said to his companions: Indeed the Apostle of Allāh ﷺ said [to me]: O my dear young son, surely you will be led to ʿIrāq; it is a land where Prophets of Allāh and Successors of the Prophets have met; It is

35 Āyatullah Sayyid Maḥmūd Ṭaleqānī, *Partuwī az Qur᾽ān*, v.5, p. 185

> a land called ʿAmūrā. And indeed you shall be martyred there together **with a group among your companions who would not sense the pain of the touch of iron**. Then Imām al-Ḥusayn (ʿa) read the verse: 'O Fire, be cool and peaceful for Ibrāhīm' (21:59). The war will be cool and peaceful on you and them.[36]

Explaining this situation of the Imām, the grand Āyatullāh Jawadī Āmulī says:

> ووفقا لرواية الامام الباقر عليه السلام **فإن جنود الحسين عليه السلام يوم عآشوراء لم يكونوا يستشعروا آلام الضرب والطعن و الجراح إلا بما تولده القرصة من ألم... لماذا؟** لأن الروح هي مصدر الألم والفرح. يصوم احدهم فيشعر بوخأة الظمأ و الجوع... و يصوم الآخر فلا نرى فيه إلا النشاط والابتهاج... اليست الظروف الفيزيائية متساوية للاثنين... فلماذا يتعذب الاول و ينطلق الآخر؟! لانّ الروح لدي الثاني مشدودة الى نقطة بعيدة عن الظروف المادية. و لقد كان ابطال كربلاء من تلك الروح العظيمة المبهورة بالغيب...
>
> According to a tradition from Imām al-Bāqir (ʿa)

---

36 Quṭb al-Dīn al-Rāwandī, *al-Kharāʾij wa al-Jarāyiḥ*, v.2, p. 848

the army of al-Ḥusayn عليه السلام did not feel the pain of the blows and wounds on the 'Āshurā' day save a pinch...why is that? This is because the spirit is the origin of pain and happiness. One of you may fast and feel the pangs of hunger and thirst...whereas another would fast but we would find in him nothing but happiness and high-spiritedness...aren't the physical conditions similar for both? So why is the first in torment while the second does not feel anything? This is because the spirit of the second is attached to a realm distant from the material conditions. Indeed the gallant warriors of Karbalā' were among those great spirits overcome by the unseen plane of existence.[37]

7. Worshippers through Awareness (*al-'Ubbād*)

The Holy Qur'ān says:

﴿مُّحَمَّدٌ رَّسُولُ اللَّهِ وَالَّذِينَ مَعَهُ أَشِدَّاءُ عَلَى
الْكُفَّارِ رُحَمَاءُ بَيْنَهُمْ تَرَاهُمْ رُكَّعًا سُجَّدًا يَبْتَغُونَ
فَضْلًا مِّنَ اللَّهِ وَرِضْوَانًا سِيمَاهُمْ فِي وُجُوهِهِم مِّنْ
أَثَرِ السُّجُودِ ذَلِكَ مَثَلُهُمْ فِي التَّوْرَاةِ وَمَثَلُهُمْ فِي
الإنجِيلِ كَزَرْعٍ أَخْرَجَ شَطْأَهُ فَآزَرَهُ فَاسْتَغْلَظَ
فَاسْتَوَى عَلَى سُوقِهِ يُعْجِبُ الزُّرَّاعَ لِيَغِيظَ بِهِمُ
الْكُفَّارَ وَعَدَ اللَّهُ الَّذِينَ آمَنُوا وَعَمِلُوا الصَّالِحَاتِ
مِنْهُم مَّغْفِرَةً وَأَجْرًا عَظِيمًا﴾

Muḥammad is the Messenger of Allāh, and those

37 Āyatullah Jawādī Āmulī, *Thawrat al-'Ishq al-Ilāhī*, p. 232

> with him are firm of heart against the unbelievers, compassionate among themselves; you will see them bowing down, prostrating themselves, seeking grace from Allāh and pleasure; their marks are in their faces because of the effect of prostration; that is their description in the Tawrāt and their description in the Injeel; like as seed-produce that puts forth its sprout, then strengthens it, so it becomes stout and stands firmly on its stem, delighting the sowers that He may enrage the unbelievers on account of them; Allāh has promised those among them who believe and do good, forgiveness and a great reward. (48:29)

Sayyid Raḍī al-Dīn bin Ṭāwūs al-Ḥasanī (may Allāh elevate his noble spirit) in his well-known *maqtal, al-Luhūf 'alā Qatlā al-Ṭufūf* narrates:

وَ بَاتَ الْحُسَيْنُ وَ أَصْحَابُهُ تِلْكَ اللَّيْلَةَ وَ لَهُمْ دَوِيٌّ كَدَوِيِّ النَّحْلِ مَا بَيْنَ رَاكِعٍ وَ سَاجِدٍ وَ قَائِمٍ وَ قَاعِدٍ . . .

> 'Al-Ḥusayn and his companions were awake the whole night [of 'Āshurā'] and **their environment resembled an area permeated with the sound of the humming of bees. [In other words all of them were busy in the remembrance of Allāh and the sound of their whisperings permeated the entire environment.] Some were in the state of *rukū'*, others in the state of *sujūd*, some standing and others sitting...** [38]

And al-Qazwinī narrates from the History of *al-A'tham al-Kūfī*:

---

38 Sayyid Raḍī al-Dīn bin Ṭāwūs, *al-Luhūf 'alā Qatla al-Ṭufūf*, p.91

إنـه مـا نـام في تلـك الليلـة الحسـين عليه السلام ولا احـد مـن اصحابه واعوانه إلى الصبح.

Surely that night neither al-Ḥusayn nor anyone of his companions and supporters slept until morning.[39]

Worship is undoubtedly a merit when it is not reduced to mere actions and recitals. The companions of al-Ḥusayn عليه السلام were men who worshipped Almighty Allāh out of awareness and knowledge. Their appellations such as *aḥibbā'Allāh (Divine lovers)*, *'ushshāq (intense lovers)* and *kushifa lahum al-ghiṭā (the curtains were unveiled for them)*, all demonstrate their knowledge and deep insight. This is because such qualities are essential corollaries of knowledge, without which they carry no meaning. It is such kind of worship that is natural and praiseworthy. Expression of utter humility near the Absolute Perfect Being can only come about naturally after one realizes whom he is infront of. Such realization is in stages. Sometimes one has conceptual knowledge about the Creator and thus he maintains a degree of humility in prayer, but that cannot be compared to one who has presential knowledge of Allāh. It is such knowledge about which Imām 'Alī عليه السلام talks in a conversation with a *rabbi*:

عَـنْ اَبـي الْحَسَـن الْمَوْصَلـي عَـنْ اَبـيْ عَبْـدِ اللّه عليه السلام قـالَ: جَـاءَ حِبْـرٌ إلى اَمِيْـرِ الْمُـؤْمنيْنَ عليه السلام ، فَقَـالَ: يـا اَمِيْـرَ الْمُؤْمنِيْـنَ هَـلْ رَاَيْـتَ رَبّـكَ حِيْنَ عَبَدْتَـهُ؟ قـالَ: فَقَـالَ: وَيْلَـكَ لَـمْ اَكُـنْ لأعْبُـدَ رَبّـا لَـمْ اَرَه، قـالَ: وَكَيْـفَ رَاَيْتَـهُ؟ قَـالَ: وَيْلَـكَ لاَ تُدْرِكُـهُ الْعُيُـوْنَ فِـي

---

39 *Al-Imām al-Ḥusayn wa Aṣḥābuhu*, v.1, p. 264

مُشَاهَدَةِ الأَبْصَارِ وَلكِن رَأَتْهُ القُلُوبُ بِحَقَائِقِ الإِيمَانِ.

Abū al-Ḥasan al-Mawṣalī narrates from Abī ʿAbdillāh [al-Ṣādiq عليه السلام] who said: A rabbi came to Amīr al-Mu'minīn عليه السلام, and said: 'Yā Amīr al-Mu'minīn, did you see your Lord when you worshipped Him? Imām عليه السلام said: 'Woe unto you! Eyes do not comprehend Him in their ocular vision, but hearts see Him through the realities of conviction.[40]

Worship without knowledge and awareness, on the contrary is insignificant and sometimes dangerous too. Consider the following traditions:

a. Imām ʿAlī عليه السلام says:

اَلاَ لاَ خَيْرَ فِي عِبَادَةٍ لاَ فِقْهَ فِيهَا

Indeed there is no good in that worship that is without understanding.[41]

b. Imām Zayn al-'Ābidīn عليه السلام says:

لاَ عِبَادَةَ إلاَّ بِالتَّفَقُّهِ

There is no worship save with understanding[42]

c. Imām ʿAlī عليه السلام says:

40 Al-'Āmilī, *al-Fuṣūl al-Muhimma fī Uṣūl al-A'imma*, v.1, p.180

41 Shaykh al-Kulaynī, *al-Kāfī*, v.1, p. 36

42 Shaykh al-Rayshahrī, *Mizān al-Ḥikma*, v.3, p. 1798

$$\text{سَـكَنُوْا فِـيْ اَنْفُسِـكُمْ مَعْرِفَةَ مَا تَعْبُدُوْنَ، حَتّى}$$

$$\text{يَنْفَعَكُمْ مَا تُحَرِّكُوْنَ مِنَ الْجَوَارِحِ بِعِبَادَةِ مَـنْ}$$

$$\text{تَعْرِفُوْنَ.}$$

Settle in your hearts the knowledge of Whom you worship so that the members that you move in worship of Whom you know can benefit you.[43]

d. Imām 'Alī ◌ says:

$$\text{لاَ خَيْرَ فِيْ عِبَادَةٍ لاَ عِلْمَ فِيْهَا}$$

There is no good in that worship which accompanies no knowledge.[44]

It is interesting to note that the expression 'They had the humming as the humming of bees' لَهُمْ دَوِيٌّ كَدَوِيِّ النَّحْلِ that has come for the noble companions of Imām al-Ḥusayn ◌ has also come with regard to the Khawārij, who were adamant in their ignorant stance and ready to fight against Imām 'Alī ◌ in the battle of Nahrawān. Jundub bin Zuhayr al-Azdī narrates:

> When the Khārijites separated from Imām 'Ali ◌, he set out to fight against them and we set out with him. I reached their camps, and found that their environment was covered with the sound of the recitation of Qur'ān. [The words used in the tradition is *lahum dawiyyun kadawiyy al-naḥl* (they had the sound of the humming of bee)]. Among them were those who wore burnoose and had calluses on their foreheads. When I saw that, doubt

---

43 *Ibid.*
44 *Ibid.*

crept my heart; so I separated myself from them, descended from my horseback, fixed my lance on the ground, and kept my shield, and placed my armor over it. And I stood in prayer while I cried: "O Allāh if fighting against them is according to Your desire, then show me something by which I know that it is the truth; and if it is not according to Your desire, then divert me from the battle. Suddenly Imām ʿAlī came and descended from the horse of the Apostle of Allāh, and stood in prayer, and then suddenly a man came and said: 'They [the Khārijites] have crossed the river. Then another one came and firmly tied his mount, and said: They crossed it and left. Thereafter Amīr al-Mu'minīn عليه السلام said: 'They have not crossed the river, nor will they cross it, and they surely will be killed near it; this has been informed to me by Allāh and His Apostle.' The Imām عليه السلام [then] said: 'O Jundub, do you see that hill?' I said, 'Yes.' He said: 'Surely the Apostle of Allāh (upon whom be peace) narrated to me that they would fight near there.' As for us, we would first send a messenger unto them, who would invite them to the Book of Allāh and the Sunna of His Prophet, and they would shoot at his face with arrows, and he would be killed. Jundub says: We went towards them and saw them still in their army not yet departed or left. So the Imām عليه السلام called his men and gathered them, then he came near their ranks saying: 'Who will take this Qur'ān and walk towards these people and call them to the Book of Allāh and the Sunna of the Prophet ﷺ? One who does so, would be killed and attain Paradise. None save a youth from Banū 'Āmir bin Sa'sa'a responded to this call. The Imām عليه السلام however, on observing his young age, said: 'Return to where you stood.' Then he made the same announcement again, and none save the same youth responded positively to his call. So the Imām ﷺ said: 'Take it [the Qur'ān], but mind you that you would be killed.' So he walked with it unto them until he came to a place where they could hear him. He called them, and they shot at him with arrows, and he returned to us, while his face resembled a porcupine (for he was surrounded with arrows). So 'Alī ﷺ said: Attack them! So we attacked them. Jundub says: The doubt [that had crept my heart earlier) came out, and I [fought] and slew...'[45]

Therefore the yardstick to judge the truly worshipful nature of a person is not by the quantity of his worship, but the quality of his worship. The Holy Qur'ān says:

﴿الَّذِي خَلَقَ الْمَوْتَ وَالْحَيَاةَ لِيَبْلُوَكُمْ أَيُّكُمْ أَحْسَنُ عَمَلاً وَهُوَ الْعَزِيزُ الْغَفُورُ﴾

...Who created death and life that He may try you–which of you is **best in deeds**; and He is the Mighty, the Forgiving. (67:2)

Ample traditions explicitly say that the value of one's worship is according to one's understanding and intellect. Observe the following:

a. The Holy Prophet ﷺ addressing a people who praised a man [for his worship] said:

كَيْفَ عَقْلُ الرَّجُلِ؟ قَالُوا: يَا رَسُولَ اللّٰهِ نُخْبِرُكَ

45 al-Rāwandi, *al-Kharā'ij,* v.2, p.755

عَنْ اجْتِهَادِهِ فِي الْعِبَادَةِ وَأَصْنَافِ الْخَيْرِ، وَتَسْأَلُنَا عَنْ عَقْلِهِ؟! فَقَالَ: إِنَّ الأَحْمَقَ يُصِيبُ بِحُمْقِهِ أَعْظَمَ مِنْ فُجُورِ الْفَاجِرِ، **وَإِنَّمَا يُرْتَفَعُ الْعِبَادُ غَدًا فِي الدَّرَجَاتِ وَيَنَالُونَ الزُّلْفَى مِنْ رَبِّهِمْ عَلَى قَدَرِ عُقُولِهِمْ.**

How is the man's intellect? They said: O Apostle of Allāh, we inform you about his struggle in worship and good actions, and you ask us about his intellect? Thereupon the Prophet ﷺ said: Indeed an idiot (*aḥmaq*) due to his silliness can perform something graver than the crimes of criminals; **and surely the servants [of Allāh] would only be elevated tomorrow in stations and reach the proximity of their Lord according to their intellects.**[46]

b. Muhammad bin Sulaymān al-Daylamī reports from his father who said:

قُلْتُ لأَبِي عَبْدِ اللَّهِ عليه السلام فُلاَنٌ مِنْ عِبَادَتِهِ وَدِينِهِ وَفَضْلِهِ فَقَالَ كَيْفَ عَقْلُهُ قُلْتُ لاَ أَدْرِي فَقَالَ **إِنَّ الثَّوَابَ عَلَى قَدْرِ الْعَقْلِ**...

I informed Imām al-Ṣādiq عليه السلام about the *'ibāda* and religiousness and merits of a certain person. **Thereupon he asked me: how is his intellect/understanding?** I said: I do not know. So he said: 'Surely reward is according to one's

46 Ibn Shu'ba al-Baḥrānī, *Tuḥaf al-'Uqūl*, p. 54

intellect/understanding.'[47]

c. The Holy Prophet ﷺ is reported to have said:

اَلْعِلْمُ إِمَامُ الْعَمَلِ، وَالْعَمَلُ تَابِعُهُ

Knowledge is the leader of action and the action is its follower.[48]

Although the Khawārij were well known for their excessive worship and recitation of Qur'ān, their ignorance never allowed them to benefit from their worship or recitation. Perhaps the following verse of the Holy Qur'ān aptly describes their example:

﴿الَّذِينَ ضَلَّ سَعْيُهُمْ فِي الْحَيَاةِ الدُّنْيَا وَهُمْ يَحْسَبُونَ أَنَّهُمْ يُحْسِنُونَ صُنْعًا أُولَئِكَ الَّذِينَ كَفَرُوا بِآيَاتِ رَبِّهِمْ وَلِقَائِهِ فَحَبِطَتْ أَعْمَالُهُمْ فَلَا نُقِيمُ لَهُمْ يَوْمَ الْقِيَامَةِ وَزْنًا﴾

Those whose endeavour goes awry in the life of the world, while they suppose they are doing good.' They are the ones who deny the signs of their Lord and the encounter with Him So their works have failed. On the Day of Resurrection We will not set for them any weight. (18:104-105)

They struggled to station themselves in the surface of religion, but were deprived of that too. They had not understood the Holy Qur'ān and thus were ready to fight against the very epitome of the Qur'ān. When Imām 'Alī عليه السلام tried to explain to them the deception that had

47 Shaykh al-Kulaynī, *al-Kāfī*, v.1, p. 11

48 Shaykh al-Rayshahrī, *Mīzān al-Ḥikma*, v.3, p. 2035

entangled them, they thought they understood religion more than one who was literally chosen by the Holy Prophet ﷺ as his *waṣī* (vicegerent). So wild had their attitude become that they had the audacity to slaughter a sincere companion of the Holy Prophet ﷺ who was loyal to his teachings, and slit the womb of his expectant wife. The latter's crime was merely loyalty to Imām ʿAlī عليه السلام.

Although this is past history for us, the Kharijī trend has remained up to this day. The Wahhābīs, due to their identical attitude, can aptly be known as the 'neo-Khārijites'.

What is interesting is that even Westerners have likened the Wahhābīs with the Khawārij. For example, Jon Kyl, a Republican Senator from Arizona writes in the *Front Page Magazine*:

> Islamic extremism as an ideology is hardly new with the first movement that resembles today's phenomenon, known as the Kharijites, appearing shortly after the birth of Islam in the 7th century.
>
> Later it was expounded on by various Islamic scholars, such as Ibn Taymiya in the 13th century, but it did not become institutionalized until the mid-18th century when the theories promulgated by the radical cleric Muḥammad ibn ʿAbd al-Wahhāb were accepted and imposed as the state religion of his realm by the founder of the House of Saud.[49]

Esposito, in his Islām and Politics writes:

> "Religious zeal and military might merged in a religiopolitical movement that waged holy war with a zeal reminiscent of the early Kharijites, viewing all

---

49 Jon Kyl, *Terrorism: Growing Wahhabi Influence in the United States*, http://www.FrontPageMagazine.com, July 3, 2003

> Muslims who resisted as unbelievers. The tribes of Arabia were subdued and united in the name of Islamic egalitarianism."[50]

The apparently worshipful attitude of the Khārijites, both present and past, should not lead one to surmise that worship in great quantity is not praiseworthy. Those who have attained realization would naturally be pulled towards constant worship. They would, in terms of a tradition, be 'amorous lovers' of worship. Consider the following tradition:

> عن أبي عبد الله عليه السلام قال: قَالَ رَسُوْلُ اللّٰه ﷺ:
> أَفْضَلُ النَّاسِ مَنْ عَشِقَ الْعِبَادَةَ فَعَانَقَهَا وَأَحَبَّهَا
> بِقَلْبِهِ، وَبَاشَرَهَا بِجَسَدِهِ وَتَفَرَّغَ لَهَا، فَهُوَ لَا يُبَالِي
> عَلَى مَا أَصْبَحَ مِنَ الدُّنْيَا عَلَى عُسْرٍ أَمْ عَلَى يُسْرٍ؟
>
> Imām al-Ṣādiq عليه السلام says: The Apostle of Allāh ﷺ said: The best of people is one who intensely loves worship (*'ashiqa al-'ibāda*), embraces it, loves it through his heart, and performs it with his body and occupies himself with it; Thereafter he does not care about the situation he faces in the world, whether it be difficult or easy.[51]

If we reflect on some historical accounts of the Holy Prophet ﷺ and his Infallible Progeny عليهم السلام we would come to realize how abundantly they engaged in worship. It was their exalted state that made them constantly absorbed in prayer. It is reported about Ḥaḍrat Zahrā' عليها السلام that she would stand in prayer so much that her feet would get

---

50 Esposito, *Islam and Politics*, page 36.

51 Shaykh al-Kulaynī, *Al-Kāfī*, v.2, p. 83

swollen[52]. And concerning Imām ʿAlī ﵇ Imām al-Ṣādiq ﵇ narrates:

وَلَقَدْ دَخَلَ اَبُو جَعْفَرٍ عَلَى اَبِيْهِ فَإِذَا هُوَ قَدْ بَلَغَ مِنَ
الْعِبَادَةِ مَا لَمْ يَبْلُغْهُ اَحَدٌ، وَقَدْ اِصْفَرَّ لَوْنُهُ مِنَ
السَّهْرِ، وَرَمِضَتْ عَيْنَاهُ مِنَ الْبُكَاءِ، وَدَبِرَتْ
جَبْهَتُهُ مِنَ السُّجُوْدِ، وَوَرِمَتْ قَدَمَاهُ مِنَ الْقِيَامِ فِيْ
الصَّلَاةِ. قَالَ: فَقَالَ اَبُو جَعْفَرٍ ﵇: فَلَمْ اَمْلِكْ حِيْنَ
رَاَيْتُهُ بِتِلْكَ الْحَالِ مِنَ الْبُكَاءِ فَبَكَيْتُ رَحْمَةً لَهُ،
وَإِذَا هُوَ يُفَكِّرُ، فَالْتَفَتَ إِلَيَّ بَعْدَ هُنَيْئَةٍ مِنْ
دُخُوْلِيْ، فَقَالَ: يَا بُنَيَّ اَعْطِنِيْ بَعْضَ تِلْكَ الصُّحُفِ
الَّتِيْ فِيْهَا عِبَادَةُ عَلِيٍّ، فَاَعْطَيْتُهُ، فَقَرَاَ فِيْهَا يَسِيْرًا
ثُمَّ تَرَكَهَا مِنْ يَدِهِ تَضَجُّرًا وَقَالَ: مَنْ يَقْوَى عَلَى
عِبَادَةِ عَلِيِّ بْنِ اَبِيْ طَالِبٍ؟!

Surely Abū Jaʿfar came to his father, while he had worshipped Allāh so much that none would equal him, and due to night vigil his complexion had turned pale; his eyes had become sore out of weeping, and his forehead had sunk in due to a lot of prostration, and his legs became swollen out of standing in prayer. Imām al-Ṣādiq ﵇ said: [Seeing this] Abū Jaʿfar [al-Bāqir ﵇] said: I could not control myself from weeping when I saw him in that state; so I wept in mercy for him. And suddenly he lay contemplating. Then after a little while, he faced me, and said: 'O my dear little son, give me some of

52 ʿAllāma al-Majlisī, *Biḥār al-Anwār*, v.43, p.84

> those manuscripts that speak about the worship of ʿAlī عليه السلام; so I gave him, and he read from it a little, and then left it in dissatisfaction and said: 'Who can worship like ʿAlī bin Abī Ṭālib عليه السلام'?[53]

These and many other incidents show how absorbed were the Ahl al-Bayt عليهم السلام in the worship of Allāh. Their worship, however, was out of insight and knowledge of the worship and the Worshipped One. So absorbed were they, that when an arrow is removed from the feet of Imām ʿAlī while he is in prayer, he does not sense any pain whatsoever.

In conclusion, it should be realized that the companions of Imām al-Ḥusayn عليه السلام were worshippers who worshipped Allāh as a natural outcome of their knowledge and vision. If such worship is done constantly and in abundance, it is highly recommended and praiseworthy. But if it is performed without knowledge, it has very little or no value at all.

8. Strangers (*Ghurabā*ʾ)

The Holy Qurʾān says:

> ﴿رِجَالٌ لاَ تُلْهِيهِمْ تِجَارَةٌ وَلاَ بَيْعٌ عَن ذِكْرِ اللَّهِ وَإِقَامِ الصَّلاَةِ وَإِيتَاءِ الزَّكَاةِ يَخَافُونَ يَوْمًا تَتَقَلَّبُ فِيهِ الْقُلُوبُ وَالأَبْصَارُ﴾
>
> Men whom neither merchandise nor selling diverts from the remembrance of Allāh and the keeping up of prayer and the giving of poor-rate; they fear a day in which the hearts and eyes shall turn about.[54]

The Holy Prophet ﷺ was once asked about *ghurabā'* (strangers in the

53 ʿAllāma al-Majlisī, *Biḥār al-Anwār*, v.46, p.75

54 Holy Qurʾān, 24:37

real sense of the word), and he ﷺ said:

اَلَّذِيْنَ يُحْيُوْنَ مَا اَمَاتَ النَاسُ مِنْ سُنَّتِيْ

> They are those who will revive what the people ruined from my Sunna.[55]

Sacrificing themselves for the revival of religion, the companions of Imām al-Ḥusayn ؑ steadfastly stood against the enemies. Earlier Imām al-Ḥusayn ؑ had permitted them to leave if they wished to, but they never dared to even think of deserting him. Among the rest of the Muslims, they were truly the *ghurabā'* whose stations others never appreciated. Imām al-Ḥusayn ؑ, however, was even more *gharīb* then them, for he occupied a station that even his companions never comprehended. It is therefore correct to call him *Gharīb al-ghurabā'* (The stranger among the strangers (his companions)). In one of the salutational recitals we address Imām al-Ḥusayn ؑ as follows:

اَلسّلاَمُ عَلىَ خَامِسِ اَصْحَابِ اَهْلِ الْكِسَاءِ،
اَلسّلاَمُ عَلَى غَرِيْبِ الْغُرَبَاء. . .

> Peace be unto you O the fifth member of the people of the cloak, Peace be unto you, **O stranger of the strangers**...[56]

55 Al-Azhari, *Mu'jam Tahdhīb al-Lugha*, v.3, p. 2646

56 Al-Mashhadī, *al-Mazār*, p. 497

CHAPTER 8

عَلَيْكُمْ مِنِّي جَمِيعًا سَلَامُ اللّٰهِ

أَبَدًا مَا بَقِيتُ وَبَقِيَ اللَّيْلُ وَالنَّهَارُ

Upon you all I invoke the peace of Allāh forever,
as long as I live and the night and day subsist

عَلَيْكُمْ مِنِّي جَمِيعًا سَلَامُ اللهِ أَبَدًا

مَا بَقِيتُ وَبَقِيَ اللَّيْلُ وَالنَّهَارُ

Upon you all I invoke the peace of Allāh forever, as long as I live and the night and day subsist.

COMMENTARY

عَلَيْكُمْ مِنِّي جَمِيعًا سَلَامُ اللهِ

Upon you all I invoke the peace of Allāh

In this phrase the predicate *'alaykum...* (upon you...) is brought before the subject '*Salāmullāh*', thus conferring the meaning of restriction (*ḥaṣr*)[1]. In simple words, the *zā'ir* is trying to say, "*Only upon you all I invoke* the peace of Allāh...". This means that it is only for the likes of Imām al-Ḥusayn عليه السلام and his noble companions that the *zā'ir* invokes *salām*. In other words, they represent those who are worthy of such invocation.

The preposition *'alā* (على), as we came to know earlier, confers the meaning of encompassment. Hence we are in reality praying for Allāh's peace to *encompass* and *envelop* Imām al-Ḥusayn عليه السلام and his loyal companions.

This sentence is a nominal sentence (*jumla ismiyya*) too, which means that our invocation is perpetual and permanent. A nominal sentence confers the connotation of continuity (*al-dawām*).

---

1 One of the grammatical rules of the Arabic language is that if the predicate (*khabar*) of a sentence is brought before its subject (*mubtada'*), it confers the meanings that the 'predicate' is exclusively for the subject.

عَلَيْكُمْ مِنِّي

Upon you, I invoke...

In the phrase *minnī* (from me) the first person pronoun يَاء *yā'* is attached to the preposition مِنْ *min* implying that the *zā'ir* is the one who invokes the *salām* of Allāh for the *mazūr* (the visited one).

عَلَيْكُمْ مِنِّي جَمِيعًا

Upon you all I invoke...

The word *jamī'an* (altogether) is a circumstantial expression (*ḥāl*)[2] for the second person plural pronoun "*kum*" in عَلَيْكُمْ *'alaykum* (upon you). Hence the meaning is 'Upon you *altogether* I invoke...'. Some commentators have also given the probability of another variable. They say that since a believer is a group in himself[3], the word *jamī'an* is not a circumstantial expression for the second person plural pronoun *kum* (you all) but rather for the first person[4] singular pronoun *yā'* affixed to the preposition *min*. It is as if the *zā'ir* says, "Upon you I invoke *with all the elements of my being,* the peace of Allāh..."

2 Mawlā ḤabībulLāh al-Kāshānī, *Sharḥu Ziyārat 'Āshūrā'*, p. 52

3 This refers to a well-known tradition that says '*a beliver is a congregation in himself.*'

4 Mawlā ḤabībulLāh al-Kāshānī, *Sharḥu Ziyārat 'Āshūrā'*, p. 52

عَلَيْكُمْ مِنِّي جَمِيعاً سَلامُ اللهِ

Upon you all I invoke the peace of Allāh

Annexing the name Allāh to *salām* either means that we are invoking a higher level of peace from Allāh or the Absolute Peace that belongs to Allāh.

Another intricacy worthy of consideration is that the Name Allāh being the all-comprehensive name (*al-ism al-jāmi'*) of God, when annexed to *salām* implies that we are seeking *salām* (protection and freedom from imperfection) in all the perfect attributes of Imām al-Ḥusayn and his loyal companions, who are manifestations of the all-comprehensive name Allāh.

أَبَداً مَا بَقِيتُ وَبَقِيَ اللَّيْلُ وَالنَّهَارُ

...forever, so long as I live and the night and day subsist.

Here the *zā'ir* implicitly tries to say that he would always remain steadfast in his love and devotion for Imām al-Ḥusayn عليه السلام. He says that his invocation of *salam* for the Imām عليه السلام and his loyal companions is perpetual. It does not matter whether he is alive in this material world or not. Expressing this kind of statement is in reality declaring one's firm and perpetual stance of loyalty to Imām al-Ḥusayn عليه السلام. This, therefore, presumes the *zā'ir's* solidified unwavering resolution.

Shaykh Mufīd (may Allāh elevate his status) narrates a tradition in the seventeenth assembly of his work *al-Amālī* that may enlighten us more about the meaning of having an unwavering resolution of attachment and devotion to the Ahl al-Bayt عليهم السلام:

Abū Muḥammad, brother of Yūnus b. Ya'qūb narrates from his brother Yūnus, who said:

كُنْتُ بِالْمَدِيْنَةِ فَاسْتَقْبَلَنِيْ جَعْفَرُ بْنُ مُحَمَّدٍ عليه السلام
فِي بَعْضِ أَزِقَّتِهَا فَقَالَ اذْهَبْ يَا يُوْنُسُ فَإِنَّ بِالْبَابِ
رَجُلاً مِنَّا أَهْلَ الْبَيْتِ قَالَ فَجِئْتُ إِلَى الْبَابِ فَإِذا
عِيْسَى بْنِ عَبْدِ اللّٰهِ جَالِسٌ فَقُلْتُ لَهُ مَنْ أَنْتَ قَالَ أَنَا
رَجُلٌ مِنْ أَهْلِ قُمْ قَالَ فَلَمْ يَكُنْ بِأَسْرَعِ مِنْ أَنْ أَقْبَلَ
أَبُوْ عَبْدِ اللّٰهِ عليه السلام عَلَى حِمَارٍ فَدَخَلَ عَلَى الْحِمَارِ
الدَّارَ ثُمَّ الْتَفَتَ إِلَيْنَا فَقَالَ أُدْخُلاَ ثُمَّ قَالَ يَا يُوْنُسُ
أَحْسَبُ أَنَّكَ أَنْكَرْتَ قَوْلِيْ لَكَ إِنَّ عِيْسَى بْنِ عَبْدِ
اللّٰهِ مِنَّا أَهْلَ الْبَيْتِ قَالَ قُلْتُ إِيْ وَاللّٰهِ جُعِلْتُ فِدَاكَ
لأَنَّ عِيْسَى بْنِ عَبْدِ اللّٰهِ رَجُلٌ مِنْ أَهْلِ قُمْ فَكَيْفَ
يَكُوْنُ مِنْكُمْ أَهْلِ الْبَيْتِ قَالَ يَا يُوْنُسُ عِيْسَى بْنِ
عَبْدِ اللّٰهِ رَجُلٌ مِنَّا حَيًّا وَ هُوَ مِنَّا مَيِّتًا

I was at Madīna, when Ja'far bin Muḥammad عليه السلام met me in one of its lanes. He said: "O Yūnus, go to the door, for a person from us the Ahl al-Bayt is at the door." He said: "I went towards the door and found 'Īsā bin 'Abdillāh sitting there. So, I said: "Who are you?" He replied: "I am from Qum." He said: "No sooner than he had said that, Abū 'Abdillāh appeared on a donkey and he entered the house riding the donkey. Then attending to us, he said: "Come through." Then he said: "O Yūnus, I believe you were not convinced when I said that Īsā' bin ʿAbdillāh is from us, Ahl al-Bayt?" I said: "It is so, may I be your ransom. For ʿIsā bin ʿAbdillāh is from people of Qum, how can he be one of you Ahl al-Bayt?" He said: **"O Yūnus, ʿIsa bin ʿAbdillāh is from us as long as he lives, and he shall be from us after he has died."**[5]

5 Shaykh Mufīd, *Al-Amālī*, 17th Assembly, p. 140.

CHAPTER 9

يَا أَبَا عَبْدِ اللهِ لَقَدْ عَظُمَتِ الرَّزِيَّةُ وَجَلَّتْ وَعَظُمَتِ

الْمُصِيبَةُ بِكَ عَلَيْنَا وَعَلَى جَمِيعِ أَهْلِ الإِسْلَامِ وَجَلَّتْ

وَعَظُمَتْ مُصِيبَتُكَ فِي السَّمَاوَاتِ عَلَى جَمِيعِ أَهْلِ

السَّمَاوَاتِ

O Aba ʿAbdillāh, I swear by Allāh, the loss is great; and the calamity on us and all the enthusiasts of Islām because of what befell you is great and severe. And the calamity that befell you is reckoned by all the inhabitants of the heavens in the heavens as great and severe.

يَا أَبَا عَبْدِ اللهِ لَقَدْ عَظُمَتِ الرَّزِيَّةُ وَجَلَّتْ وَعَظُمَتِ
الْمُصِيبَةُ بِكَ عَلَيْنَا وَعَلَى جَمِيعِ أَهْلِ الإِسْلَامِ وَجَلَّتْ
وَعَظُمَتْ مُصِيبَتُكَ فِي السَّمَاوَاتِ عَلَى جَمِيعِ أَهْلِ
السَّمَاوَاتِ

O Abā ʿAbdillah, I swear by Allāh, the loss is great; and the calamity on us and all the enthusiasts of Islam because of what befell you is great and severe. And the calamity that befell you is reckoned by all the inhabitants of the heavens in the heavens as great and severe.

COMMENTARY

يَا أَبَا عَبْدِ اللهِ...

O utterly obedient servant of Allāh...

Once again we *call* Imām al-Ḥusayn ﵇, although we realize that he can listen to us and behold our presence wherever we are. And why employ the vocative particle *yā* to call him? We said in the beginning that *yā* is used for a person who is quite far. The reason is that we would like to express our deep veneration for his exalted self. This is because although he may ontologically be very close to us, his exalted spirit is utterly remote from our inferior level. The most important thing, however, is to be able to see his noble self when we address him. If we purify our souls and behold the realm beyond this world we may be able to vision what most of the people are deprived of due to their accumulation of sins. The very fact that we *address* Imām al-Ḥusayn ﵇ presumes that the *mukhāṭab* (addressee) is present before us. Otherwise why don't we employ the third person pronoun and invoke *salam* on his exalted being? And since the traditions of the Ahl al-Bayt ﷺ teach the believers to always aspire for the best, whenever we recite this salutation we must crave to attain the station that can facilitate a direct communication with Abā ʿAbdillāh al-Ḥusayn ؑ. When such an encounter is made possible, the heart breaks and the rivers of tears flow and the believer melts down before *al-witr al-mawtūr.*

يَا أَبَا عَبْدِ اللّٰهِ لَقَدْ عَظُمَتِ الرَّزِيَّةُ

O utterly obedient servant of Allāh, by Allāh, the loss is great.

Some commentators of this sacred *Ziyārat* say that the vocative particle *yā* is once again brought in this verse to renew the feelings of sorrow for what befell on Imām al-Ḥusayn ؑ. Al-Kashānī supporting this view says, "*Juddida nidā'uhu litajdīd al-ḥuzn...*"[1] (calling the Imām was renewed due the renewal of sorrow...).

لَقَدْ عَظُمَتِ الرَّزِيَّةُ

By Allāh, the loss is great.

The letter '*lām*' (لَ) in لَقَدْ *laqad* is employed for taking an oath. And since the particle قَدْ '*qad*' here appears before a past tense verb *'aẓumat* (*is great*), it denotes emphasis. Hence *laqad 'aẓumat* would mean 'By Allāh, surely great has been...'. The origin of the word '*raziyya*' (رَزِيَّة) is the word *razī'a* (رَزِيْئَة) with a *hamza* (ء) after the letter *yā*. Some have

1 Mawlā HabībulLāh Kashānī, *Sharḥu Ziyārat 'Āshurā'*, p. 53

merely translated it as a calamity. However, it denotes a specific kind of calamity: calamity due to loss. Al-Kashānī in his commentary says that it specifically refers to the calamity of the loss of the dear and beloved ones[2]. However, it is also used for a calamity of loss in the general sense. Before his departure from this mortal world, the Holy Prophet ﷺ in his state of illness sought a paper and pen to write something very important for the Muslim Umma. An ignorant man nearby said, "Indeed pain has overtaken the Messenger of Allāh, and you have the Qur'ān with you. The Book of Allāh is sufficient for us". This followed a difference of opinion among people near the Holy Prophet ﷺ. On seeing this chaotic state of affairs, he told them to disperse from there. 'Abdullāh bin 'Abbās in reference to the impediment that hampered the Holy Prophet ﷺ to write down the important direction, would employ the word *raziyya* and say:

إِنَّ الرَّزِيَّةَ كُلَّ الرَّزِيَّةِ مَا حَالَ بَيْنَ رَسُوْلِ اللهِ صَلَّى اللهُ عَلَيْهِ وَسَلَّمَ وَبَيْنَ أَنْ يَكْتُبَ لَهُمْ ذَلِكَ الْكِتَابَ...

Surely the calamity, a total calamity hindered the Messenger of Allāh from writing for them that testament..[3]

The verb رَزَءَ *raza'a* or *razi'a* literally means 'he lessened' or 'he diminished'[4]. Al-Fīrūzābādī in his *al-Qāmūs al-Muḥīṭ*, giving an example of how this verb is used, says:

مَا رَزِئْتُهُ بِالْكَسْرِ مَا نَقَصْتُهُ

---

2 *Ibid.*

3 Al-Ṭabarī, *Al-Mustarshid*, p. 682

4 E.W. Lane, *E.W. Lane Arabic-English Lexicon*, under the root word *raza'a*

> *Mā razi'tuhu* means I have not lessened[5]

Therefore *laqad 'aẓumat al-raziyya* means 'By Allāh, indeed the loss is great.'

This phrase talks about the greatness and intensity of the calamity that the believers faced by losing an Infallible Imām of the Ahl al-Bayt ﷺ who enjoyed a very exalted rank near Allāh and represented Allāh on earth. Only those who comprehend the greatness of such a Divine leader can tangibly feel the loss. Amīr al-mu'minīn 'Alī ؑ says in a meaningful tradition:

> فَكُلَّمَا عَظُمَ قَدْرُ الشَّيْءِ الْمُتَنَافَسِ فِيهِ عَظُمَتِ الرَّزِيَّةُ لِفَقْدِهِ
>
> ...so, the greater the value of the envied entity the greater the calamity of its loss.

And since the sanctity of Imām al-Ḥusayn ؑ is such that its essence is incomprehensible, the gravity of losing his personality is likewise incomprehensible. In addition, the difficult circumstances that Imām al-Ḥusayn ؑ and his noble progeny faced and the manner in which their sanctity was violated leave such wounds in the hearts of his lovers that make them tearful forever. Ibrāhīm bin Abī Maḥmūd narrates from Imām al-Riḍā' ؑ:

> اِنَّ يَوْمَ الْحُسَيْنِ اَقْرَحَ جُفُوْنَنَا وَاَسْبَلَ دُمُوْعَنَا وَاَذَلَّ عَزِيْزَنَا، بِاَرْضِ كَرْبٍ وَبَلاَءٍ، وَاَوْرَثَتْنَا الْكَرْبُ وَالْبَلاَءُ اِلى يَوْمِ الاِنْقِضَاءِ، فَعَلَى مِثْلِ الْحُسَيْنِ فَلْيَبْكِ الْبَاكُوْنَ، فَاِنَّ الْبُكَاءَ عَلَيْهِ يَحُطُّ الذُّنُوْبَ

5 Al-Fīrūzābādī, *Al-Qāmūs al-Muḥīṭ*, v.1, p. 122

الْعِظَامَ

Surely the day of al-Ḥusayn wounded our eyes and made our tears pour down and dishonored our venerated ones in the land of sorrow and tribulation, and thereby it **made *us inherit sorrow and calamity until the final day***, and therefore the mourners must weep for the likes of al-Ḥusayn, for surely weeping over him wipes out major sins ...[6]

Imām al-Mahdī عليه السلام in his well-known *Ziyārat al-Nāḥiya* addressing Imām al-Ḥusayn عليه السلام cries:

فَلَئِنْ أَخَّرَتْنِـي الـدُّهُوْرُ، وَعَاقَنِيْ عَـنْ نَصْـرِكَ الْمَقْدُوْرُ، وَلَمْ أَكُنْ لِمَنْ حَارَبَكَ مُحَارِبًا، وَلِمَـنْ نَصَبَ لَكَ الْعَـدَاوَةَ مُنَاصِبًا، فَلَأَنْـدُبَنَّكَ صَبَاحًا وَمَسَاءً، وَلَأَبْكِينَّ عَلَيْكَ بَدَلَ الـدَّمُوْعِ دَمًا، حَسْـرَةً عَلَيْكَ وَتَأَسُّفًا عَلَى مَا دَهَاكَ وَتَلَهُّفًا، حَتَّى أَمُوْتَ بِلَوْعَةِ الْمُصَابِ وَغُصَّةِ الِاكْتِيَابِ

But as I have been hindered by the course of time and as (Allāh's) decree has prevented me from helping you, and as I could not fight those who fought you, and was not able to show hostility to those who showed hostility to you, I will, therefore, lament you morning and evening, and will weep blood in place of tears, out of my anguish for you and my sorrow for all that befell you, until I meet death from the pain of the catastrophe and the

---

6 Sayyid Raḍī al-Dīn bin al-Ṭāwūs, *Iqbāl al-Aʿmāl*, v.3, p. 28

choking grief.[7]

لَقَدْ عَظُمَتِ الرَّزِيَّةُ

By Allāh, the loss is great.

Before one tries to swear and say that the loss is great, one must have knowledge about the same. Although we cannot even imagine the magnitude of the loss that the Ahl al-Bayt عليهم السلام encountered in the plains of Karbalā, it is important for us to search for authentic information about the same, so that we may naturally express our sorrow as we recite this particular phrase.

An Unparalleled Incident

One of the reasons that make this calamity outstanding and unique is that those who joined al-Ḥusayn عليه السلام knew very well what awaited them. Despite that, they chose with complete volition on their side, to undertake this sacred journey and meet the calamities with open arms. Imām al-Ḥusayn عليه السلام made it very clear to them when he resolved to embark on his journey to ʿIrāq that martyrdom is what awaits him:

مَنْ كَانَ فِينَا بَاذِلاً مُهْجَتَهُ، مُوَطِّناً عَلَى لِقَاءِ اللهِ نَفْسَهُ فَلْيَرْحَلْ مَعَنَا فَإِنِّي رَاحِلٌ مُصْبِحاً إِنْ شَاءَ اللهُ تَعَالَى...

Whosoever is ready to sacrifice his soul for us, and has stationed himself for meeting Allāh, he must leave with us, for surely I will leave tomorrow

7 Muḥammad bin al-Mashhadī, *Al-Mazār*, p. 500

> morning Inshā Allāh...[8]

It is such a move in complete awareness of the horrendous massacre that singles out the tragedy of Karbalā. The late eminent scholar ʿAllāma Muḥammad Taqī Jaʿfarī in response to a question asked as to why the Karbalā event is the most sorrowful of all events in history, said:

> The important factor in the story of al-Ḥusayn عليه السلام which cannot be compared to any other event whatsoever is that it was out of complete awareness and choice. At no moment did they lose their free will. Furthermore, historical analysis shows that even at the very last moment if the Imām عليه السلام would say 'yes' [to Yazīd], not only would the difficult situation be over, but he would be saved from that place, and perhaps the next era would be his era...[9]

وَجَلَّتْ وَعَظُمَتِ الْمُصِيبَةُ بِكَ عَلَيْنَا وَعَلَى جَمِيعِ أَهْلِ الإِسْلامِ

...and the calamity on us and all the enthusiasts of Islām because of what befell on you is great and severe...

The past tense verb جَلَّتْ '*jallat*' mentioned in the above phrase is commonly translated in the same way as the verb *ʿaẓumat* (is great). Some lexicographers however state that there is a fine difference between the two verbs: whereas *ʿaẓumat* can apply for both material as well as spiritual intensity, *jallat* is only correct for spiritual greatness[10]. Therefore this phrase implies that the calamity on us is spiritually great.

---

8 Al-Shaykh ʿAbdullāh al-Baḥrānī, *al-'Awālim (al-Imām al-Ḥusayn ('a))*, p. 216

9 Muḥammad Riḍā Jawādī & ʿAlī Jaʿfarī, *Dar Maḥzar-e- Ḥakīm ʿAllāmeye Jaʿfarī*, p. 18

10 Al-Muṣtafawī, *Al-Taḥqīq fī Kalimāt al-Qur'ān al-Karīm*, v. 2, p. 102

All that the Imām عليه السلام and his noble family members as well as sincere companions faced has enormously hurt our spirits and the spirit of every lover of Islām. In revealing the magnitude of the tragedy, Imām al-Ḥasan عليه السلام addressing his brother says:

لاَ يَوْمَ كَيَوْمِكَ يَا أبَا عَبْدِ اللّه

There is no day like your Day O Abā ʿAbdillāh.[11]

And Imām Zayn al-'Ābidīn عليه السلام in one of his sermons says:

وَهَذِهِ الرَّزِيَّةُ الَّتِيْ لاَ مِثْلهَا رَزِيَّةٌ.

...and this is a calamity the like of which there is no calamity.[12]

And ʿAbdullāh bin al-Faḍl narrates from Imām al-Ṣādiq عليه السلام:

إنَّ يَوْمَ قُتِلَ الْحُسَيْنُ عليه السلام أعْظَمُ مُصِيْبَةً مِنْ جَمِيْعِ سَائِرِ الأيَّامِ...

Indeed the day of the martyrdom of al-Ḥusayn is a day of greater calamity then all other days...[13]

وَعَلَى جَمِيعِ أَهْلِ الإِسْلامِ

and on all the members of the enthusiasts of Islām

The genitive construction *Ahl al-Islām* denotes 'those who are intimate

11 Al-Baḥrānī, *al-ʿAwālim (al-Imām al-Ḥusayn عليه السلام)*, p. 154

12 *Ibid.*,, p. 448

13 *Ibid.*,,p. 516

and attached to Islām'. The literal meaning of the word *ahl* according to some lexicographers is *uns* (intimacy) coupled with specific relationship and attachment[14]. The word Ah al-Bayt refers to the people of a house, because they are intimate, attached, and have a specific relationship to the house.

Therefore when we say that the loss and calamity is great on all the Ahl al-Islām we mean that all those who really have intimacy, attachment and relationship with Islam suffer with great loss and calamity. This is where we must try to analyze ourselves and see whether we are from the Ahl al-Islām or not.

The main reason why the Ahl al-Islām must express sorrow is that Imām al-Ḥusayn عليه السلام is the epitome of Islām. Naturally therefore, all the lovers of Islam would tangibly feel sorrowful when any kind of calamity befalls him.

In one of his counsels to his contemporary, Imām al-Bāqir عليه السلام describing the Ahl al-Bayt عليهم السلام, says:

وَنَحْنُ مَوَاضِعُ الرِّسَالَةِ وَنَحْنُ الدِّيْنُ. . .

> And we are the places of the Divine Message, and we are the Religion...[15]

And in another tradition, Imām al-Ṣādiq عليه السلام informs his companion Dāwūd:

يَا دَاوُدَ نَحْنُ الصَّلاَةُ فِي كِتَابِ اللَّهِ عَزَّ وَجَلَّ وَنَحْنُ الزَّكَاةُ وَنَحْنُ الصِّيَامُ وَنَحْنُ الْحَجُّ وَنَحْنُ الشَّهْرُ الْحَرَامُ وَنَحْنُ الْبَلَدُ الْحَرَامُ وَنَحْنُ كَعْبَةُ اللَّهِ وَنَحْنُ

14 Al-Muṣṭafawī, *Al-Taḥqīq fī Kalimāt al-Qur'ān al-Karīm*, v. 1, p. 169

15 Al-Daylamī, *Irshād al-Qulūb*, v.2, p. 418

قِبْلَةُ اللّه . . .

O Dawūd, we are the prayer (*al-ṣalāt*) in the Book of Allāh, the Invincible and Exalted, and we are the poor rate (*zakāt*), and we are the fast (*al-ṣiyām*), and we are the pilgrimage (*al-ḥajj*) and we are the sacred month (*al-shahr al-ḥarām*) and we are the sacred city (*al-balad al-ḥarām*) and we are the Kaʿba of Allāh and we are the *qibla* of Allāh...[16]

These traditions inform us that the Imāms of the Ahl al-Bayt عليهم السلام were epitomes of religion. Therefore love for religion in the true sense is love for them, and vice versa.

وَجَلَّتْ وَعَظُمَتْ مُصِيبَتُكَ فِي السَّمَاوَاتِ عَلَى جَمِيعِ أَهْلِ السَّمَاوَاتِ

And the calamity that befell on you is reckoned by all the inhabitants of the heavens in the heavens as severe and great.

In this phrase we confess that not only was the calamity great for the earth and its inhabitants, the heavens and their inhabitants likewise were overtaken by sorrow and grief for what transpired on a representative of Allāh on earth.

Imām ʿAlī bin Mūsā al-Riḍā عليه السلام addressing to Ibn Shabīb says:

وَلَقَدْ بَكَتِ السَّمَاوَاتُ السَّبْعُ وَالأَرَضُونَ لِقَتْلِهِ . . .

Certainly, the seven heavens and earths cried because of his martyrdom (i.e. of al-Ḥusayn عليه السلام)..

16 ʿAllāma Majlisī, *Biḥār al-Anwār*, v.24, p. 303

And Imām al-Ṣādiq ﷺ is reported to have said:

إِنَّ أَبَا عَبْدِ اللَّهِ الْحُسَيْنَ عليه السلام : لَمَّا قَضَى بَكَتْ عَلَيْهِ السَّمَاوَاتُ السَّبْعُ وَالأَرَضُونَ السَّبْعُ وَ مَا فِيهِنَّ وَمَا بَيْنَهُنَّ وَمَنْ يَنْقَلِبُ فِي الْجَنَّةِ وَالنَّارِ مِنْ خَلْقِ رَبِّنَا وَمَا يُرَى وَ مَا لاَ يُرَى

> Indeed when Abā ʿAbdillāh al-Ḥusayn bin ʿAlī ﷺ left this world, the seven heavens and the seven earths and whatever is in and between them, and whosoever moves in Paradise and Hell Fire from the creation of our Lord and what can be seen and what cannot be seen wept for him.[17]

It should be known that it has been established in its own place that every existential entity has a share in comprehension (*shuʿūr*), glorification (*tasbīḥ*), laudation (*ḥamd*), love (*ʿishq*), and lamentation (*bukāʾ*). Those, however, who have not contemplated on the Holy Qurʾān and the traditions of the Ahl al-Bayt ﷺ well, may consider this as far fetched. In order to grasp this reality intellectually, they should refer to works on the Transcendent Philosophy (*al-ḥikmat al-mutaʿāliya*) propounded by leading philosophers such as Mullā Ṣadrā and Mullā Hādī Sabzawārī (may Allāh elevate their noble spirits).

Following is a verse of the Holy Qurʾan that clearly informs us about the possibility of the sky weeping:

﴿فَمَا بَكَتْ عَلَيْهِمُ السَّمَاءُ وَالأَرْضُ وَمَا كَانُوا مُنْظَرِينَ﴾

> So neither the sky wept for them, nor the earth; nor

---

17 Shaykh al-Kulaynī, *Al-Kāfī*, v.4, p. 575

> were they granted any respite. (44:29)

Commenting on this verse, Imām al-Ṣādiq عليه السلام is reported to have said:

> لَمْ تَبْكِ السَّمَاءُ عَلَى أَحَدٍ مُنْذُ قُتِلَ يَحْيَى بْنِ زَكَرِيَّا، حَتَّى قُتِلَ الْحُسَيْنُ عليه السلام، فَبَكَتْ عَلَيْهِ
>
> The sky did not cry over anyone ever since Yaḥyā bin Zakariyya was slain, until al-Ḥusayn عليه السلام was slain, whereupon it cried over him.[18]

And Imām Muḥammad al-Bāqir عليه السلام is reported to have said the following about the abovementioned verse:

> مَا بَكَتِ السَّمَاءُ عَلَى أَحَدٍ بَعْدَ يَحْيَى بْنَ زَكَرِيَّا، إِلاَّ عَلَى الْحُسَيْنِ بْنِ عَلِيٍّ عليهما السلام، فَإِنَّهَا بَكَتْ عَلَيْهِ أَرْبَعِينَ يَوْمًا
>
> The sky did not cry for anyone after Yaḥyā bin Zakariyyā save on al-Ḥusayn bin ʿAlī عليه السلام, for surely it cried over him for forty days.[19]

The verse as well as the comments of the Ahl al-Bayt عليهم السلام clearly reveal to us that the sky manifests sorrow and expresses its lamentation as well.

---

18 Al-Baḥrānī, *Al-Burhān fī Tafsīr al-Qur'ān*, v. 3, p. 701.

19 *Ibid.*

۞

وَجَلَّتْ وَعَظُمَتْ مُصِيبَتُكَ فِي السَّمَاوَاتِ عَلَى جَمِيعِ أَهْلِ السَّمَاوَاتِ

And the calamity that befell on you is reckoned by all the inhabitants of
the heavens in the heavens as severe and great.

۞

The article *al* that precedes *al-samāwāt* (السماوات) confers the meaning
that all the heavens are taken into consideration.

And heavens and skies should not transport us to their material
extensions. Scholars of authority opine that they refer to the higher
levels of the universe of contingent existence.

The phrase *ahl al-samāwāt* can refer to the angels who inhabit the
heavens and all the exalted departed souls who witnessed or came to
know about the tragedy of Karbalā.

Consider the following traditions:

Imām al-Riḍā عليه السلام tells Ibn Shabīb:

وَلَقَدْ نَزَلَ إِلَى الْأَرْضِ مِنَ الْمَلَائِكَةِ أَرْبَعَةُ آلَافٍ

لِنَصْرِهِ فَوَجَدُوهُ قَدْ قُتِلَ فَهُمْ عِنْدَ قَبْرِهِ شُعْثٌ غُبْرٌ

إِلَى أَنْ يَقُومَ الْقَائِمُ فَيَكُونُونَ مِنْ أَنْصَارِهِ

وَشِعَارُهُمْ يَا لَثَارَاتِ الْحُسَيْنِ

Four thousand angels descended on earth to aid
him, but (when they were allowed to reach there)
they found him martyred. **So they remained at his
grave, dishevelled and covered with dust, and will
remain there until the rising of al-Qā'im** (Imām al-
Mahdī عليه السلام, whereupon they will aid him. Their
slogan will be, 'Vengeance for the blood of al-
Ḥusayn عليه السلام!'

Imām al-Ṣādiq عليه السلام tells a companion called Fuḍayl:

مَا لَكُمْ لاَ تَأْتُونَهُ يَعْنِي قَبْرَ الْحُسَيْنِ عليه السلام فَإِنَّ أَرْبَعَةَ
آلاَفِ مَلَكٍ يَبْكُونَ عِنْدَ قَبْرِهِ إِلَى يَوْمِ الْقِيَامَةِ.

What is the matter with you that you do not visit him [the grave of Imām al-Ḥusayn عليه السلام]? Surely four thousand angels constantly weep near his grave, [and will do so] until the Judgment Day.[20]

As for the departed souls, one of the traditions that break the hearts and make us realize how grave is the matter of al-Ḥusayn عليه السلام is the following conversation between Imām al-Ṣādiq عليه السلام and Abū Baṣir, his loyal companion, who had lost his physical eyesight, but was endowed with spiritual effulgence:

يَا أَبَا بَصِيرٍ إِذَا نَظَرْتُ إِلَى وُلْدِ الْحُسَيْنِ عليه السلام أَتَانِي
مَا لاَ أَمْلِكُهُ بِمَا أَتَى إِلَى أَبِيهِمْ وَآلِهِمْ يَا أَبَا بَصِيرٍ إِنَّ
فَاطِمَةَ عليها السلام لَتَبْكِيهِ وَتَشْهَقُ. . . فَلاَ تَزَالُ
الْمَلاَئِكَةُ مُشْفِقِينَ يَبْكُونَ لِبُكَائِهَا وَيَدْعُونَ اللَّهَ
وَيَتَضَرَّعُونَ إِلَيْهِ إِلَى أَنْ قَالَ قُلْتُ جُعِلْتُ فِدَاكَ إِنَّ
هَذَا الأَمْرَ عَظِيمٌ قَالَ غَيْرُهُ أَعْظَمُ مِنْهُ مَا لَمْ تَسْمَعْهُ
ثُمَّ قَالَ يَا بَا بَصِيرٍ أَ مَا تُحِبُّ أَنْ تَكُونَ فِيمَنْ يُسْعِدُ
فَاطِمَةَ عليها السلام فَبَكَيْتُ حِينَ قَالَهَا فَمَا قَدَرْتُ عَلَى
الْمَنْطِقِ وَمَا قَدَرْتُ عَلَى كَلاَمِي مِنَ الْبُكَاءِ.

Imām al-Ṣādiq عليه السلام said: O Abā Baṣīr, when I look at

20 ʿAllāma Majlisī, *Biḥār al-Anwār*, v. 45, p. 222

the progeny of al-Ḥusayn عليه السلام, I am overcome due to what happened to their father and his family; O Abā Baṣīr, Indeed Fāṭima عليها السلام constantly weeps for him (al-Ḥusayn عليه السلام) and sighs [out of deep sorrow]....So the angels constantly sympathize and weep due to her weeping and pray to Allāh and express their humility to Him.... Abū Baṣīr said: May I be made your ransom. Indeed the matter is great. Thereupon the Imām عليه السلام said: What you have not heard other than this is even greater. Thereafter the Imām عليه السلام said: O Abā Baṣīr: Don't you want to be among those who assist Fāṭima عليها السلام? Abū Baṣīr says: When he said this, I started weeping and could not utter a word, nor could I speak due to my weeping...[21]

This tradition clearly hints to us that whatever we have heard and known about Imām al-Ḥusayn عليه السلام cannot be compared to that which we do not know. ❁

---

21 Shaykh al-Nūrī, *Mustadrak al-Wasā'il*, v.10, p. 314

Also published by World Federation

1. *Islamic Laws - English Version of Tawḍḥīul Masā'il* by Āyatullāh al-ʿUẓmā al-Ḥājj as-Sayyid ʿAli al-Ḥusaynī as-Sīstānī; translated by the late Mulla Asgharali M.M. Jaffer

2. *A Restatement of the History of Islam and Muslims* by the late Sayyid Ali Asghar Razwy

3. *al-Amālī - Dictations of Shaykh al-Mufīd* by Shaykh Muḥammad ibne Muḥammad al-Nuʿman; translated by the late Mulla Asgharali M.M. Jaffer

4. *Nahjul Balāgha Revisited* by the late Mulla Asgharali M.M. Jaffer

5. *The Role of Ahlul Bayt in the Preservation of Islam* by ʿAllāmah Sayyid Murtaḍā ʿAskarī; translated by the late Mulla Asgharali M.M. Jaffer

6. *Fiqh and Fuqahā* by the late Mulla Asgharali M.M. Jaffer

7. *Pearls of Wisdom* by the late Mulla Asgharali M.M. Jaffer

8. *The Collection and Preservation of Qur'ān* by Āyatullāh al-ʿUẓmā al-Ḥājj as-Sayyid Abūl Qāsim al-Khū'ī; translated by the late Mulla Asgharali M.M. Jaffer

9. *Anecdotes for Reflection - Part I* by Sayyid Ali Sadaaqat; translated by Shahnawaz Mahdavi

10. *The Islamic Moral System: Commentary of Sūrah Ḥujurāt* by Āyatullāh Jaʿfar Subḥānī; translated by Saleem Bhimji *Published in co-operation with the Islamic Humanitarian Service [www.al-haqq.com]*

11. *Tafsir of the Noble Qur'ān: Sūratul Jinn* by Āyatullāh al-ʿUẓmā al-Ḥājj ash-Shaykh Nāṣir Makārim Shīrāzī; translated by Saleem Bhimji *Published in co-operation with the Islamic Humanitarian Service [www.al-haqq.com]*

12. *40 Ḥadith: Month of Ramaḍān* by Shaykh Mirmanafi; translated by Shahnawaz Mahdavi

13. *40 Ḥadith: Tablīgh* by Shaykh Mirmanafi; translated by Shahnawaz Mahdavi

14. *40 Ḥadith: ʿAzādārī* by Shaykh Ray Shahri; translated by Shahnawaz Mahdavi

15. *40 Ḥadith: Qur'ān* by Sayyid Majid Adili; translated by Arifa Hudda and Saleem Bhimji

16. *Islam and Religious Pluralism* by Āyatullāh Murtadhā Muṭahharī; translated by Sayyid Sulayman Ali Ḥasan *Published in co-operation with the Islamic Publishing House [www.iph.ca]*

17. *Guiding the Youth of the New Generation* by Āyatullāh Murtadhā Muṭahharī; translated by Saleem Bhimji

18. *40 Ḥadith: Prophet 'Isā*; translated by Shahnawaz Mahdavi

19. *Anecdotes for Reflection - Part II* by Sayyid Ali Sadaaqat; translated by Shahnawaz Mahdavi

20. *Jesus on Ethics* - compiled by the Islamic Education Board of the World Federation; translated by Dr. Muḥammad Legenhausen

21. *Manifestations of the All Merciful* by Abu Muḥammad Zainul Abideen

22. *A Short Treatise on the Divine Invitation* by Muḥammad Khalfan

23. *Essence of Worship: Ṣalāt [40 Ḥadith]* by Shaykh Ray Shahrī; translated by Shahnawaz Mahdavi

24. *Lofty Status of Parents [40 Ḥadith]* by Shaykh Ray Shahrī; translated by Shahnawaz Mahdavi

25. *The Spiritual Journey – Ḥajj [40 Ḥadith]* by Maḥmud Mahdīpūr; translated by Saleem Bhimji

26. *Completion of Islām – Ghadeer [40 Ḥadith]* by Maḥmud Sharifī; translated by Saleem Bhimji

27. *180 Questions – Volume 1* by Āyatullāh al-'Uẓma al-Ḥājj ash-Shaykh Nāṣir Makārim Shīrāzī; translated by Shahnawaz Mahdavi

28. *Anecdotes for Reflection - Part III* by Sayyid Ali Sadaaqat; translated by Shahnawaz Mahdavi

29. *Jesus on Ethics [Second Edition]* - compiled by the Islamic Education Board of the World Federation; translated by Dr. Muḥammad Legenhausen

30. *Islam and Religious Pluralism [Second Edition]* by Āyatullāh Murtadhā Muṭahharī; translated by Sayyid Sulayman Ali Ḥasan

31. *Introduction to the Science of Tafsir of the Qur'ān* by Āyatullāh Ja'far Subḥānī; translated by Saleem Bhimji

32. *Faith and Reason* by The Porch of Wisdom Research Institute; translated by a Group of Muslim Scholars

33. *180 Questions – Volume 2* by Āyatullāh al-'Uẓma al-Ḥājj ash-Shaykh Nāṣir Makārim Shīrāzī; translated by Shahnawaz Mahdavi

34. *The Savior of Humanity: Imām al-Mahdi in the Eyes of the Ahlul Bayt [40 Ḥadith]* by Abdul Rahim Mugahi; translated by Saleem Bhimji

35. *From Marriage to Parenthood: The Heavenly Path*, compiled by Abbas and Shaheen Merali

36. *The Sacred Effusion* written by Muhammad M. Khalfan

37. *Zakāt [40 Ḥadith]* compiled and translated by Muhammed Reza Tajri

Notes